Journal of Contemporary History: **2**

THE LEFT WING INTELLECTUALS BETWEEN THE WARS 1919-1939

♫ Journal of Contemporary History

Edited by Walter Laqueur & George L. Mosse

Published:

Volume 1: INTERNATIONAL FASCISM, 1920-1945. TB/1276
Essays by: Gilbert D. Allardyce
Paul M. Hayes
Ludwig Jedlicka
Adrian Lyttelton
George L. Mosse
Erwin Oberländer
Hugh Seton-Watson
Robert J. Soucy
Hugh Thomas
Eugen Weber
Llewellyn Woodward

Volume 2: THE LEFT-WING INTELLECTUALS
BETWEEN THE WARS, 1919-1939. TB/1286
Essays by: Jens A. Christophersen
Paul Ignotus
James Joll
Kemal A. Karpat
Norbert Leser
Martin Peretz
Stuart Samuels
Robert S. Short
Hans-Albert Walter
David Wilkinson
Stuart Woolf

In Preparation:

Volume 3: 1914: THE ORIGINS OF WORLD WAR I

Edited by **WALTER LAQUEUR & GEORGE L. MOSSE**

THE LEFT WING INTELLECTUALS BETWEEN THE WARS 1919-1939

ROBERT S. SHORT

JAMES JOLL

DAVID WILKINSON

STUART SAMUELS

MARTIN PERETZ

HANS-ALBERT WALTER

NORBERT LESER

JENS A. CHRISTOPHERSEN

PAUL IGNOTUS

KEMAL A. KARPAT

STUART WOOLF

HARPER TORCHBOOKS ❦ **The Academy Library**
Harper & Row, Publishers, New York

THE LEFT WING INTELLECTUALS BETWEEN
THE WARS, 1919-1939.

Copyright © 1966 The Institute for Advanced Studies in
Contemporary History.

Printed in the United States of America.

This book was first published under the title "Left-wing
Intellectuals between the Wars," as Volume 1, Number
2 1966, of the *Journal of Contemporary History*, edited
by Walter Laqueur and George L. Mosse, by Weiden-
feld & Nicolson, Ltd., London. It is here reprinted by
arrangement.

First HARPER TORCHBOOK edition published 1966 by
Harper & Row, Publishers, Incorporated,
49 East 33rd Street,
New York, N.Y. 10016.

Contents

The Politics of Surrealism, 1920–36

Robert S. Short

> *'Transformer le monde', a dit Marx;*
> *'Changer la vie', a dit Rimbaud; ces deux mots*
> *d'ordre pour nous n'en font qu'un.*
>
> ANDRÉ BRETON

Including as it did at one time or another writers and artists of the calibre of Louis Aragon, André Breton, Paul Eluard, René Char, Michel Leiris, René Crevel, Robert Desnos, Antonin Artaud, Raymond Queneau, Tristan Tzara, Pierre Naville, Max Ernst, André Masson, and Alberto Giacometti, to mention just a handful of the hundred or so who joined its ranks, the Surrealist group probably exercised a greater influence on the intellectual climate of the inter-war period in France than any other comparable movement. As such the political history of the Surrealists, who participated collectively in many of the organizations of the revolutionary left, deserves attention.

Not that the Surrealists ever had a decisive effect on the course of political events, or made any original contribution to political theory. The interest of the movement's political history lies in its tenacious efforts, set forth in some highly articulate polemical writing, to associate its intellectual, artistic, and moral preoccupations with the aims and methods of international communism. The issues at stake may be reduced to three: the reconciliation of a generalized spirit of revolt with revolutionary action; the reconciliation of the idea of a 'spiritual revolution' and its accompanying insistence on ethical 'purity' with the practical necessities of political effectiveness; the reconciliation of an independent revolutionary art with the demands for propaganda and didacticism made by the communist party. An examination of them will show how the evolution of the theory of Surrealism, an enterprise which was initially and

3

essentially poetic, led the movement to call for the transformation of society; and an account of Surrealism's ventures into politics and of the repeated setbacks these met with, will suggest some of the reasons why the Surrealists failed to translate their metaphysical and spiritual ambitions into social terms, and, more specifically, why they failed to find a permanent place within the communist movement.

While in the narrow sense, according to the definition in Breton's *Manifesto* of 1924, Surrealism appeared to be no more than a new poetics, a linguistic experiment and a novel method of 'forcing inspiration', in the broad sense it implied an ethics, a philosophy, and a politics. Bringing together Rimbaud's 'Lettre du Voyant', Hegel's dialectical method, and Freud's analysis of the unconscious, the Surrealists began by making a drastic revaluation of the poetic image. They believed that the series of images which they brought to light by using automatic techniques represented the 'real process of thought'. They devoted themselves to the exploitation of the untapped resources of the unconscious, hitherto ignored or suppressed by a culture obsessed by technological progress and material comforts. For the Surrealists, poetry was not a cultivated form of escapism; it was an instrument of discovery. In so far as the source of poetic inspiration was the unconscious mind, a faculty which, like Descartes' reason, was common to all men, they believed that poetry could be 'made by all' and not just by the technically accomplished *littérateur*. It had ceased to be a 'means of expression' and had become 'an activity of mind'.

From the moment poetry was conceived as a spiritual activity accessible to all men, it ceased to be a purely aesthetic matter and became an ethical one. In Paul Eluard's words: 'Toute véritable morale est poétique, la poésie tendant au règne de l'homme, de tous les hommes, au règne de notre justice.' Surrealism thus affirmed the ethical basis of all expression and the 'communism' of poetry. At the same time, poetry's roots in the unconscious meant that it was the expression not only of primal mental activity but of man's deepest desires as well, for the unconscious was also the seat of the instincts and the libido. As such, poetry could not remain at the abstract level of 'fine art'. As the expression of desire, it involved choices and demands which sought satisfaction in the real world. Far from being a compensation for an inadequate and unworthy reality, poetry represented that towards which reality should progress. The Surrealists were confident that once the mind had a vision of what was possible, the will would struggle to achieve it, and that the 'interpretation' of man and of the world would inevitably be accompanied by their transformation. The poet would lead the struggle to raise man's spiritual and social state up to the level of his dreams. In so far as the disparity between that which existed and that which was desired was the result of alterable social conditions rather than of an immutable human condition, the Surrealists came to demand a radical social upheaval: a revolution.

This, very schematically, was the chain of reasoning that linked the Surrealist conception of art to an attitude of revolt against society and towards political commitment. This sequence of ideas was reflected in the intellectual evolution of the group in the seven years following the first world war.

The word 'revolution' punctuated the writings of the Surrealists with great regularity between 1922 and 1925 but it had not yet acquired political connotations. As a document from April 1925 stated:

The immediate sense and purpose of the Surrealist revolution is not so much to change anything in the physical and manifest order of things as to create an agitation in men's minds.[1]

At this stage, they believed in a 'revolution' in experience to be brought about by the mind and the imagination once the fetters of rationalism and habit had been struck off. Aragon challenged his audience in Madrid: 'Do you believe, yes or no, in the infinite powers of thought? We will prevail against all odds.' Ignoring social and political forces, the Surrealists claimed to be able to set off their revolution unaided, since it was not something rendered inevitable by the laws of social evolution so much as something ardently desired which, if willed with sufficient passion, was bound to occur. Their first task was to rejuvenate language, the instrument and substance of thought and hence the key to their 'subjective idealist' revolution. Putting to advantage their earlier apprenticeship among the Dadaists in the art of provocation and scandal, the Surrealists turned on the regime whose conventions had crippled and stunted language. They denounced the wretchedness of everyday life, the cults of family and fatherland, the necessity to work,

[1] Maurice Nadeau, *Documents Surréalistes* (Paris, 1947), p. 44.

masochistic Christianity, and the whole system of values which had permitted the war in which they themselves had unwillingly sacrificed their youth. As André Breton put it: 'We were possessed by a will to total subversion'. They extolled all forms of anti-social behaviour – crime, drug-addiction, suicide, insanity – as so many expressions of human freedom and revolt. They preferred the criminal to the political militant since crime seemed to be a self-sufficient act implying no fresh determinations. As an indispensable preliminary to the reconquest of liberty, they called for a crime on an international scale: a second 'Terror' or a new wave of barbarian invasions from the East. But these remained poetic symbols of menace. The Surrealists refused as yet to serve any real revolutionary cause because they conceived liberty as an absolute and commitment would have imposed intolerable limitations on their *disponibilité*. 'Je meurs si je m'attache', said Breton.

The distance that separated the Surrealists from young communist intellectuals was revealed in a controversy between Aragon and the editors of *Clarté*, Marcel Fourrier and Jean Bernier, over *Un Cadavre*, a tract published by the Surrealists on the death of Anatole France. The Clartéists had approved the general spirit of this lampoon but objected to Aragon's use of the phrase 'Moscou la gâteuse' (doddering Moscow) in his comment on a telegram of condolence sent by the Kremlin to the French nation on its loss. Aragon replied to the Clartéists:

If you find me antagonistic to the political spirit . . . it is because, as you cannot fail to see, I have always valued and continue to value the spirit of revolt far more highly than any politics . . .. As for the Russian Revolution, you'll forgive me for shrugging my shoulders. Measured by the yardstick of ideas, it is nothing more than a trivial ministerial crisis.[2]

Other Surrealists shared Aragon's contempt for communism. Eluard called it 'a mediocre regime which, just like capitalism, depends on the crude and repulsive order of physical labour'. The group did not yet see revolutionary politics as the means of satisfying their grievances against the world; Breton told Jacques Baron: 'We just don't bother ourselves with politics.'

It was not until the summer of 1925 that the Surrealists began to reassess their resources and what they meant by 'revolution'. The public had remained cheerfully immune to threats of the Terror and an Oriental scourge however vividly these horrors were evoked

2 *Clarté*, 1 December 1924.

in the columns of *La Révolution Surréaliste*. Breton realised that the social order was not going to yield before mere invective whose extravagant violence rendered it ridiculous. If their revolution was not to deteriorate into an impotent nonconformism it had to be given some tangible content, if necessary social content, and join forces with other revolutionary intellectuals. Critics like Marcel Arland had been quick to pigeon-hole the Surrealists' revolt as a symptom of a *'nouveau mal de siècle'* or to identify the group as a latterday generation of 'poètes maudits'. To avoid this forcible assimilation into a literary avant-garde which they despised, no better means was to hand than affiliations with proletarian politics. The press furore aroused by the Surrealists' behaviour at the banquet in honour of the poet Saint-Pol-Roux, where they had shouted overtly political slogans for the first time, proved that this was the way to make the public take notice of their protest.

The outbreak of hostilities between the French army under Pétain and the Riffs in Morocco precipitated the Surrealists into politics. It was 'le grand choc' which suddenly clarified a highly ambiguous intellectual position. Their admiration for Eastern and particularly for primitive peoples, their hatred of militarism and of the 'professional patriots', the academic intellectuals who celebrated France's civilizing role abroad – all directed their sympathies towards Abd-el-Krim. Nineteen of the group put their signatures to Henri Barbusse's protest: 'Appel aux Travailleurs Intellectuels. Oui ou non condamnez-vous la guerre?', which appeared in *L'Humanité* on 2 July 1925.

For Breton, the first step towards conversion to communism was reading Trotsky's biography of Lenin. He set about convincing his friends, anticipating their objections that the Russian Revolution hardly satisfied the exigencies of Surrealism by insisting that it was not yet over or complete and that on the moral plane there was no incompatibility between the ideas of Lenin and their own. It was necessary, he said, to abandon the myths of revolution for the reality. Communism might represent a minimum programme, but it was the only force in existence capable of bringing about the social revolution which in turn was the necessary condition of 'une révolution dans les esprits'. The autumn of 1925 saw the political conversion of the group *en masse*. Michel Leiris admitted that the individual by himself, however passionate and profound his sense of revolt, was impotent when it came to social action. Aragon was soon writing with the conviction and facility of a lifelong Marxist. In articles such as 'Le Prolétariat de l'esprit', he showed how capital could turn ideas themselves into commodities.[3] The Surrealists seem to have undergone a kind of intoxication with communism; the hyperbole and naïve enthusiasm of their early political writings, their panegyrics on the Cheka and the Ogpu, cast doubt on the permanence and seriousness of their conversion. Breton appeared one morning at the Café Cyrano with a workman's cap over his long curls to demonstrate his solidarity with the proletariat. André Masson, recalling the atmosphere of the group's meetings, admits: 'When I was present at these things I kept saying to myself: "But I'm dreaming. I must be dreaming".'[4]

The passage towards politics was eased by the instruction and encouragement the Surrealists received from the young editors of *Clarté*. But the national movement that Barbusse had founded in 1919 was now only a shadow of its former self. *Clarté* had long been suffering from shortage of funds, loss of readers, and repeated changes of policy as its successive editors struggled to determine the role that a communist cultural review independent of the communist party could usefully play in a period of prolonged anticipation of the revolution. Despite some misgivings, the Clartéists decided to collaborate with Breton's group, many of whom were brilliant and already notable writers, in the hope of saving their review. *Clarté* was to adopt an editorial policy very close to that already undertaken in part, though for less consciously political motives, in *La Révolution Surréaliste*: 'the systematic denunciation of bourgeois thought'. On their side, the Surrealists saw in *Clarté* a useful half-way house on their road towards commitment and one which, unlike membership of the PCF, did not deprive them of their independence.

The *Clarté* 'alliance', made up of the Surrealists, the *Clarté* writers, and the 'Philosophers' (Georges Politzer, Pierre Morhange, Henri Lefebvre, Norbert Guterman, and Georges Friedmann) formed a distinct new generation of communist adherents. They differed greatly from the original post-war intellectual sympathizers with the October Revolution, such as Barbusse, Romain Rolland, Anatole France, Marcel Martinet, and Paul Vaillant-Couturier.

[3] *Clarté*, 30 November 1925.
[4] Georges Charbonnier, *Entretiens avec André Masson* (Paris, 1958), p. 108.

They were emphatically not humanitarians, pacifists, or 'men of good will'. Both the Surrealists and the 'Philosophers' came to communism in the course of an independent spiritual quest. The 'Philosophers', who were pioneer existentialists, rebelled against the idea of an irreducible dualism between the human and the absolute which had been taught them by their Sorbonne professors. They retorted: 'Our thought is earthbound and concrete. It is no longer Thought with a capital T.'[5] One way of making their thought concrete seemed to be to make it political. As for the Surrealists, communism served to give some positive justification to an idealistic revolt which had been turning in a vacuum, propelled only by the energy and passion it consumed. A curious feature common to these novice fellow-travellers was their lack of confidence in the revolutionary will of the French proletariat. They wrote of the 'sickening passivity' of the working class and its contentment with a few wretched improvements in its standard of living. As Marcel Martinet pointed out, it was grotesque for self-styled Marxists to express contempt for the one and only instrument of the social revolution. The reason was that this second generation had not digested the materialism in the Marxist equation. They had come to communism, as one of their number, Roger Vailland, admitted, to save their souls.[6]

Nevertheless, it seemed at first that the *Clarté* alliance would earn the blessing of the PCF. Its inaugural manifesto, 'La Révolution d'abord et toujours', was welcomed by Albert Treint in *L'Humanité* (21 September 1925), where the presence of several Clartéists on the staff guaranteed an initial friendly reception. Lunacharsky, the Soviet Commissar for Education, gave his approval:

The Surrealists have rightly understood that the task of all revolutionary intellectuals under a capitalist regime is to denounce bourgeois values. Their efforts deserve to be encouraged.[7]

On 19 October, the alliance proved its courage by republishing on its own responsibility a text titled 'Aux soldats et aux marins', which called on the troops in Morocco to fraternize with the Riffs and which had earned its original authors arrest and imprisonment.

5 Henri Lefebvre, 'La Pensée et l'esprit', *L'Esprit*, May 1926.
6 Marcel Martinet, 'Contre le Courant', *Europe*, 15 May 1926; Roger Vailland, *Drôle de Jeu* (Paris, 1961), p. 21.
7 Quoted by Clement Vautel in *Le Journal*, 1 January 1928.

From September 1925 until the following March, writers from the alliance such as Péret, Victor Crastre, and Marcel Noll dominated the cultural pages of *L'Humanité*.

The break-up of the alliance began in the spring of 1926 after *La Guerre Civile*, the projected review in which the groups hoped to pool their resources and set forth their revolutionary position, failed to appear. No real cohesion or ideological agreement had been forthcoming. The contributions of each to the reviews of the others always seemed incongruous. As Marcel Fourrier put it: 'To tell the truth, a lot went on between individuals but practically nothing collectively.' Determined to preserve the autonomy of Surrealism, Breton had refused to accept the replacement of *La Révolution Surréaliste* by the new review. Differences of temperament and formation had also played their part, the imaginative effervescence of the Surrealists never finding harmony with the stolid seriousness of the journalists.

In January 1927, five of the Surrealists: Breton, Aragon, Eluard, Péret, and Pierre Unik, applied for membership of the PCF. In 'Au Grand Jour', the five explained that they wanted to give final proof of the sincerity of their communist convictions which were still an object of distrust within the party, and to dispel the ambiguities of their fellow-traveller status. They had long believed that the Hegelian dialectic was the key to the resolution of conflicts in the real world and that Hegelianism found its own historical resolution in Marxism. This logic, they said, brought them face to face with the communist party to which, as Surrealists, they had no alternative to offer.[8] They felt bound to lend their full support to the party whose leaders were harassed and imprisoned by Chiappe and Tardieu, the party which Sarraut had identified as 'the vanguard of an Asian movement against Europe'.

The welcome offered by the PCF to the Surrealists was not a warm one. Breton was summoned five times before its Control Commission and asked to explain why he still needed to call himself a Surrealist now that he had become a communist. The contents of *La Révolution Surréaliste* caused consternation and moral outrage among his interrogators. Despite Breton's promise to change the review's equivocal title and to make other concessions, the persecution of the five did not cease after they had been allocated to their respective party cells. They all beat a hasty retreat

[8] Maurice Nadeau, *op. cit.* pp. 97–109.

when Breton, who found himself posted among the gas-workers in the rue Lafayette, was asked to make a statistical report on the state of that industry in Italy. 'I couldn't do it', he confessed.[9]

It is ironical that it was precisely those characteristics in the communist party of the later twenties which had impressed the Surrealists that caused the PCF to give them the cold shoulder. The party's 'gauchisme', for instance, which led it to refuse any kind of cooperation with the socialist leaders and which the Surrealists admired as fine revolutionary intransigence, or the noisy invective of a Jacques Doriot singing the 'Carmagnole' in front of Ministers of State – all these went hand in hand with 'ouvrièrisme', an instinctive hostility to intellectuals whom the workers' party held responsible for its own troubled birth. The party had been completely 'bolshevized'. It was now unquestioningly obedient to orders from Moscow and about to enter its notorious 'third period'. Under the shady direction of the Barbé-Célor faction, it showed less interest in militancy than in the imposition of strict internal discipline and the stifling of all criticism and ideological argument.

Whatever the intellectual shortcomings of the party may have been, the communists had ample enough grounds for being suspicious of the Surrealists, whose record of ideological vicissitudes in the previous three years was hardly a recommendation for reliability – and the communists had not forgotten Aragon's quip about 'doddering Moscow'. Nor could they ignore the comfortable bourgeois origins of the majority of the Surrealists. In general the communists believed that Surrealist writing and art had no appeal to the masses and that their social activity suffered for the sake of their premature artistic experiments. Anticipating charges later made by Sartre, Pierre Naville, himself a former Surrealist, argued that Surrealist speculation about the mind at a time when it was conditioned by innumerable social factors all of which would be changed by the revolution, suggested that they believed in some form of spiritual liberation anterior to and independent of the abolition of bourgeois conditions of life.[10] Ilya Ehrenburg affirmed quite simply that the Surrealists used their vaunted revolutionary activities as a cloak for immorality; but the proletariat was not deceived.[11]

9 André Breton, *Second Manifeste* (Paris, 1930).

10 Pierre Naville, *La Révolution et les Intellectuels. Que Peuvent faire les Surréalistes?* (Paris, 1926), pp. 29–31.

11 Ilya Ehrenburg, *Vus par un écrivain de l'URSS* (Paris, 1934), pp. 55, 64.

The Surrealists themselves never made it very clear what functions they could fulfil once they were admitted to the party. They complained that the communists would not use the talents they had to offer, yet it is difficult to see what purpose these talents could have served apart from a purely Surrealist one – and the five stressed the fact that they were joining the party as ordinary individuals and not as Surrealists. They did not conceal their ignorance of economics and Breton behaved as if he had been insulted when he was asked to compile the Italian gas industry report. They were unwilling to take on the journalistic work offered by the party press. Breton had told Marcel Fourrier quite bluntly: 'Literary work is dirty work such as we have never undertaken in any circumstances.' The only task they were prepared to accept, and which they claimed was their special duty, was the defence of the 'moral truth' of the revolutionary cause. To quote Maxime Alexandre: 'In politics, it is our duty to watch over the moral implications of the revolution with all the energy we can summon up.' To a political party concerned first and foremost with the mobilization of the working class and the day-to-day problems of running a mass movement, a proposition of this kind was totally unacceptable. It was clear that such a moral guardianship was more likely to devote its energies to finding fault with the party itself than with its enemies.

The Surrealists' entry into the PCF thus remained a gesture only and one that was not repeated. Relations with the party were not broken off, however. For the next six years, writes Jacques Fauvet, 'un équilibre qui tourne parfois en équilibrisme s'instaure entre eux et le parti'.[12] The Surrealists were waiting patiently, said Breton in the *Second Manifesto* of 1930, for the better days when the militants would recognize their own.

From 1927 to 1933, Surrealist political activity, apart from attendance at strike meetings, demonstrations on behalf of Sacco and Vanzetti, and the physical 'correction' of slanderers of the Soviet Union, took the form of pamphleteering – in the pages of *La Révolution Surréaliste*, in its successor *Le Surréalisme au service de la Révolution*, in numerous tracts and in books such as Aragon's *Traité du Style* (1928), René Crevel's *Le Clavecin de Diderot* (1932),

[12] Jacques Fauvet, *Histoire du Parti Communiste Français*, vol. 1 (Paris, 1963), p. 100.

and Benjamin Péret's *Je ne mange pas de ce pain-là* (1934). The Surrealists denounced each successive ministry of the Third Republic, saving their most savage insults for Poincaré, Paul-Boncour, and Tardieu. They claimed to be unable to distinguish between the condition of Italy under Mussolini and of France 'where the cop is king'. They vilified the army and reactionary ex-servicemen's organizations. They condemned colonialism and racial discrimination, and helped in the preparation of the PCF's riposte to the Colonial Exhibition of 1931. But in the early thirties, their campaign against the church and religion eclipsed all the rest. As Crevel put it: 'For a revolutionary intellectual of bourgeois origin, there can be no revolutionary activity without anti-religious activity.'[13] They praised the splendid example set by Russia, where hundreds of churches were dynamited or turned into workers' clubs. From fascism, bourgeois mores, capital punishment, the press, lunatic asylums, to professional sport; the objects of Surrealist polemics paralleled those in the communist party but in range extended far beyond them, finding targets in every section of the superstructure.

Surrealist pamphleteering was predominantly destructive because Surrealist politics remained what they had been from the beginning: the politics of protest. Satire and insult were its main weapons. It proceeded by contradiction and not by argument. It was haphazard and undisciplined, shifting its ground from one phrase to the next. Its tone was invariably violent and tended to swing feverishly between the outraged and the outrageous. It expressed unmistakably the political views of poets – of idealists impatient beyond all endurance at the failure of the real to emulate the imaginable. It reflected an Olympian view of the problems of society: indifferent to all that lay between the poetic image and the Absolute, pitiless towards human weakness, and inexorable in its condemnation of compromise. The technique of Surrealist political writing was also that of poets. When it adopted the verse form, it did not become satire pure and simple, nor did it deteriorate into 'poésie de circonstance'. Its sources were in automatism rather than in dialectical materialism.

A striking series of contrasts may be drawn between communist propaganda and the Surrealist literature of protest. While the former was addressed to those who might one day make the revolution, the latter was written for its potential victims. The Surrealists' aim

13 René Crevel, *Les Pieds dans le Plat* (Paris, 1933), p. 277.

was to demoralize their readers and to provoke a class-betrayal on the model of their own. As René Crevel wrote of his most recent book: 'I don't care to see *Êtes-Vous Fous?* as anything more than a modest contribution to public demoralization.' While the communists interpreted contemporary events in the light of the inevitable economic collapse of capitalism, the Surrealists exposed the moral and cultural symptoms of the same *débâcle*. Communist theory explained the substructure of the social system and the Surrealists denounced and ridiculed the decrepit superstructure. They sought not so much to convince as to move – not so much to argue the cause of a particular programme as to arouse the feeling of revolt and to prompt the demand that *something* must be done. While the communists instructed the proletariat in the strategy of revolution, the Surrealists were trying to bring about the emotional climate in which the revolution might break out.

Spasmodic demonstrations and pamphleteering did not solve the fundamental problem of effectiveness. As communists outside the party, the Surrealists' only *raison d'être* could be that the dissemination of their ideas in some way hastened the advent of the revolution. Yet their scanty finances compelled them to publish their works in limited editions which were bought mainly by bibliophiles. The average circulation of their reviews was only 2000, and the quality of their audience as dubious as its size was small. By 1930, there was no escaping the truth of Aragon's warning: 'The snobs are here'.[14] Certain elements in Surrealism – its taste for scandal, for blasphemy, for the bizarre and the erotic – attracted the anarchistic and bohemian set among the aristocracy and bourgeoisie. This unwanted public sought to detach the artistic aspects of Surrealism from their moral and implicitly revolutionary base.

To these threats to neutralize their revolt, the Surrealists replied by enforcing a rigid self-discipline and by eliminating everything in their works that could provide an excuse for misinterpretation. Breton decided to purge the group of those adherents who were seeking to exploit for their own ends the artistic techniques that Surrealism had discovered and those whose revolt was sentimental, anarchistic, or a pretence. In February 1929 an ultimatum in the form of a circular letter was sent out to 70 members of the group asking them what form of collective enterprise they were prepared

14 Louis Aragon, 'Introduction à 1930', *La Révolution Surréaliste*, 15 December 1929.

to collaborate in. Many of the addressees did not reply. Some, like Antonin Artaud, who had already been expelled, thought that the social revolution was irrelevant to the problems which Surrealism had originally made its own and that the human condition was incapable of improvement by social means. Others, like Philippe Soupault, refused to submit to a Surrealist discipline after having joined the group with the express intention of escaping that imposed on them by their families in their youth. By the end of 1929, Jean Miro, Robert Desnos, Roger Vitrac, André Masson, Michel Leiris, and Raymond Queneau among many others had been banished or had left the group of their own accord.

The extreme bitterness of these internal disputes reflected the habits of a PCF cell rather than of a literary group. Votes of confidence and interrogations of members were universal characteristics of revolutionary organizations such as the Surrealists aspired to become. At the Bar du Château reunion in March, in their reception of the young *Grand Jeu* group, Breton and Aragon adopted inquisitorial techniques, and a sectarian vocabulary and ritual identical with those of which they had themselves been the victims at the hands of the PCF Control Commission only two years before.

Breton's efforts to make Surrealism an effective revolutionary force while maintaining its independence by steering a course between the Scylla of assimilation into the art world and the Charybdis of absorption by the communist party, caused casualties on the left of the group as well as on the right. The most serious defections occurred in 1932 when Aragon, Luis Buñuel, Georges Sadoul, Maxime Alexandre, and Pierre Unik left the group for the party. Under the influence of Mayakovsky and Elsa Triolet, whom he had met in 1928, and of his experiences in Russia at the Kharkov Conference of Revolutionary Writers in 1930, Aragon had rejoined the PCF; he became editor of *La Lutte Antireligieuse*, and was encouraged by Maurice Thorez to undertake progressively more responsible work for the party. He was also subject to increasing moral pressure to break with the Surrealists. On 5 January 1932, *L'Humanité* announced the founding of the 'Association des Ecrivains Révolutionnaires' (AER), which would be open only to intellectuals who were already party members. Such regulations might have been deliberately calculated to disunite the Surrealists, some of whom were practising PCF members and some not.

Matters came to a head when Aragon was prosecuted for sedition on account of his most unsurrealistic propaganda poem 'Front Rouge'. The Surrealists rallied to his defence and distributed a petition which soon gathered over two hundred signatures, including those of many prominent poets, novelists, painters, and musicians. The terms of one paragraph of this petition suggested that the Surrealists expected all poetry, no matter how subversive its implications, to be immune from legal proceedings. Romain Rolland, André Gide, Jules Romains, and Roger Martin du Gard refused to sign the petition, believing that the Surrealists were trying to shirk their responsibilities now that they were threatened with serious retaliation from the regime. Breton was in fact restating a point made in the *Manifesto* of 1924, that the Surrealist poet was a mere 'recording machine' of the voice of his unconscious for the utterances of which he could not be held legally or morally liable. Though this may have been true of much Surrealist writing, it was clearly irrelevant in the case of 'Front Rouge', which was a very deliberately composed *poème de circonstance* and as such an example of a genre abominated by the Surrealists. As the affair progressed, it became less a matter of defending Aragon from prosecution than of defending the Surrealist conception of poetry against those who, in Breton's opinion, were prepared to sacrifice the integrity of art to the needs of propaganda. The contradiction in Breton's pamphlet, *Misère de la Poésie*, lay in its attempt to exculpate 'Front Rouge' in the name of an idea of poetry of which this particular work was the very negation. Though Breton may have succeeded in extricating Aragon from the grip of the law, he drove him straight into the arms of the communists. Breton's public critique of the party's policy towards artists, a critique he had long restrained himself from making despite constant provocation from Léon Moussinac and Jean Fréville in *L'Humanité*, forced Aragon to make the choice about which he had been hesitating for the previous twelve months. On 10 March, a note appeared in *L'Humanité*, in the name of the AER, announcing Aragon's disavowal of all connections with the Surrealists and his denunciation of their position as 'objectively counter-revolutionary'.

The 'Aragon affair' revealed a disagreement between communist and Surrealist ideas about the writer's role in the revolutionary struggle that had grown deeper as the era of comparative tolerance towards intellectuals, fostered by Trotsky and Lunacharsky, was superseded in the USSR by that of domination by RAPP, the Association of Proletarian Writers, and of the imposition of the dogma of 'socialist realism' in 1934. Since 1928, Breton had argued that there could be no such thing as a 'proletarian art' under a capitalist regime, and that the culture which developed after the revolution would be classless rather than proletarian – the first 'human' culture. The twentieth-century artist, he affirmed, whether in Russia or the capitalist West, was subject to a determinism imposed by the necessary evolution of art in the recent past as well as to the laws of economic determinism. Both were equally ineluctable and it was from its 'situation' in their framework that the artist's work derived its authenticity.[15] As an example of what he meant by 'une culture résolument libératrice', Breton traced out an artistic tradition which went back through Picasso, Lautréamont, Rimbaud, Borel, Courbet, and Sade, the work of all of whom was at once an attack on the absurdities of the existing social order and a vision of a new world. He claimed that art would lose its authenticity if it was made to serve immediately political ends and adopted an alien subject matter. The revolutionary artist had to preserve his freedom *as* an artist. If not he was likely to be lost not only as an artist but as a revolutionary. By the very fact that art strove to be totally human it was bound to be subversive in a society that was intrinsically inhuman.[16]

Ultimately, the differences between Breton on one side and Aragon and the communists on the other were about the nature of communication. For Breton, a writer's 'meaning' lay in the words he wrote and the intention behind them; their subversive value was latent within them. For Aragon, meaning lay solely in the interpretation made by the reader or by the majority of society at any given time. Once Aragon became convinced of the ineffectiveness of Surrealist protest, he was driven to seek a uniquely social remedy. If words were vain, it was necessary to change the reader or society as a whole. Aragon concluded that unswerving service to the revolution was the writer's first duty not merely for the sake of his ideals as a man but for the sake of the validity of his writing.

The middle thirties, which saw a whole new generation of French

---

[15] André Breton, 'Reply to Enquiry about Proletarian Literature,' *Monde*, 8 September 1929.

[16] André Breton, *La Position Politique du Surréalisme* (Paris, 1935).

intellectuals flocking towards the PCF and its 'front organizations' in recognition of its stand against fascism and its recently adopted 'Popular Front' strategy, coincided with the growing disillusionment of the Surrealists. They had joined the AER, now re-christened the Association des Ecrivains et Artistes Révolutionnaires (AEAR), when it was partially liberalized by Vaillant-Couturier following Stalin's dissolution of the sectarian RAPP, on which it had been modelled. Breton and his friends edited tracts, helped to judge a workers' poetry competition, and did their share of routine work in the organization. But harmony was short-lived. Breton found himself voting regularly with the minority at committee meetings. He was called to answer for articles in the Surrealist review, and it was one of these, a letter from Ferdinand Alquié deriding the puritanism of Soviet society, that led to the expulsion of all the Surrealists, save Crevel and Tzara, from both the Association and the PCF in July 1933.

By now the Surrealists had given up their pretence of the twenties that the Russian Revolution had not yet said its last word. They were no longer reluctant to voice their disappointment with the social pattern that was emerging in the Soviet Union. The suicides of Essenin and Mayakovsky were evidence that the atmosphere in Russia was profoundly uncongenial to poetry and spiritually barren because, as the Surrealists put it, the problem of material necessity had been allowed to ride roughshod over human necessity. They were appalled by the communists' obsession with material productivity and by the premium they put on the virtues of industry. Before the picture of Russia presented by Soviet propaganda, Breton found it difficult to avoid the reaction: 'Ce n'est que cela!'[17]

The communists' reversal in May 1934 of the 'class against class' strategy with which they had persevered for the previous six years further alienated the Surrealists, who saw the decision to co-operate with the socialist leaders in the Popular Front as a treacherous concession to the bourgeois democratic system. Another blow was the Stalin-Laval pact of mutual assistance in the spring of 1935. This volte-face, after years of propaganda about imperialist war-mongering against the workers' fatherland, meant that French communists were virtually ordered to put an end to their attacks

[17] André Breton, *Les Vases Communicants* (Paris, 1932), p. 169.

on the national military build-up and jettison the watchword of 'revolutionary defeatism' which had first attracted the Surrealists to communism at the time of the Moroccan War. It seemed to them that the aims of the International were being sacrificed for the sake of the security of the Russian state, and that the latter was behaving with the selfish cynicism of any bourgeois regime.

The Surrealists' final repudiation of Stalinist communism came in the summer of 1935 and was occasioned by a cultural rather than a political issue. Breton was deprived of his right to speak at the International Congress of Writers for the Defence of Culture (as a punishment for boxing the ears of the visiting Russian delegate, Ilya Ehrenburg). René Crevel committed suicide on the eve of the Congress after vain efforts to get this right restored to Breton. In the pamphlet *Du Temps que les Surréalistes avaient raison*, the group gave free rein to their long pent-up anger about the Congress, the recent Pact, socialist realism, the Stalinist personality cult, and communist party intolerance. The pamphlet ended with the words: 'Ce régime, ce chef, nous ne pouvons que leur signifier formellement notre défiance.'

The break did not mean that the Surrealists ceased to participate in politics. (The group is still politically active to this day.) In the later thirties, they were prominent anti-fascists, sent some of their number to serve the Republic in Spain, formed two ephemeral revolutionary organizations: Contre-Attaque and the Fédération Internationale des Artistes Révolutionnaires Indépendants (FIARI), and established close relations with the Trotskyists. Nevertheless from 1935 onwards it was clear that they had failed to achieve the three reconciliations referred to at the beginning of this article. They could no longer associate the cause of 'spiritual revolution' with that of international communism, the only credible agent of social revolution. The group's artistic and political activities were definitively separated. Lacking their own review after 1933, they had begun to contribute to fine art magazines such as *Minotaure* or to friendly literary periodicals, while the only outlets for their politics were sporadic tracts drawn up in response to particular events. As the notoriety of the movement became international and as one exhibition of Surrealist painting succeeded another, the plea that it was essentially different from other avantgarde 'isms' became increasingly difficult to sustain. Ideological rigour in the group had relaxed to such a degree that even Salvador Dali, who did not hide his fondness for Hitler and Franco, was tolerated until the eve of the war. Except in rare instances, political action arose from individual rather than collective initiatives. The Surrealists' main preoccupation was now the defence of art's independence against the only political movement they had believed in. The intellectual unity which Breton had struggled to maintain for so long was shattered. Not only had the Surrealists to reconcile themselves to a division of labour between those whose watchword was 'change life' and those who worked to 'transform the world'; they had to face the fact that, in the political circumstances of the time, these two forces were working in diametrically opposite directions.

Although it was ostensibly the particular character that communism assumed under Stalin that accounted for these setbacks, there were many other factors that would have prevented any lasting association between the Surrealists and the militants. The Surrealist argument, for instance, that the common roots of both Surrealism and Marxism in the Hegelian dialectic would make them readily conciliable was highly dubious. On the philosophical plane, the Surrealists grossly distorted their original ideas in order to make them acceptable to the Marxists. Jules Monnerot writes of the unfortunate efforts they made to fit themselves into 'a sort of pseudo-Hegelian orthopoedic apparatus'.[18] It was these efforts which explain the misuse or excessive use of Marxist jargon in Surrealist works. They recited the rubrics of Marxism-Leninism like a catechism. They swallowed down the bitter pill of materialist determinism even though, as taught by contemporary communists, it involved a dualism of the kind which it was the avowed aim of Surrealism to surmount. The sincere will to believe was not sufficient to bring faith. Surrealist Marxism was condemned either to remain superficial or to distort Surrealism more profoundly. To quote Breton: 'Personally, the violence that I had to inflict on myself did not enable me to toe the line for very long.'[19]

The Surrealist conception of the mechanism of revolution was different from that of the Marxists. In order to justify Surrealist artistic and psychological speculation in the name of revolutionary

[18] Jules Monnerot, *La Poésie Moderne et le Sacré* (Paris, 1945), p. 76.
[19] André Breton, *Entretiens* (Paris, 1952), pp. 69–70.

utility, Breton was compelled to stress the relative independence of the superstructure and to play down the effects of materialist determinism. He made extensive use of Engels' letter to Joseph Bloch to this effect. Only if the superstructure was independent to some degree could the Surrealists demand that art *should* be free. For this demand presupposed that art *could* be free. If their position was compatible with the ideas of Marx and Engels, it was not so with those of Lenin, who rejected the possibility of any kind of liberation within the terms of the existing substructure since such a hypothesis would make its overthrow less urgent. Breton claimed, on the contrary, that greater awareness of the unused and stifled potentialities of man would make the demand for revolution still more urgent. Psychological awareness would fortify social awareness. Changing the picture which men had of the laws governing the world would make still more necessary the transformation of the substructure. The existing social order, far from being an insuperable barrier beyond which, if it was finally broken down, lay a land where all man's problems would be solved, was for the Surrealists no more than a fragile screen standing between man and the real problems which he had yet to face. Furthermore, unless the business of the 'interpretation of man' went on simultaneously with that of the 'transformation of the world', there was every likelihood that the social order finally emerging from the revolution would not be very different from the one that had been destroyed.

There was a crucial difference between the ends envisaged by Surrealists and by Marxists. If both saw the revolution as the prelude to the founding of a world based on the desires of men, their ideas about the content of these desires were not the same. For the Marxists they were material while for the Surrealists they were primarily subjective and spiritual. The resulting human 'goods' in the view of the latter would be individual rather than social. The joys of 'la poésie faite par tous' would be experienced in privacy even when they were accessible to all. As André Masson remarked: 'What is Surrealism if not the collective experience of individualism?'

The Surrealists set little store by the economic effects of the revolution and by the remedying of social injustice. They were more deeply offended by the stupidity and presumption of the ruling classes than moved by the sufferings of the victims of exploitation. The *idea* of social injustice repelled them far more than its real effects. Paul Eluard once confessed:

For my part I don't love the wretched, not in the least. I don't feel any love for the man I come across begging at the entrance to the Metro. It revolts me, I think it absurd and disgraceful that things can be so. But I feel no pity, no love.[20]

In *Nadja*, Breton declared that it was not the misery of the workers that disposed him in their favour but the vigour of their protest against it.

The Surrealist revolution was conceived, in effect, on a different plane of experience from that of the Marxists. A new 'October' was envisaged as the prelude to the 'changing of life' rather than as an organic element in it. Only the ambiguous definitions of the word 'revolution' permitted the prolonged Surrealist misunderstanding that there was real common ground between their aims and those of the Marxists. Their own Marxism could never be more than a 'placage', a flimsy façade tacked on to a philosophy that was different in kind. Their attempt to unite the two meant either the tortured readjustment of Surrealist ideas or the forcible addition to Marxism of ideas that had no place in it. Both alternatives were tried and found impracticable.

If the Marxism of the Surrealists was a 'placage', then their joining the communist party, as Pierre Drieu La Rochelle had been the first to warn them,[21] was a coincidence rather than an intellectual and moral necessity. The stalwarts of the PCF Central Committee had more reason to be suspicious of the Surrealists' adherence than that of other intellectuals, since the former had a private revolutionary purpose while the latter, on the whole, did not. The Surrealists' role, ostensibly artistic but refusing to be qualified as such, apparently not political but demanding to be considered as such, made negotiations fruitless. The communists did not want adherents who already identified themselves either as writers or as revolutionaries, but only individuals who were prepared to serve as the party required them. Unlike other fellow-travellers, the Surrealists were conspicuously resistant to what David Caute calls 'the law of compensations', according to which intellectuals who began to support the communists on one issue

[20] Jean Duval, 'Avec Paul Eluard', *Europe*, November–December 1962.
[21] Pierre Drieu La Rochelle, 'Troisième Lettre aux Surréalistes', *Les Derniers Jours*, 8 July 1927.

usually came to support them on all points. The Surrealists, as we have seen, jealously maintained their right to freedom of criticism within the party and outside it.

Their stress on the maintenance of the moral rigour of the revolutionary ideal is perhaps the key to their relations with the communists. Such moral rigour was meant to meet a need not only in the communist cause but in Surrealism itself, and its exercise was to be in two directions rather than one. First, and most obviously, the Surrealists claimed to watch over the ideals represented by the communist revolution. Secondly, and no less important, the communist revolution was required to act as a guarantor of the real effectiveness of Surrealism. It is for this latter reason that the political history of Surrealism leaves the impression that the Surrealists were using communism for ends of their own. Communism was their shield against absorption by the Paris literary and artistic world, against a decline into dilettantism and bohemia. It seems that, rather than looking forward to the prospects of sustained commitment within the party or its subsidiary organizations, the Surrealists were always looking back over their shoulders to see the effects of their step on their own group and its situation in the cultural scene. Communism was at the furthest remove from aestheticism; it set the seal on an intellectual revolt which the bourgeoisie persisted in not taking seriously. It is noticeable that questions of political principle were invariably raised by André Breton at moments when the group seemed to be on the point of yielding to the temptations of artistic irresponsibility, individualism, and gratuitousness. At these moments the degree of political commitment of its members was taken as the test of their integrity as Surrealists. Communism was thus the touchstone by which to judge the health of Surrealism. It offered a means of maintaining discipline and cohesion in the group which would have been most difficult if Surrealism had remained completely unpolitical. But communism could be a touchstone only so long as the Surrealists were outside the party. Hence the perpetual game of advance and retreat which was endemic to the group's relations with communism. Breton's movement derived its very existence from the tension, in constant need of readjustment, between the world of art and the party of the proletariat.

It may be that the term 'politics' when applied to Surrealism is a misnomer. The Surrealists seldom advanced beyond the stage of political *agitation*, since they rejected or were incapable of the sustained application which commitment demanded. Breton was the first to confess, to Pierre Naville, this lack of concentration:

You know the degree to which we are the slaves of impatience. The slightest delay in the achievement of something which we've regarded once and for all as inevitable affects us far more than some other much more serious defeat.

Time and time again they took up a political cause with fire and enthusiasm, pursued it for a while and then let it drop, leaving to others the spadework which could alone lead to any real achievement. The very diversity of the action which they defended as serving the revolution makes one suspect its relative importance. They frequently maintained that, under the existing regime, all kinds of behaviour – interrupting meetings, raiding newspaper-offices, insulting priests and soldiers – was of revolutionary value. They never showed satisfactorily, however, that this kind of action possessed an effectiveness equal to that of the militants whom they refused to join. It seems that they committed themselves to little tasks in order to avoid commitment to bigger ones.

Perseverance in any single line of political action would ultimately have been contrary to the very spirit of Surrealism. In the simplest terms: action, which was relative and contingent, was bound to betray the Surreal, which was absolute. Prolonged action belittled or infringed the global nature of Surrealist desires. Agitation, on the other hand, by virtue of its ephemeral character and constant susceptibility to change (it could be taken up and abandoned at will), seemed to escape these limitations. It did not contradict what Julien Gracq calls Breton's 'manie cavalière et intriguante de s'absenter'.[22] It provided a compromise, however disappointing in its final results, in answer to the cruel dichotomy between an end which promised every release (the revolution) and the means which demanded every discipline (militant communism).

Despite all their declarations to the contrary, it still remains uncertain whether the Surrealists ever chose definitely between the alternative means of saving the human spirit: rescuing it from the world of reality (a metaphysical or 'religious' solution), or creating a new reality in which it could flourish (a social and political solution). In the *Second Manifesto*, Breton referred to 'the supreme

[22] Julien Gracq, *André Breton* (Paris, 1948), p. 202.

24

irony which applies to everything including political regimes'. Apparently the Surrealists, even in the period of their greatest political activity, never lost their original pessimism or their awareness of the eternal gap between the aspirations of man and his achievements. Such intrinsic pessimism did not stop them believing in the necessity to struggle for reform, but it did make them strangers to the single-minded optimism that was the strength of the communist militants.

If these are some of the explanations of the failure of Surrealist attempts at active participation in politics, they do not invalidate the fundamental aims of the Surrealist adventure or detract from its unique interest. The Surrealists' demands for a society based on the psychological needs and desires of mankind rather than imposed by the dictates of utility, logic, and mindless economic determination, are still profoundly relevant. So too are their efforts to overcome the divorce between the artist and society and to improve the spiritual quality of life. The Surrealists, says André Masson, had to *dream* politically or cease to be. But they were unable at the same time to *act* politically. Perhaps it is unjust to blame them for this failure. As Victor Crastre writes, and his remarks about Breton may be applied to the Surrealists as a whole:

The debate between politics and mysticism is an eternal one: the pure revolutionary and the creator of new social forms are never the same man . . . The man who combined the two vocations would be a sort of monster (of perfection). From this point of view what might be considered as Breton's failure has been on the contrary the condition of his salvation.[23]

[23] Victor Crastre, 'André Breton et la Liberté', in Marc Eigeldinger, *Essais et Témoignages à André Breton* (Neuchâtel, 1950).

The Front Populaire—After Thirty Years

James Joll

On 14 July 1935 a mass meeting was held in the Buffalo Stadium at Montrouge on the outskirts of Paris. It was under the auspices of the Communists, Socialists, Radicals, CGT, and a number of other political groups, and it marked in effect the launching of the Front Populaire. The proceedings ended with an oath 'to remain united to defend democracy, to disarm and dissolve the factious leagues, to place our liberties out of reach of fascism. We swear', the oath continued 'on this day which reminds us of the first victory of the Republic, to defend the democratic liberties conquered by the people of France, to give to the workers bread, to the young people work, and to the world a great human peace'. And in the afternoon a crowd, estimated by the police at 100,000 strong, marched in procession from the Bastille to the Cours de Vincennes.

The foundation of the Popular Front raised hopes and fears which were to increase over the next year; and the Fourteenth of July celebrations a year later, in 1936, were a festival that seemed to mark the triumph of the Front Populaire, though it was a triumph soon to turn to disappointment. In the thirty years since July 1935, the aims, achievements, and failures of the Popular Front have not ceased to be the subject of lively controversy, while the character and policies of its leader, Léon Blum, continue to interest both politicians and historians. For some Léon Blum was one of those responsible for the defeat of 1940 – *L'homme qui a sapé l'armée française*', as Marshal Pétain called him.[1] For others the government of the Front Populaire marked the first stage of an overdue social revolution in France, the effects of which are still being felt. On the left, Blum and his government have been criticized by writers such as Colette Audry and Daniel

[1] J. R. Tournoux, *Pétain et de Gaulle* (Paris, 1964), p. 166.

27

Guérin[2] for missing the chance of making a true revolution and for selling out at a crucial moment – from cowardice or from an over-scrupulous regard for constitutional niceties. Again, the record of the Front Populaire has been examined by those wishing to point out the dangers of any cooperation with the communists, and its history is still influential in the attempts to produce a candidate of the left as an alternative to General de Gaulle.

However, although the brief period of Léon Blum's government – a bare twelve months from June 1936 to June 1937 – remains a topic for political controversy, we have seen in the last few years a revival of more strictly academic interest in the events of the 1930s. This is indeed an international phenomenon; but in France especially, the period of the Front Populaire illustrates perhaps more vividly than any other the forces at work in the Third Republic and provides material for an analysis, the scope of which extends beyond the single year of Blum's government or even the two preceding years during which the Front Populaire was being formed. Thus, to name only a few of the studies published in the last few years, we have had a full-length history of the Front Populaire by the veteran socialist historian, M. Georges Lefranc, a study of the elections of 1936 by M. Dupeux, and a remarkable investigation by M. Antoine Prost[3] of the strength, distribution, and structure of the French trade union movement at the time of the Front Populaire. Abroad, Professor Joel Colton, Professor Ehrmann, and Professor von Albertini have studied important aspects of the period, while Professor Gilbert Ziebura of the Free University of Berlin has published the first volume of a massive and exhaustive biography of Léon Blum.[4] At the same time, more source material is becoming available; Léon Blum's own articles and speeches from this period have been reprinted in the latest volumes of L'Oeuvre de Léon Blum,[5] while Professor Renouvin is

[2] Colette Audry, *Léon Blum ou la Politique du Juste* (Paris, 1955); Daniel Guérin, *Front Populaire – Révolution manquée* (Paris, 1963).

[3] Georges Lefranc, *Histoire du Front Populaire* (Paris, 1965); Georges Dupeux, *Le Front Populaire et les Elections de 1936* (Paris, 1959); Antoine Prost, *La CGT à l'Epoque du Front Populaire* (Paris, 1964).

[4] e.g. Joel Colton, 'Léon Blum and the French Socialists as a Government Party', *Journal of Politics*, XV, 1953/4; H. W. Ehrmann, 'The Blum Experiment and the Fall of France', *Foreign Affairs*, 1941; Rudolf von Albertini, 'Zur Beurteilung der Volksfront in Frankreich (1934–1938)', *Vierteljahrshefte für Zeitgeschichte*, February 1959; Gilbert Ziebura, *Léon Blum*, vol. i (Berlin, 1963).

[5] *L'Oeuvre de Léon Blum*, 1934–7, 1937–40 (Paris, 1964, 1965).

engaged on selecting for publication the Foreign Ministry documents of the 1930s, some of which have already appeared.

In this paper I want to look at some of the questions raised by these re-assessments of the Popular Front and to discuss briefly what it achieved and why it failed. First, then, a word about the origins of the Front Populaire. Who wanted what from it, and why did the groups which adhered to it do so?[6] Perhaps the most important thing to remember about the Popular Front is how much it owed to a movement of the working class from below.[7] Just as in an earlier crucial period for the French socialist movement – the years immediately after the first world war – there was a rush to join working-class organizations. Thus in the years 1934–7 trade union membership increased from 755,000 to nearly four million. It is hard to evaluate the different reasons for this activity; the economic situation is obviously the most important, when France was feeling the effects of the world crisis just at the moment when the other industrial countries of the world were emerging from it; and, as M. Prost has suggested, it was in those industries where work was casual, unskilled, and unstable that the greatest militancy was to be found. Again, the general political situation was alarming; in Germany and Austria the socialist movement had been totally defeated in 1933 and 1934; in Spain in 1934, the Asturias miners had been savagely repressed by the new Republic; and in France itself the political crisis of the early months of 1934 had led to the riots of 6 February which, even if, as Professor Beloff has shown,[8] they were not a fascist attempt at a coup d'état, were nevertheless widely believed to have been so. Finally, the movement towards a popular front and a more militant attitude created its own momentum, so that by the spring of 1936 there was a genuine and widespread belief that, as Marceau Pivert, the leader of the revolutionary left in the Socialist Party, exultantly put it, *'Tout est possible!'*[9]

6 For a more detailed discussion, see James Joll, 'The Making of the Popular Front', in *The Decline of the Third Republic*, ed. J. Joll, *St. Antony's Papers*, No. 5 (London, 1959); and John T. Marcus, *French Socialism in the Crisis Years* (New York, 1958).

7 See especially Arthur Mitzman, 'The French Working Class and the Blum Government', *International Review of Social History*, 1964.

8 Max Beloff, 'The Sixth of February', *St. Antony's Papers*, No. 5.

9 Marceau Pivert, 'Tout est possible', *Populaire de Paris*, cf. G. Lefranc, *op. cit.* pp. 450–3.

Without this impetus from below, the movement towards unity and a popular front in the weeks and months after February 1934 would never have been successful. Many of the socialist leaders were hesitant, and one often has the impression that they were in the position of Ledru-Rollin in the revolution of 1848, *'Je suis leur chef; il faut que je les suive'* – or, as Léon Blum himself said in June 1935, *'Pour animer les masses, il faut montrer aux masses que vous êtes des animateurs'*.[10] The socialist leaders were in fact in a difficult position, which was to remain fundamentally unchanged throughout the next three years. They had not long emerged from a painful crisis which had led to the splitting off of the Neo-Socialists, that curious grouping of old reformists like Renaudel with men on the way to fascism such as Déat and Marquet, who wanted to substitute, as Blum put it, 'authority and order' for 'liberty and justice' as the party's watchword.[11]

Even though the long-term parliamentary effects of the split were not very grave, there was, from 1934 on, a potential threat from the right of the party if the leaders went too far in the direction of a pact with the communists or of a revolutionary programme, while on the left there was, particularly in Paris and its suburbs, a vociferous minority demanding radical measures and immediate unity of the working class. It needed all Blum's political skill and personal prestige to maintain the balance between the two wings, and, of course, once the Popular Front had been formed and Blum had become leader of the government, this balancing act had to take account not only of the different trends in Blum's own party, but also of the different interests and presuppositions of the other groups and parties supporting the government.

Thus Léon Blum, in the long drawn out negotiations with the communists, was always anxious to spell out his position, to make it quite clear to what it was that he was committing himself. He wanted a detailed and specific programme rather than the vague outline which the communists regarded as sufficient, and he was to remain very conscious of the limits within which he would be operating if the Front Populaire once came to power. The socialists, he repeated again and again, were not making a revolution; they were preparing to exercise power within a capitalist and constitutional framework; and, to the rigid distinction which he had

[10] Blum at Mulhouse Congress, 10 June 1935, *Le Populaire*, 11 June 1935.
[11] *La Vie Socialiste*, 24 July 1933. cf. Marcus, *op. cit.* p. 29.

elaborated over the past fifteen years between the conquest of power and the exercise of power, he added the notion of the 'occupation of power' to meet a specific emergency. It was from this subtle but not unrealistic distinction that most of the disagreements with his left-wing critics were to arise.

If the socialist leaders were somewhat reluctantly obliged by pressures from below to move towards association in a common front with the communists, the communist leadership did not, it might be thought, given the rigorous disciplines of the party, have to worry about such considerations. Nevertheless, it is worth noting that, at the moment when the party line switched from unremitting hostility to the socialist leaders to willingness to collaborate with them, one of the communists' most forceful figures, Jacques Doriot, was expelled from the party for having prematurely advocated just this, with, it appeared, considerable response from the rank and file. If the change over to the policy of the Popular Front was not the result of pressure from below, it at any rate coincided with it. In fact, however, it seems likely that the impetus to the change came from the usual source of such switches of line, namely from Moscow. For it was at this moment that Stalin seems to have realized that Hitler had come to stay and that the Soviet Union might have something to gain from a policy of collective security in association with the western powers. On 31 May 1934 – over two months after the first moves from the socialist rank and file for a common anti-fascist front – *L'Humanité* was quoting an article from *Pravda* 'We would be committing a crime against the working class not only by opposing the desire for a common front, but by underestimating it',[12] and going on to approve the idea of negotiations with the socialist leaders. And in August 1935, at the Comintern World Congress, the formal seal of approval was given to the change of tactics and the French communist leader Maurice Thorez was explicitly praised for having 'grasped the need of the hour'.[13]

However, the communist policy involved difficulties. On the one hand, from May 1934 they were working for a common front with the socialists explicitly directed against the government. But, on

[12] Jacques Fauvet, *Histoire du Parti Communiste Français* (Paris, 1964), p. 143.
[13] *VII Congress of The Communist International*. Abridged stenographic report of Proceedings (Moscow, 1939), p. 552.

the other hand, by the early months of 1935 the Soviet government was actively negotiating with the French government for an alliance finally signed on 2 May, and celebrated by a visit to Moscow by Laval, when he obtained from Stalin the notorious declaration that the Soviet leader approved the French government's re-armament programme – a programme of which the French Communist Party had been the severest critic.

The communist interest in joining the Popular Front, therefore, seems to have been twofold. On the one hand, the Front Populaire enabled the French Communist Party to play a large part in directing French opinion towards support for the aims of Soviet foreign policy – an alignment with France in order to resist nazi Germany. But, at the same time, by appearing as the confident leaders of the move towards popular unity, the PCF – as the elections of 1936 and the growth in membership of the CGT, now newly reunited with the communist CGTU, which had been formed some years earlier, were to show – was able to place itself at the head of a mass movement and to win mass support of a kind it had failed to attract in the fifteen years of its existence.

If the socialist leaders somewhat apprehensively embarked on the Popular Front policy because they felt that they must meet the demands for solidarity in the face of fascism, and that the Popular Front might give them a chance for the exercise or the occupation of power and so enable them to put at least part of their programme into practice, and if the communists were anxious to serve Stalin's foreign political aims as well as to stake a claim for the leadership of a growing mass movement, what did the Radicals hope to gain from joining the Popular Front ? Once again their participation was largely the result of the feeling that a party which, in spite of everything, stood for republican liberties, could not afford to dissociate itself from a great popular movement of the left which looked like winning a considerable body of electoral support. Of course, the very looseness of structure of the Radical Party, and the fact that there were always two or three prominent leaders able to adopt different political lines, made it very easy for the Radicals to pursue opportunistic tactics and follow a flexible policy. However, in 1934-5 their freedom of manoeuvre was somewhat limited because one of their most respected leaders, Edouard Herriot, was a member of Doumergue's government and was also to be Minister of State under Laval. Any move to the left, therefore, involved either Herriot's resignation from the government or an unthinkable breach between him and his party.[14]

Herriot himself, like another senior Radical leader, Albert Sarraut, who was actually Prime Minister at the time of the 1936 elections, was firmly opposed to any close alliance with the socialists. The Socialist Party had challenged his position in his own fief of Lyons and had, in 1929, nearly succeeded in shaking his position as virtually permanent Mayor of the city. One of Sarraut's nominees had run against Léon Blum in Narbonne; and relations between radicals and socialists had not been improved by the socialist rejection of radical overtures after the elections of 1932 and after their vote against Daladier's government in October 1933 – an occasion on which, it is reported, Daladier turned white with rage.

However, the crisis of February 1934 had led to a rapprochement between Blum and Daladier, and it was Daladier who, with the support of some of the younger radicals, took the lead in the move towards the left and the Popular Front. The crisis in the party came at the end of 1935, when the pressure on Herriot to leave Laval's government was such that he resigned from the post of president of the party, leaving the way clear for those radicals who were ready to work for the creation of the Popular Front and the drafting of its programme. (After the Blum government was formed, Herriot became President of the Chamber of Deputies and thus the party avoided the problems which his position might have otherwise caused.) The paradox of the radicals' role in the popular front was that in many ways they found it easier to get along with the communists than with the socialists, for the communists' general left-wing slogans, their constant references to the traditions of the revolution and to the need for republican solidarity, were not far from the commonplaces of radical oratory, whereas the dogmatic assertions of the socialists about economic policy and the measures which would be required to restore the French economy were far from the deflationary policies of the radicals. This was demonstrated by the radicals' own programme for the elections of 1936, in which they expressed a desire simultaneously for 'monetary stability, a condition of security indispensable for initiative, and the spirit of enterprise', and for 'a struggle against under-

14 See especially Michel Soulié, *La Vie Politique d'Edouard Herriot* (Paris, 1962), pp. 469–78.

consumption by the increase in the purchasing power of the masses' – an uneasy juxtaposition of traditional radical financial policy with a gesture towards the policies of the Popular Front programme. Indeed, the fact that the radicals were an indispensable component of almost any government of the 1930s and that their differences with their allies on the left were masked but not resolved by appeals to republican solidarity against fascism, was to prove perhaps the most fatal weakness of Léon Blum's government when it eventually took power in June 1936.

In the programme of the Front Populaire published in January 1936, none of its constituent elements got quite all they wanted, but it remained nevertheless a blueprint for fundamental changes in French society and a document that owed much to previous programmes of the Socialist Party. And certainly the elections of April and May, with their high poll, served to demonstrate both the demand for change among the electorate and the effectiveness of the Front Populaire in organizing mutual support among its member parties. That the working-class parties should be successful was perhaps not surprising: but an examination of the electoral results such as that conducted by M. Dupeux seems to show that in many rural areas the electors increased their support for the socialists and even for communist candidates – a measure perhaps of the extent to which the economic crisis had hit peasants and small shopkeepers even harder than it had the working class. And in the rural areas with a strong radical allegiance, the fact that the radicals were now looking to the left was of some importance, though it is significant that, of the parties allied in the Front Populaire, it is the radicals who had the least success.

The agreement between the parties adhering to the Front Populaire to stand down in the second ballot in favour of the Popular Front candidates with the most votes produced problems in practice between the first and the second ballot. In 59 of the 424 constituencies in which there were second ballots, candidates representing Popular Front parties ran against each other, though in the event only six seats were lost as a result of these breaches of discipline, which mostly reflect local rivalries which were too deep-rooted – especially in the case of radicals and socialists – to be forgotten in a mood of new-found solidarity.[15] However, the rifts

[15] G. Dupeux, *op. cit.* pp. 132–4.

revealed by such cases were soon forgotten when it was seen how overwhelmingly the new Chamber was dominated by the Front Populaire, though it was also clear that within the Popular Front itself, the centre of gravity had moved to the left. What was the Front Populaire going to make of this opportunity? Or, as Léon Blum himself is reported to have remarked, 'How can I know how I will do a job I have never done before?'[16]

These questions bring us to the centre of the controversies about the Popular Front and its achievements and failures, but here I want to limit myself to a brief discussion of three aspects of the history of Léon Blum's government – the stay-in strikes which ushered in the new ministry, the dilemma in which the government was placed by the outbreak of the Spanish Civil War, and the extent to which the government's economic and social policies contributed to its fall.

Many years before, Blum had pointed out one of the dangers which would face the socialists if they ever came to 'exercise' power within the existing social and constitutional framework instead of 'conquering' it and so making the revolution. 'The danger of the exercise of power', Blum had told a party conference in 1926, 'is precisely that it may be confused with the conquest of power, so that the proletariat is encouraged to expect from the former the totality of results which can result only from the latter'.[17] In fact, this is just what seems to have happened in 1936. There was, constitutionally, an uneasy pause of some weeks before the newly-elected parliament met and before Blum, as Prime Minister designate, could present his government to the Chamber. Blum refused to accept the views of some of his supporters that he should insist on taking office immediately, regardless of the constitutional situation, and would not recognize a *vacance du pouvoir* created by the elections. The government of Albert Sarraut therefore continued in office till 4 June.

Meanwhile, however, in the second half of May, a great wave of strikes spread throughout France, notable because of the new technique which they employed – that of the stay-in, the occupation of the factories by the workers, who simply remained there instead of going home in the evening. The method seems to have been used first – at Le Havre and at Toulouse – in the course of

16 Geoffrey Fraser and Thadée Natanson, *Léon Blum* (London, 1937), p. 250.
17 *La Revue Socialiste*, nos. 38–39 (1950), p. 60.

ordinary industrial disputes during the second week of May; but when it spread to many key industries in the region of Paris and, perhaps even more dramatically, to the great department stores of the capital, it was clear that the strikers hoped for some total revolutionary change in their whole social and economic situation.

The mood in the factories has often been described – notably in a famous passage by Simone Weil:[18] it was one, nearly all the witnesses are agreed, of happiness, excitement, almost of festivity. But it was also a mood in which, as the left pointed out, anything was possible, even, as Trotsky himself remarked, a new French Revolution. The Blum government took office, that is to say, at a moment of extreme tension, with exaggerated hopes being entertained on the left and perhaps exaggerated fears on the right. The most remarkable thing about the strikes is that they seem to have been genuinely spontaneous in origin, even though inevitably, both at the time and since, people have ascribed them to the machinations of agitators – communists, anarchists, Trotskyists, even fascists aiming at embarrassing the government. Actually, everybody, including the communists and the leaders of the CGT, seem to have been taken by surprise at their extent and efficacity. There were, of course, a few voices raised among the revolutionary left urging the socialist and trade union leaders to make the revolution at once. They believed, as one of their leaders, Marceau Pivert, put it some years later, 'If Blum had wanted, he had only to say the word and workers' and peasants' militias would have sprung up even in the smallest villages'.[19]

However, understandably enough, the main preoccupation of Blum and the trade union leaders was to bring the strike movement back under control. Indeed, on the very first evening the ministers took over their offices – even before their investiture by the Chamber – they were faced with a shortage of bread in Paris unless fuel for the bakeries could be released in time from the occupied fuel oil depots; and it is characteristic that when a leading trade unionist and a representative of the government went to the depot they were hard put to it to establish their credentials, and that, when the strikers had finally agreed to release some fuel oil, they did so only on condition that it was fetched in civilian trucks and not in the army lorries which were waiting ready, and that they

[18] Simone Weil, *La Condition Ouvrière* (Paris, 1951), pp. 168–74.
[19] D. Guérin, *Front Populaire* (Paris, 1963), p. 112.

were provided with a requisition order duly signed, which they could produce eventually to their *patrons* should they have to give an account of their stewardship.

It was in this atmosphere of emergency, when even the communists (who were not, of course, members of the government) were attributing the strikes to Trotskyists and were soon to proclaim '*Il faut savoir terminer une grève*',[20] that Léon Blum succeeded in bringing off what was perhaps the greatest achievement of his government – the Matignon agreements signed on 7 June. The speed with which these negotiations between the government, the CGT, and the representatives of the employers were concluded is a sign of the panic felt by the latter in the face of the strikes, and the fact that the actual contents of the agreements and of the social legislation that followed them went further than anything in the programme of the Popular Front is evidence that the upsurge from below had, as in the original emergence of the Front Populaire, been a more powerful force than many of the political leaders had expected.

The Matignon agreements were an enormously important stage in the improvement of the status of the French working class; there was, after all, something in the feeling that things would never be the same again, for after the restoration of the Republic in 1944, the gains obtained under the Blum government – collective contracts, holidays with pay, the 40 hour week, a system of industrial arbitration – were confirmed and expanded. Although the Matignon agreements did not immediately put an end to the strikes, they and the programme of social legislation passed by the government in its first weeks of office, even if not wholly satisfying the revolutionary left, did much to suggest that the hopes placed in the Popular Front would not be disappointed. That they were to be so nevertheless was due in part to the general economic situation in France, but also to a large extent to the unexpected shock to Blum's government which was given by the outbreak of the civil war in Spain on 18 July.

There is no need to tell the sad story of the failure of the policy of non-intervention in Spain. For the history of the Front Populaire, two aspects are important. First, it was the Spanish war which first showed how tenuous were the bonds binding together the various

20 Maurice Thorez at meeting on 11 June 1936. See Jacques Danos and Marcel Gibelin, *Juin 36* (Paris, 1952), p. 118ff.

components of the Popular Front; and, second, it is an example of how a government can, from rational motives and with the best intentions, embark on a policy which seems to many of its supporters to be a betrayal of everything in which they believe. When, on 20 July, the Spanish government asked the French government to sell them aircraft, Blum immediately agreed and informed the ministers concerned of his decision. On the next day he left for London, with Delbos, the Foreign Minister, for general discussions with the British government. These had been arranged some time previously, and did not in fact cover the Spanish situation at all. Professor Renouvin reports that the official minutes contain no reference to Spain, and the most that Eden seems to have done is to advise Blum very informally not to get involved. However, while Blum was in London, the right-wing press had learnt, from supporters of Franco in the Spanish embassy in Paris, of Blum's decision about the delivery of aircraft, and thus Blum found on his return from London that he had a major cabinet crisis on his hands, with the majority of his radical colleagues anxious to stop the delivery of arms, and with the Foreign Ministry making its own position clear in a communiqué to the press on 24 July, which ran, 'No delivery of arms can be made to a foreign power without the Quai d'Orsay being consulted. The Ministry of Foreign Affairs has received no request of this kind'.

While Blum was looking for ways of supplying the Spanish government without breaking up his own – he was investigating the possibility of nominally transferring aircraft to the Mexican government instead of directly to the Spaniards – he was forced on 27 July to yield to the pressure of his colleagues and to issue a formal ban on the export of any war material whether by the state or by private firms. However, within a few days the question was re-opened by the fact that, on 30 July, an Italian plane bound for Spain was forced to land in French North Africa. This clear evidence of Mussolini's intervention on Franco's behalf obviously obliged Blum to think again; and it was this that led him to prepare a non-intervention agreement. The proposal, M. Renouvin tells us, was originally made simply to London and to Rome, and it was on the suggestion of the British Foreign Office that it was also addressed to Germany, the USSR, and Portugal. From that moment, indeed, a non-intervention agreement was as much an aim of British as it was of French foreign policy.

Blum's motives for accepting a policy that he himself seems to have thought of as second-best are clear enough. In the early stages of the war, it really did look as if the government could suppress the rebellion once Franco's hopes of immediate success had been thwarted, provided that the insurgents received no help from outside. And, as Fernando de los Rios and other Spanish Republicans pointed out, for the French popular-front government to fall over the issue of arms for Spain would be a direct and bitter blow to the popular-front government in Spain. However, it was quite clear in any case that, if France were to become involved in a war with Germany or Italy arising out of intervention in Spain, she was even less likely to obtain British support than she had been a few months earlier when Germany had denounced the Locarno agreements and remilitarized the Rhineland. It has been suggested that the British made a formal statement to the French government to this effect; and one Spanish source even maintains that Baldwin sent a personal message to the President of the French Republic. If the latter seems out of keeping with what we know of Baldwin's passivity with regard to foreign affairs and would perhaps have been his only recorded initiative in this field – a few weeks later Eden was complaining that he had had 'only one letter and one telephone call this month, and these about my spending a weekend with him in South Wales'[21] – there is in any case no reason to think that the French government were not perfectly aware of the British position. And, indeed, Admiral Darlan – at this period, in spite of his later career, one of the few senior officers with some sympathy with the Front Populaire – had wholly failed to convince the British Admiralty of the dangers to the British and French naval position in the Mediterranean if the Spanish Republic lost the war.

It was this conviction that at all costs France must remain aligned with Britain that made Blum continue the non-intervention policy even when it was clearly a failure – this, and also the feeling that it would take very little to plunge France into a civil war as disastrous as that in Spain. It is still uncertain how far there were people in the French army who were prepared to emulate Franco and stage a coup against the government; but again, as with the riots of 6 February, what is important is that the atmosphere of the time was such that it certainly *seemed* possible; and it is certain that, even before Franco's rising, right wing journalists and politi-

[21] Lord Avon, *Facing the Dictators* (London, 1962), p. 404.

cians in France had been pointing out the similarities between the situation in the two countries.

Moreover, the moment of panic which had induced the French *patronnat* to accept the Matignon agreements soon passed, and during the autumn and winter of 1936–7 the opposition to the government from the right revived, while, on the left, Blum was being criticized both because of his non-intervention policy and because it looked as though the employers were reluctant to recognize the workers' newly-won rights of collective bargaining and minimum wage agreements. These difficulties with the left were exemplified in December, when the communists abstained from voting in support of the government's foreign policy. Blum talked of resigning, and it seems that during the next few months the idea of giving up the premiership was often in his mind. Some of his left-wing supporters were now in open opposition; Marceau Pivert resigned from Blum's secretariat in February, while, in March, police fired on participants in an anti-fascist demonstration at Clichy – an affair which has still not been wholly explained – and Blum said, 'It is impossible for me to admit that while I am the responsible head of the government, the police have shed the blood of the workers'.[22] If he stayed in office, it was no doubt because once again he felt that he might be able to restrain the revolutionary left from precipitating similar situations to that at Clichy elsewhere in France.

If the more politically militant of Blum's supporters were attacking his Spanish policy and suggesting that he was preventing a revolution, it was his economic policies which were worrying his radical allies and conservative opponents, without, as prices continued to rise, really satisfying the working class either, and by the spring of 1937 renewed labour disputes were adding to the government's difficulties. Blum's own analysis of the economic situation was fairly clear. The most important thing was to increase purchasing power and thus increase industrial production and decrease unemployment. Measures such as holidays with pay and the 40 hour week were primarily to serve a social need; but the government also hoped that they would contribute to the increase of spending power and the absorption of unemployed labour. Arrangements for the marketing of grain through the newly established *Office du Blé* aimed at improving the situation of the peasants. The

[22] G. Lefranc, *op. cit.* p. 237.

Bank of France was to be brought under stricter government control.

Although some of these measures were at least partially successful, the degree of recovery was never as great as Blum had hoped. In spite of assurances to the contrary, he had been obliged to devalue the franc on 26 September 1936, and although this was followed by a brief period of increased production, the government was never able to regain or retain the confidence of financial circles. Nor was Blum successful when, in the hope of winning this confidence, he announced a 'pause' in his social and economic programme. The real trouble was that many of Blum's economic difficulties were inherited from previous governments, in a number of which his radical associates had played a prominent part; and many of the radicals were still distrustful of the socialist economic programme. As long as the radicals remained loyal, the government's majority in the Chamber was not in doubt; but it was in the Senate that the government was hardest pressed – it had a majority of only 10 in the debate on devaluation – and it was there that radical hesitations and doubts were more clearly expressed. But if the radicals could cause the government trouble from within, it was the forces outside parliament that did most to make its policies ineffective. As long as Blum was unable either to impose his will on industry and big business – as he had been able to do briefly in the moment of crisis and panic in June 1936 – or to win their confidence as he hoped to do by declaring the 'pause' in February 1937, then the flight of capital continued and the confidence in the government's loans diminished, so that it became increasingly hard for the government to carry out a coherent economic policy.

When, on 20 June 1937, Blum presented his request for full powers – mainly to stop the export of capital – to the Senate, he asked his opponents, 'Is it a shift in the majority you want or is it the overthrow of the government?' In fact, by defeating him personally, the Senate in a sense got both. For the Chautemps ministry which followed, although theoretically for six months still a government of the Front Populaire, was, in spite of the participation of the socialists and the support of the communists – who according to some sources went so far as to offer Chautemps the participation in the government which they had refused to Blum – simply another Radical government, powerless to carry further the programme of the Front Populaire or to fulfil the hopes of 1936. Blum has been much criticized for acquiescing in this situation and for accepting a defeat which was for him as much a personal as a political one, instead of provoking a division in the country and risking perhaps a civil war. But he had never been a man for the *politique du pire*; and he was too much a man of the Third Republic to want to overthrow it. What he had tried to do, and to some extent succeeded in, was to suggest the possibility of a social-democratic France within the existing constitutional arrangements and to start the transformation of French society which began again after the end of the second world war.

(*I am most grateful to the Fondation Nationale des Sciences Politiques in Paris for an invitation to take part in a* Colloque *on Léon Blum's Government, in March 1965. This essay is largely based on the contributions made at this meeting, which are shortly to be published in the* Cahiers de la Fondation Nationale des Sciences Politiques.)

Malraux, Revolutionist and Minister

David Wilkinson

For seven years now André Malraux has been Minister of State for Cultural Affairs in the Fifth Republic. In this capacity he has played a bureaucratic role, and a dramatic one: he administers culture to the French people; he is also a high priest of their history. To explain the existence of these posts to 'Anglo-Saxons' would be the task of the commentator on this particular ministry; to explain why Malraux fills them and to what end, the task of a biographer of Malraux the Minister. But to one with some knowledge of Malraux's activities (and perhaps less of his writings) only up till 1939, the first question to occur would not be what does Malraux do as Minister, or why; but, how in the world did he get there? What could prevail on a leftist cosmopolitan adventurer, a lover of action and revolution, to become a *Minister*; a Minister of *Culture*; a Gaullist, and a French nationalist?

Of course these questions were asked, and in some measure answered, immediately after the second world war, when Malraux first became a Gaullist minister and showed his change of front. The significance of his conversion is no longer a subject of political and literary gossip, and so much the better; but the light that this episode in his biography can shed on Malraux's thought, and his own thoughts on this change, are of enduring interest.

Party schisms, the lure of office, an unsuspected and buried sentiment: these often explain why left-wing public figures have made surprising evolutions. But where the political liaisons of thinkers are concerned, these typical factors have less application. We may recall the striking changes in the public lives of Sorel and Barrès, figures difficult to label as 'left', but of importance nevertheless (and in more ways than this one) for understanding Malraux. Sorel seemed to pick up political attachments across the spectrum, from revolutionary syndicalism to reactionary royalism, from Mussolini to Lenin. Barrès began too nihilistically to have any political character, became a Boulangist without illusions, and ended as a voice of French nationalism and traditionalism, raising the memories of the dead even as Malraux does. Indeed, the analogies merit further pursuit. Beginning with the first, we can see how Malraux the Marxist could become Malraux the Gaullist; returning to the second, we can see what nationalism can mean to one who believes only in Man.

Under all of Georges Sorel's inconstant allegiances there is a constant moral norm. Neither this norm, an image of the good life for man, nor Sorel's best-known political prescription – that of the *Reflections on Violence* – is as surprising as the fact and manner of their combination: capitalist virtue is to be generated by class struggle.

Sorel as moralist envisages the good life as clearly as the bad: one is the bourgeois ideal, the other the bourgeois reality. The bad is the mediocre and decadent: repetition, routine, material fulness and emptiness of the spirit, parasitic non-productivity or stupefied production followed by demoralized consumption, ultra-refined stupidity, timorous peacefulness. The good life, for the many, combines the ideals of capitalism and of religious enthusiasm: passionate individualism, hard and productive work done with zeal, vigorous energy, thrift, the rigid values of family life (chastity, fidelity, and solicitude for the weak). For the few, the image of the captain of industry and the Homeric hero are merged; let them view life as a struggle, not a pleasure, and seek energy in action and victorious attack on moral evils; they are war-like creators of productive forces, bold captains, insatiable and pitiless conquerors, of indomitable energy.

If Sorel were merely a moralist, he would have preached these lives to others, and endorsed or condemned their choice according to how it was exercised. As he was a political thinker, he asked how these virtues might be brought to birth, what mechanism might ensure the preservation of the highest morality. His answer was always some form of social struggle, notably that of the revolutionary working people against the decadent exploiters. Strikes and violence would be the key, perhaps to overturning the exploiters, perhaps to their awakening to their own class sentiment and struggle for survival; perhaps to the political power of the workers, perhaps to their secession from society, but surely to their morale, their new culture. Real violence and its mythology would support the myth of a future, apocalyptic general strike: accepting this myth (an expression of the determination to act), the revolutionaries would undergo a patient apprenticeship, acquire an extraordinary ardour, an 'entirely epic state of mind' which would be their true reward.[1]

But it did not have to be the proletariat which was thus regenerated by myth, struggle, and violence. Any political movement, provided it was a mass-based movement, might in its struggles for power (if not after its victory) be the source of virtue. And so for Sorel attachment to syndicalism, or to something else, was not a matter of principle. The question, at any given moment, was what was the force whose struggle might (even unintentionally) produce the desired effect? Hence his seeming faithlessness to causes whose stated goals were to him not goods in themselves, but instrumental energizing myths which might or might not do the job in hand; whose struggles were means not to ultimate victory, but to immediate virtue.

At the most general level there is an identity between these thoughts of Sorel's and Malraux's attitude towards political forces – a sort of philosophical opportunism. The goal is the creation of a certain state of feeling and action in men: the method is to attach them to a force in conflict, whose impact will make them become as they ought to be. But Malraux's choice of forces, seemingly more simple than Sorel's, is in fact more complex. For the political struggles of revolutionaries (and others) seldom lead to Sorel's frozen and balanced tableau wherein 'a united and revolutionary proletariat confronts a rich middle class eager for conquest' – and indefinitely sustains the confrontation.[2] Rather they lead to defeat and to victory – classic problems to which the philosophers of action, conflict, and revolution are then forced to attend.

These are the problems that underlie Malraux's move from apparent apologies for communism in *Days of Wrath* (1935) to public denunciations of communism at the side of de Gaulle, from 'Marxist humanist' at the Soviet writers congress in Moscow in 1934 to Gaullist minister in 1945, agitator in 1948, minister again

---

1 Georges Sorel, *Reflections on Violence*, trans. T. E. Hulme (New York, 1941), p. 294.

2. Ibid., p. 91.

in 1958. This is the notorious change in his politics, the one which has given rise to the argument of a discontinuity in his thought, beneath which lie all too often the emotional accusations of 'sellout' and 'fascist'. A variation on this theme finds a deeper continuity in Malraux: he was always a fascist in spirit, or at least a nihilist: he has never got beyond his initial perception of the world's absurdity, for all his principal characters are nihilists, and all their lives are empty cycles of struggle and death; they engage in struggles of the will, which are demoniac, and this delights him, which is fascistic.[3] If we seek in Malraux's novels the representative hero-figures who win arguments (if there are any) and attribute their views to Malraux, we may find (with some difficulty) a consistent character from Perken's straight-out nihilism and action in *The Royal Way* (1930) to Möllberg's intellectual rejection of action, intellect, and meaning. From the man of total action to the man of sheer intellect, from unthinking superman to passive intellectual, there is a straight line: do they not show the same belief in the meaninglessness of human existence, the same incompleteness as persons, at last the same defeat in life? Indeed: but what matters is that Malraux, too, understands this, and, through Claude Vannec and Vincent Berger, passes judgment upon these figures, who stand for an attitude towards life which Malraux in the beginning and the end rejects.

Since Gaullism as a movement has shown itself to have no recognizable doctrine of race or class, indeed to be situational and pragmatic almost beyond comprehension, the cry of fascist politics has faded. But its exciting quality served to obscure Malraux's elucidations. It has also served to make the explainers forget what Malraux has repeatedly said, that, had Leon Trotsky won his battle with Stalin, he himself would have become a Trotskyist communist,[4] and that, while de Gaulle was in the wilderness after the failure of the RPF, Malraux was not unwilling to associate himself with Mendès-France.[5] These episodes suggest that Malraux has never put his total allegiance anywhere, not in official communism nor in nationalism, nor in the person of de Gaulle. If we see Malraux's

[3] See 'Malraux Man', *Times Literary Supplement*, 26 November 1964, and H. A. Mason in *Scrutiny*, Spring 1947, pp. 162–71.

[4] This did not prevent Natalya Sedova-Trotsky denouncing him for suppressing the Trotskyite press in France while he was Minister of Information (*New York Times*, 10 March 1948).

[5] *L'Express*, 25 December 1954, 29 January 1955.

alliance with communism as essentially tactical, dictated by a philosophy which was his own and which, despite appearances, communism never shared, then we can understand his lack of total devotion more easily. The proper terms of this understanding are not those of self-advancement, but of tactics: at one point, the goals of the parties to an alliance coincide, and the alliance increases their chances of success; at another, this is not so, and tactics dictate the replacement of the old alliance by a new one. 'I have not changed. It is the world, and most of all the communists, who have changed.'[6]

What Malraux has sought in his political career is a political force which will, knowingly or not, yield certain ethical and political goods; but the goods he has sought have altered over the years as his thought has developed. A successful revolutionary movement can yield power to its leaders: this power Garine of *The Conquerors* (1928) sought and received by attaching himself to the Canton communists; as Malraux judged, it was not enough. Even an unsuccessful revolution can break the existential isolation of the revolutionaries at the level of sentiment: this is the discovery and the victory of Kyo Gisors in *Man's Fate* (1933). He is no Marxist: he finds his fraternal bond with revolutionaries who happen to be communists, that is all. But for a leader it is not enough to fail gloriously: having animated others with a mythic future where their dignity will be assured, and having as it were gained one's own freedom by imbibing their hope, it is no longer satisfying to be a defeated hero fraternally joined to others equally doomed. One must live instead to create the future, to build the social order that will ensure the brotherhood of man: this is the understanding that emerges from the complex dialectic of *Man's Hope* (1937). It is incidental to this period, but not to Malraux's later role, that the better order was seen by him less as a certain set of ideal relations between men and the economy than as a certain set of ideal attitudes of men towards other men. That the ideal order is psycho-political rather than politico-economic should be no surprise, since the virtue that order is intended to create is one of sentiment and not of material well-being. Again, Sorel is in point here. On the one hand one must accept the conditions of organization and authoritarian discipline that are required if a revolution is to be more than

6 T. S. White, 'The Three Lives of André Malraux', *The New York Times Magazine*, 15 February 1953.

a presently absorbing struggle with a doomed future – so the anarchists are no longer a politically valid force; on the other, the chance of victory attracts sadists and racketeers to the movement, and one must ask if the movement truly can and will make good the myth of hope on which it has operated when victory is won – so the communists become thoroughly suspect as allies. *Man's Hope* was still able to distinguish between the Pradases and Kurtzes of the communist party on the one hand – the dogmatists, factionalists, and spies – and the Manuels on the other, men who were not wholly in opposition to what Malraux stood for. The Hitler-Stalin pact made it somewhat clearer which types were in control, and marked the final parting in what was never more than a match of convenience.

For Malraux, the second world war was a continuation of the Spanish Civil War, offering the same personal rewards when there was no hope and the same opportunity for institutionalizing fraternity when victory came in sight. In France, where he fought, the war was at first and became again more a national than a civil war. In the Resistance as with the Republic, a tenacious and desperate struggle offered at its darkest moments the intense emotional bond that the same society at peace could not provide. In *Altenburg* (1943) victory is no longer in sight, and the goal of fraternity is returned from the future to the present; but those who share it are no longer revolutionaries. This is characteristic: wherever the real world seems to resist and reject all attempts to transform it, there appears in Malraux the figure of the defeated hero for whom the justification of action is internal rather than external to himself. When men are defeated, dying, or in prison, when their struggle has become hopeless, an experience or a sentiment overshadows the failure to achieve concrete results. In *Altenburg*, the attainable human good is fellowship; the force that supplies it is fighting France; then, defeated France.

But the Resistance was ultimately successful, and Malraux, at the head of the Alsace-Lorraine Brigade, shared the victory. In the struggle, as he puts it, 'I married France'. What this meant, however, was that Malraux demanded that France possess herself of the 'universal humanism' he still advocated. France ought to take advantage of her moment of unity to make herself over, to create the social order in which the dignity and the brotherhood of man would be ensured. This was in line with the myth of national regeneration that had animated the Resistance. That myth was, in turn, in line with the mystique of de Gaulle: towards the end of the war Malraux sought to achieve his goals through exploiting the spirit of the Resistance and the prestige and leadership of de Gaulle.

No doubt something beyond tactics drew Malraux to the side of this figure. It might be a form of Pygmalionism: de Gaulle is an ideal-type of Malraux's devising made real but enlarged. He is the active intelligence, the hero combining mind and will. But he was, and was again to become, the hero without the morbid touch of inner and outer failure that afflicts most of Malraux's own literary creations. Even in real history Saint-Just, Trotsky, T. E. Lawrence, are the men of action over whom Malraux reflects; all welded fragmented nations into victorious armies; all, of course, tasted defeat after victory. De Gaulle resembled them; now he has gone them one better. There is a psychological as well as a tactical reason for Malraux's adherence to his cause. But the tactics predominated.

Factionalism, the parties, and the old order combined to frustrate de Gaulle and the Resistance-mystique alike. The latter dissolved into impotence; Malraux took part in founding a party, the RPF, for the benefit of the former. De Gaulle could not win at the polls and would not cross the Rubicon of revolution; Malraux drifted away and thought that Mendès-France might do the job. But it was de Gaulle whom the death of the Fourth Republic called back to power; and with him, but not as one of his chief servants, came Malraux. He is in a sense irreplaceable; he fills a role no one else of any stature could. But the role is more necessary to Malraux than to de Gaulle. The incantatory part of that role may be understood by contrast to Barrès, to whose idea of history (as to Sorel's tactical ethics) Malraux is profoundly in debt.

Again, though, the comparison must be kept within limits. Unfortunately Barrès journeyed from egoism to nationalism, and Malraux made the same journey. This lends itself to overstatement. The two ends of Barrès' evolution are indeed close and relevant to Malraux's; the path is entirely dissimilar. Barrès begins (in *Le Culte du Moi*) with a Cartesian isolation of the ego, and a non-Cartesian devotion to it. Among all false gods and spurious religions, the self is the one tangible reality. Therefore defend this sole value and nourish it. Defend it against the others, the non-ego, who would 'constrain or impede or distort' its development; nourish it on self-exploration, and employ study and travel and action to create new and obscure emotions to be explored.

The next step is taken when novelties no longer seduce but pall, when the self dries up under its own microscope. To save its life, Barrès concludes, to unplug the spring of emotion, the ego must find a love and a purpose, and this is achieved through a different sort of self-knowledge: I ask, what made me, what determined what I am? Barrès' answer, in general, is 'your roots' – race, surroundings, and time. The land and the dead created you – your land and its dead. To survive and flourish, then, return to your roots (which you share with *some* others). You cannot be nourished by a universal civilization: you have a specific moral patrimony from your country, your province, your community, and your family. Take the inheritance that is yours, see yourself as one of a series, look at the lives of your forebears to determine what you ought to do: follow in the footsteps of the fathers. Construct your life, then, as a work of art, to be worthy of the past and productive for the future: find your narrow social sphere, or create a situation for yourself, and, rooted there, persevere in the service that discharges the example and the duty inherent in your rank, place, and ancestry. The inheritance is all that sustains your ego; those who threaten the inheritance – innovators, revolutionaries, foreign and hostile communities – are your sworn enemies. Whoever would undo the work of the dead would destroy the only means of life. He who is destined for political service ought then energetically to sustain the noblest traditions, uphold the old national mission, renew the national strength, and repel the enemies of them all.

Malraux's novels are explorations of the means of defending the self against the pall of sterility that frustrated Barrès' individualism. But the defences that satisfy Malraux do not lead to a landed proprietor's conservative ideal, and do not include the search for roots. Rather the individual can break his ultimately deadly isolation through political action, the fraternal bond of common struggle, the myth of human dignity that ennobles a conflict of power, and the possibility of a future social order yielding actual dignity – dignity being a sort of negative freedom, the absence of oppression and of humiliation. Or he may do so through artistic creation, the transmutation of destiny into tragedy. For through the creation and contemplation of works of art, Malraux claims (or rather, deeply believes) men can be made aware both of their isolation and destiny, and of the great human ideals by means of which men can come to terms with their predicament. He is as pragmatic about the ethical contents of art as he is about political allegiance: whatever ideals will produce the desired psychological changes are those which the artist is obliged to transmit; if he has a sense of history, he will know whether the appropriate myths are religious or humanist, revolutionary or nationalist. Such ideals and myths have their fitting uses and appropriate moments, but only the predicament against which they protect endures. When action fails, the artist can redeem the failure by shaping the memory of action and preserving the ethic for future dreams.

This ideology of art and action diverges from Barrès' significantly enough, but offers no readily apparent justification for the appearance of Malraux in the thoroughly Barrèsian role of high priest of history for France and intellectual aide-de-camp to a general more discreet and more fortunate than Boulanger. Nationalism and Gaullism are, as we have seen, opportune means and instruments for Malraux where both are absolutes and ends for de Gaulle, while Barrès' nationalism was a commitment deduced from rather than instrumental to prior principles, and Boulanger a momentary instrument. Not only is the source of attachment to France unlike for Malraux and Barrès, but also the function of nationalist propaganda: Barrès wrote to evoke a will to action, to defend France (or rather, to defend men's roots) against her inward and outward enemies as he understood them. Malraux, in a manner less magnificent but no less magniloquent than de Gaulle's, seems to have been trying to create France.

This is essential: for Barrès the nationalist there is a France which is threatened and needs to be preserved. For Malraux the nationalist, the France that would be worthy of defence does not yet exist: it is still to be born. For de Gaulle France exists – occasionally. Barrès means by 'France' the traditions of a nation. De Gaulle means, primarily, its unity (and consequent pride). Malraux means its unity and its humanism. France, since the Revolution, has had a disunity of spirit far larger than that between the American North and South since the civil war. As between Right and Left (and, less violently, as among many fragments of each) there have been few experiences of common struggle and many of mutual hatred; few shared heroes, many figures idolized on the one hand and detested on the other. Those nationalists, however, whose myth of France includes all Frenchmen without regard to class or party, have sought to evoke figures and episodes of the French past that do not involve the retrospective humiliation of some living and historically conscious Frenchmen. The American secular cults of Washington and Lincoln, popular sentimental symbols of national unity, serve as equivalents of the common memories these French nationalists seek. De Gaulle is such a nationalist. For him the full existence of France, its unity in pride, depends upon a charismatic leader who is such a symbol and who evokes the symbols of the past. For him the key figure of French history is Joan of Arc: restorer of national unity, strength, territory, leadership, and honour.

For Malraux, the unity of France need not pass with de Gaulle, nor indeed depend upon him, so long as the symbols of the past are evoked by someone. These symbols are the land and the dead, interpreted so as to yield unity and not division. Malraux's speeches display and promote the intention of unifying a nation. Or at any rate some of them do. Those about Frenchmen and French places are directed at national unity. Those about foreign lands and about policy, however, go beyond the goal of unity to the goal of national humanism. The youth of France are to receive from the Republic not only the myths of France, but also the myth of Man.

As the voice of French history Malraux evokes the past, vividly and passionately: at Orleans Joan of Arc; at the Parthenon Jean Moulin, Resistance leader; at Metz, the Alsace-Lorraine Brigade; at Rennes, the first meeting of Free French and Resistance leaders, and the liberation of Paris. The dead must not be forgotten, they must be called up to create common memories for the young. The memories of a mystical national unity and fraternity, past action transformed by the orator's art into present consciousness, become the basis for present unity even in the absence of a great common struggle. 'The history of a people is made of illustrious deeds, but its soul is made of forgotten deeds which would disappear as a cloud drifts if they were not mysteriously brought together again.'[7] And places contain a file of such memories: 'Chateaus, cathedrals, museums, are the fraternal and successive landmarks of the im-

[7] Speech at Metz, 14 May 1961 (France: Ministry for Cultural Affairs; mimeographed copy).

mense and lively dream pursued by France for nearly one thousand years . . . Our monuments are the greatest dream of France. That is why we want to preserve them . . . for the emotional response of the children . . . It is for them that the battles, the hatreds, and the fervours which make up our history unite, transfigured, on the fraternal ground of the dead'.[8]

In 1924, when no-one would have called him a nationalist, Malraux analyzed the concept of the nation: 'The mind supplies the idea of a nation, but what gives this idea its sentimental force is a community of dreams. Our brothers are those whose childhood develops according to the rhythm of epics and legends which dominates our own. We have all felt the freshness and the haze of the morning of Austerlitz. . . . What images white men need to give them a national spirit!'[9] It is these images Malraux now resurrects: having then analyzed the nation, he now espouses it.

Where Barrès invoked French history to remind Frenchmen both of the limits beyond which they must not go if they were to have the only identity they could ever attain, and of the enemies whom being French required them to defy, Malraux awakens history to let Frenchmen feel that their isolation as men is overcome by the fraternity that being French permits them to share with the dead, and with the living to whom the same dead belong. Still, the construction of personal identity by an appeal to men and places, to the land and the dead, is the same enterprise for Barrès and Malraux. What sets Malraux farther apart from Barrès as from de Gaulle is simply his refusal to declare that the national tie is the primary or the ultimate bond among men.

This retention of humanism atop nationalism is expressed by Malraux's equal willingness to evoke the spirit of French and non-French places, and to discuss the 'meaning' of Athens or of Brasilia to man as well as to Frenchmen: Brasilia, where man's struggle against the land is given worthy forms; Athens, which, like Malraux himself, unites the spear and the intellect, in the statue of Pallas and the person of the citizen-soldier-poet. But the humanist Malraux is better represented by his official Ministerial role as overseer of French cultural affairs than by his rhetorical preserva-

---

[8] Debate, National Assembly, 14 December 1961. France: *Journal officiel, Débats parlementaires, Assemblée nationale* (hereafter cited as DPAN), 1961, p. 5637.

[9] *La tentation de l'occident* (Paris, 1926), Letter VIII, p. 96.

tion of the spirit of history. Neither Barrès nor Malraux, after all, has written a history of France: that is what full devotion to their antiquarian and monumental approaches to history would require. But Barrès was satisfied with his limited role as mediator between Frenchmen and their past, for he believed that the order of society was basically sound: if only men did not uproot themselves and did not let others cut off the past, little urging would be needed to keep them faithful to the land and the dead; if they did their duty, they would keep their healthy egos. Malraux has consistently considered most established means of defending the ego fruitless and unsound (*Man's Fate* is the catalogue of unsound methods): the old human virtues were not available in normal life, only to unusual individuals, in extreme situations, or in a new order of things. His programme as Minister for Cultural Affairs reflects an extremely gradual approach to that new order, which is really more an order of thoughts than of things, of culture than of society.

It is possible to illuminate Malraux's political route by reference to Sorel, and his rhetorical role by allusion to Barrès. His cultural policy has no such parallel. This policy is expressed in the development of the institutions through which the French government has traditionally patronized the arts. If there is a discrepancy between Malraux's vision and the concrete progress of his policy, that is not to be wondered at: nevertheless, in practice the administrator has dominated the cultural revolutionary, and in a way one may regret this. France is not the only country to have a cultural policy, but it is perhaps the first to have an 'existentialist' cultural policy that proceeds deductively from the principles of an ethical thinker. The full expression of those principles would have been more than merely interesting. It could have been, for good or ill, exemplary for the rising number of contemporary thinkers who concern themselves less with the attainment of general opulence than with the quality of life in the prosperous society. But Malraux's experiments retain some interest, for their motivation and theory more than for their gradualist and reformist scale.

The theory can be briefly summarized: it is the last stop on Malraux's philosophical journey. Every man is in the same human predicament (a premise by now familiar). For the few, violent political action or artistic creation may serve to break the isolation of the ego and to create 'communion'. The only means of defence in principle available to all is the consumption of culture.[10] Whether an individual is or is not able to employ this means depends on two social conditions: his access to the contemporary culture; and its quality. Both of these are in turn, according to Malraux, subject in part to conscious control exercised by the state.

The distribution of culture in modern industrial societies is, he says, doubly faulty. To the intellectual elite, ample access is provided to cultural objects of the highest quality. The rest get little access to the best, and a deluge of shoddy trash. This is true for bourgeois society, as in the United States, where there is no political leadership in the cultural field, and where by and large culture is accessible to a man in proportion to his wealth. It is true also for totalitarian society. Soviet Marxism declares that art is nothing but the expression of the political orientation of the artist (reactionary or progressive), and that the dominant art of a society is nothing but its reflection. There is then no distinction to be drawn between artistic creation and artistic production, between the masterpiece and the fourth-rate. This is an ideology which conceals the fact that in modern culture, East or West, the *creator* of art is not in harmony with his world, and 'art is opposed in its profoundest sense to the society within which it is born'.[11] Once this is denied, a totalitarian state can conscientiously suppress creativity and promote production: rubbish for all, when in the West it is rubbish for some. But it is in the reform of the Western system that Malraux is concerned, and the rest of his analysis relates to it alone.

In the West, limited access to true culture has turned the majority into a cultural proletariat. This is concealed by the general access to so-called 'mass art', novels and paintings and films which indeed command a mass audience, but which constitute anti-art. There was once a 'popular art', truly of and for the people, as well

10 Malraux avoids economic metaphors in this context. I shall employ them even though they suggest a crude approach that Malraux does not take, because they also suggest a parallel to certain programmes of economic reform through welfare-state action. This parallel will in turn suggest standard criticisms of the competence of men of intellect and men of affairs to deliberate upon and to control the consumption of other members of their society. The fact that Malraux is discussing art raises added questions of their competence in matters of taste, and questions of the relative propriety of moral education under the surveillance of the state and character formation by an ethical free market.

11 Malraux, 'What Stand Will You Take?' *Confluence*, September 1952, pp. 3–11.

as for the few, intimately bound to the central values of the contemporary society. But modern society has no stable values; the people have dissolved into the rootless urban mass. Authentic art serves some chosen part of man, relates him to time or to eternity, or to some ethic of human nobility. Authentic art in a civilization united by an ethic, a goal, or a myth, transmits that vision to all and makes them not masses but brothers. Where such a civilization is absent, anti-art flourishes. Anti-art is a non-expressive something whose purpose is to sell itself for a profit, and which concerns itself therefore not with transmitting values but with catering to pleasures. It creates in men not profound emotions but superficial and puerile ones: 'the sentimentalities of love or religion, the taste for violence, a touch of cruelty, collective vanity and sensuality'.[12]

Anti-art distracts mass taste; it obscures the cultural impoverishment of the majority. The uncontrolled proliferation of an imagination not grounded upon values, through pop fiction, radio, records, cinema, and television, does worse than this. The mechanization of dreams for the tastes of a free market composed of men out of communion with values and with one another reinforces what is least human and most animal in men: sex and death, instincts in their most primitive form – the urge to dominate, to exploit (viz. Ferral and Valerie in *Man's Fate*), and to kill – even if expressed in the imagination. Others than Malraux often take this line, of course. But because they speak from a socially conservative and religiously traditionalist position, their programme is not like Malraux's: they propose a return to 'the sentimentalities of love or religion' which are in Malraux's view equally elements of anti-art.

Culture influences human nature. There are available in human nature, according to the Manichean psychology that appears marginally through Malraux's works on art, elements that tend to ennoble man, to lead him to self-transcendence and communion, and elements which tend to animalize, isolate, and destroy him.[13] If we

[12] Malraux, 'A Universal Humanism', *Liberté de l'Esprit*, June–July 1950, pp. 97–100.

[13] Before one criticizes this psychology for its unscientific and simplistic dualism, one should recall that Malraux *means* by psychology not a scientific appraisal of human nature but an artistic creation, a mythology which changes with culture and artists; and that this mythology has antecedents in the late Freudian dichotomy of Eros and Thanatos, and in the Nietzschean 'human, all-too-human' and 'human, superhuman'.

wish to know what these are, we should contemplate the gods and demons of religious cultures, for the divine and the diabolical principles are constant: 'the demons of Babylon, of the early church, and of the Freudian subconscious have the same visage'.[14] The anti-art of mass 'culture' appeals to and encourages the demonic in human nature.

A reform in access might amend this: authentic art cannot be mass-produced, but it can be mass-distributed; let the masses have access, then, to modern artistic creation, and they can be liberated. But here the question of quality again enters in: even authentic art, in a civilization where the artist is not in harmony with society, where it is a matter of chance what values he inherits, may be a source of corruption rather than of regeneration. 'Every authentic work of art devotes its means (even the most brutal) to the service of some essential part of man passionately or obscurely sponsored by the artist.'[15] But the dark, demonic side of man's nature is as elemental as the divine. Western civilization is displaying a disturbing tendency to interrogate and to rend the divine, to advance the diabolical, even at the highest levels of authentic art. Modern artistic creation is in part consciously following the same damaging line as that unconsciously pursued by mass anti-art. Mass distribution of modern authentic art cannot then provide men with the defence they need. Men must receive art of a certain quality.

Malraux's vision of the (cultural-reformist) future politics of art has, consequently, three phases. Let us call them the new human type, the systematic resurrection of the past, and cultural democracy. The artist-politician must strive to humanize the art of the present, revive the 'divine' art of the past, and make the one and the other available to all.

1. *Tragic humanism:* Humanism is Malraux's term for his own final philosophical position. It is to him at once an ideology and the name of a cultural style that expresses the ideology. The nineteenth century was the zenith of optimistic humanism: God was dead, but the kingdom of Man had replaced Him; the world was the sphere of progress in manners and morals, customs and arts, under the guidance of reason and of science. But in the two wars, with their suffering, their horrors, and their human degradation, that happy

---

[14] Malraux, *The Voices of Silence*, trans. Stuart Gilbert (New York, 1953), p. 541.

[15] Ibid., p. 524.

world was slaughtered along with its inhabitants. The best that we can find in man, the maximum value that we and our culture can possess, is a tragic humanism: this is the alternative to demonism in art (or to anti-art and totalitarian art, which peddle themselves or the will to dominate of the ruling class).[16] Tragic humanism combines the belief that no change in the material or political conditions of life can substantially alter the terrible isolation of every man with the belief that under certain political conditions men can choose to make political and ethical commitments which will in turn produce emotions and memories by means of which their predicament will be from moment to moment mitigated or abated.

In his own view, Malraux is not the lonely advocate of the philosophy which he calls 'tragic humanism': this humanism is a new culture, struggling to be born. It will be born when the West reconstructs for itself the idea of man. Every great *politique* creates its new human type,[17] a myth around which human ideals orient themselves: the next great human type is the liberal hero. 'Symbolic types of this sort are born from the merging, at certain moments of history, of attitudes which seemed up to that time irreconcilable'.[18] Such a type provides the individual with a clear understanding of what his civilization expects from him. But Malraux has never delineated the liberal-hero type. In all probability, however, this character reflects the best of an earlier Malraux hero-type, the Bolshevik, a combination of 'tremendous energy, of violence, and of humanitarian ideology', to which is added a new reflectiveness, a new intimacy with art, in consonance with Malraux's postwar views.[19]

[16] Malraux, 'Man and Artistic Culture', *Reflections on Our Age* (New York, 1949), pp. 84–9.

[17] On such types, cf. Nicolas Berdyaev: 'The War ... produced a new spiritual type, a type inclined to transfer war-time measures to the ordering of life in general, prepared to put the theory of violence into practice, and with a love of power and a great respect for force ... a new anthropological type, a new facial expression ... a different gait, different gestures ... This is a world-wide phenomenon; it is seen equally in communism and in fascism.' *The Origins of Russian Communism* (London, 1937), pp. 122–3.

[18] André Malraux and James Burnham, *The Case for de Gaulle* (New York, 1948), p. 62.

[19] Thus Malraux offered as a slogan for French youth 'culture and courage', a purely natural outgrowth of his own concern with reconciling aesthetic perception with political activism. This liberal hero resembles one of his fictional heroes, but not so much as he resembles Malraux himself – or the Malraux-myth.

The emergence of such a positive hero – and accordingly a liberating rather than a corrupting effect, a humanist rather than a negative style – in authentic modern art is necessary if that art is to bring men the rewards that Malraux considers possible. But having rejected the idea of an official style, he allows no decisive role to the state in reforming artistic creation: all that it can do is to promote and support art which it must not closely control. His own works and rhetoric, however, preach his gospel: no doubt this is the most radical political action he conceives as tolerable in the creation of the new human type. It cannot satisfy the impatient, and threatens to be ineffectual.

2. *The resurrection of the past:* It is, however, possible to affect the men and the style of the arts of tomorrow while ignoring or short-circuiting those contemporary creators who are not humanists. It is a leading premise of Malraux's aesthetics that art feeds on art, that each artist develops his unique style first by imitating, then by revolting against, some predecessor or predecessors. (These need not be men of the previous generation, or even men of his own culture.) And a second main premise is that, because of anthropological and aesthetic research, the attitude of cultural relativism, and the large-scale technology of artistic collection and distribution represented by museums, photography, and the ethnological cinema, in the twentieth century all previous styles of all previous artists and cultures have become potential predecessors. The preservation and distribution of past culture is a large-scale organized operation: therefore it is suitable for state action in a way individual creativity is not.

Hence the key theme in Malraux's political speeches of the young and the dead: 'we intend' to form the taste of the young by systematically giving them the chance to know the great films of the past: we shall recapture all of the human past, we shall render accessible the largest possible number of *capital* objects-of-art; true culture requires a communion, a '*presence*, in our lives, of what should belong to the dead', and an emotion in that presence. So our job is to make the genius of humanity not merely known, but to make it loved; to create our exemplary man and to shape our new past, we must conquer all forms of love, art, personal greatness and thought that, during the millennia, have allowed men to become less enslaved; let our culture be the resurrection of the *noblesse* of the world. In political terms, let the state undertake not only a promotion of uncontrollable creativity, but also a selective preservation of the creations of the past.[20]

3. *Cultural democracy:* It is not enough, however, to shape the tastes of tomorrow's creators. To them, and to the past, a mass public must be restored. The cultural distribution system must be reformed so that every man has access to authentic and defensive art as well as to anti-art. To Soviet totalitarian culture and American bourgeois culture, France will counterpose a democratic culture. This was impossible in the nineteenth century, not simply because culture was synonymous with refinement, but because twentieth-century technology has invented mass reproduction and mass distribution techniques. The works of humanity will be rendered accessible to all; even the poorest man must be able to know art, and every child of sixteen is to have a real contact with the glory of the human spirit. 'From the university level down to places that are quite defenceless today, within thirty years ... every human being must have the means to defend himself, and we must afford him those means.' In the past, the museums won the elite away from the anti-arts; in the future, the general distribution of works of art and photographic reproductions will win back the masses. And this is all a democratic process, in the sense that a facility is created that anyone may use, but the masses are not forced 'through another political rolling mill'. Again, state intervention is required, to break the cash nexus and the class discrimination of the cultural distribution system.[21]

At the theoretical level, then, the state is justified in assuming a major or even a dominant role in the promotion, preservation, and distribution of culture. Since Malraux found the French state already so involved, he was able to move piecemeal to turn that involvement to the service of his theories.

More state action in a given area normally translates itself into a bureaucratic demand for more appropriations and higher priority. Under Malraux, expenditures for culture have been increased and

[20] Debate, Senate, 23 November 1960. France: *Journal officiel, Débats parlementaires, Sénat* (hereafter cited as DPS), 1960, p. 1844; Debate, National Assembly, 23 July 1962. DPAN 1962, p. 2776; Speech, Brasilia, 23 August 1959 (France: Ministry for Cultural Affairs: mimeographed copy).

[21] Debate, National Assembly, 17 November 1959, 6 October 1961, 9 November 1963, DPAN 1959, p. 2500, 1961, p. 3148, 1963, p. 7091; Debate, Senate, 8 December 1959, DPS 1959, p. 1569; *The Case for de Gaulle,* p. 69.

the budgetary priority of cultural affairs raised: the cultural affairs budget has been given autonomy instead of being the least important item in the education budget; and episodic appropriations have been regularized by means of a 'cultural five-year plan', or rather a place in the fourth national plan of modernization.

The various areas of French cultural life have been unevenly organized by the state. Where intervention has been lacking, Malraux has initiated it on a small scale: thus a commission of officials and specialists in music has been set up to consider the needs of music; money has been sought to commission representative contemporary artists to create prototypes in the decorative arts (especially furniture), so as to revive that industry.

France's promotion of contemporary artistic creation encompasses measures to foster the physical well-being of artists (projects of relief and social security for writers, painters, sculptors, decorators; of construction of housing-and-studios for artists), and to increase their numbers (more scholarships and endowments for the national and regional schools of music, drama, architecture, art, and decorative arts), as well as more direct approaches. In each of the arts, and for all, there are special measures for the preservation of masterpieces, for production support and quality control, and for decentralization.

In the cinema, France has organized an international film festival at Cannes, a cinemathèque or library of great films of the past, a commission for research into technical improvement, an institute for advanced filmic studies, federations of cineclubs, and special programmes in scientific and ethnological cinema. Malraux has worked to reduce taxes on the industry, to subsidize the modernization of studios, and to get the national film-distribution organization to favour quality films by diffusing the prize-winning films from international festivals. Automatic state support for film production has been replaced by selective aid (in the form of advances and guarantees of receipts) to productions judged by an advisory commission, on the basis of scenarios or previews, to be of high artistic merit – a system which has supported many international prize-winning films.

In the national theatre, Malraux has sought to alter the repertory and enlarge the audience. The national theatre, in his view, was suppressing the national and human patrimony – Racine, Shakespeare, Greek tragedy – in favour of popular comedy: a classic, traditional, and tragic repertory has been reinstated. For private theatres Malraux has sought tax relief; those that reduce their prices for students and members of cultural groups are aided; in particular productions are subsidized, on consideration of the value of the work, author, direction, and actors, by repayable advances. State aid has been afforded directly to permanent, itinerant, and young provincial troupes, and new ones have been encouraged and become established; the attempts of provincial towns to subsidize tours by Parisian troupes have been seconded; aid to the provincial dramatic festivals has been increased and made more selective.

In architecture, a national inventory has already classified at least 20,000 structures of historical, artistic, or archeological interest which it is desirable to preserve. The next step is to compile and make public photographs of all these structures. Meanwhile the repair and restoration of the neglected monuments is under way, with a vast dirt-removal campaign to restore their original appearance, and full restoration undertaken for a few great structures. Not only have individual structures received attention: the preservation of entire streets and quarters, through external restoration and internal modernization, is under way.

Distribution has largely been equated in practice with decentralization; that is to say, the problem is seen not as getting culture from the elite to the masses so much as getting it from Paris to the provinces. A cultural diffusion centre catalogues all the 'manifestations' (dramatic, musical, filmic, literary, and sporting events, artistic exhibitions, conferences, etc.) that can be put on tour, and affords aid to mayors and cultural leaders for their procurement. A special project of Malraux's own devising is the organization of fixed and mobile *maisons de la culture* in the provinces, for the deposit of collections of reproductions of phonographic, cinematic, and other artistic masterpieces.[22]

One may concede the impressiveness of this practical programme and its superiority to that of other nations. It seems better to aid the arts than to talk about aiding them; the French approach is probably superior to either pure free enterprise or pure state control. This does not mean that the pertinent questions of unintended effects, of the corruptions of power, and of the adequacy of means to ends should not be raised. Judgments of quality in a work of art

[22] *The Case for de Gaulle*, p. 68.

contain the danger of political flattery or of cliques and academicism, depending upon whether politicians or artists do the selection: who is to judge? Regulation of private enterprises is often reversed: under a less forceful successor, may not its wider audience-appeal lead to pressures, in the name of profits and of democracy, for the subsidization of 'anti-art'? How does one ensure that statistics showing an increased audience reflect the awakening of masses, rather than an increased interest on the part of the existing consumers? And, if the object of all this activity is to bring about a change in men's attitudes and consciousness, how can success or failure be measured, when statistics reflect only a physical presence? Malraux has evaded the first problem by referring most selections to committees of 'experts'; he has not, to my knowledge, dealt seriously with the rest either. But eventually they must and will be forcibly raised, and he or his successors will have to confront them. We need not confront them here except to note that while they remain unanswered, Malraux's practical achievements cannot be considered either to have achieved or to have validated his cultural utopia and theory, which must still be judged as provisional hopes, not as established facts. We do not know whether all Frenchmen will become Malrauxs; we are permitted to wonder whether they can.

As with Sorel, Malraux's shifting allegiances prove to be of merely transient importance. Since the true politics of these men was not represented by any one contemporary movement, they attached themselves year by year to whatever force of the moment seemed most likely to create the state of mind or the state of affairs at which they were avowedly aiming. It is this private purpose that we must comprehend if we are to sense the significance and insignificance of their political involvements. For Malraux, a losing political struggle was still the good fight if only it could break the parallel solitudes of the fighters. To win was more dangerous; victory could be justified only by the intention to experiment with the social order, so that it might increase the availability of the spiritual and artistic means of promoting human fraternity. Otherwise a stable social order would be an evil order without that result ever being planned. For war and revolution, the normal opportunities for men to step outside themselves, would be banished without a substitute.

Since the victory of de Gaulle, Malraux has tried, in a Cabinet composed of men not particularly sympathetic to his style of thought, to justify that victory, or rather to make it justifiable. His attempt has been made in a rhetorical mode which recalls the rhetoric of Barrès by its evocation of historic places and dead heroes and its intention to induce in men by an intensely emotional appeal the state of mind previously generated only by violent action. It has also been made in a bureaucratic mode: the Minister of Culture seeks by administrative action to insure the exposure of all of France to those masterpieces which, he believes, will permit those who perceive art rightly to experience that same psychological escape from and conquest of the human predicament that the grosser instrument of political struggle surely allows.

It would be a bold man who would presume to judge the validity of Malraux's diagnosis of the psychological malady of modern humanity, or who would care to forecast with much certainty the eventual outcome of his policy. All that needs to be said at this point is that André Malraux, after a varied but internally consistent and comprehensible career, has obtained an enviable opportunity. Unlike most political thinkers he has secured the power to test his theories and to realize, if they can be realized, his dreams. He has tried. Now we must wait on the outcome of the experiment.

The Left Book Club

Stuart Samuels

> Forced to make the choice themselves,
> Our rude forefathers loaded shelves
> With Tennyson and Walter Scott
> And Meredith and Lord knows what!
> But we don't have to hum and ha,
> Nous avons changé tout cela –
> Our books are chosen for us – Thanks
> To Strachey, Laski, and Gollancz!
> (Poem in a bookseller's window)

In the Britain of the nineteen-thirties it was easy to identify a left-wing, anti-fascist, pro-Soviet, anti-war, popular-front intellectual. The sign of identification was not necessarily a party card, a lapel button, or a signature at the bottom of a revolutionary manifesto, but the colour of the bindings on his bookshelves. This was neither red nor pink, but the omnipresent orange of the limp, cloth-bound volumes published by the Left Book Club. For in the thirties the Left Book Club became the giant umbrella under which most progressive, left-wing activists found shelter.

The first proposal for a Left Book Club was made in May 1935, when John Strachey was asked by a representative of the Workers Bookshop, the foremost communist bookseller in London, to 'sit on the selection committee of a Left Book Club which was to choose books from any publisher's list'.[1] The bookshop devised and circulated to those already publishing left-wing volumes a plan for supplying books. The response was disheartening. All these publishers refused to put up any capital for the venture, and only Victor Gollancz accepted the scheme. No further progress was made on the proposal until Gollancz revived the idea in early 1936.

Gollancz and Strachey were called to a meeting organized by

[1] John Strachey, 'Left Book Club', *New Statesman and Nation*, 15 May 1937.

Sir Stafford Cripps to consider the establishment of a left-wing journal, *Tribune*, as a popular-front weekly. When leaving this meeting, Gollancz suggested to Strachey that the publication of a popular-front weekly was not sufficient. What was needed was a Left Book Club. Strachey agreed and Gollancz recommended that he and Strachey with the addition of Harold Laski should constitute the Club's selection committee. On 6 March 1936, an advertisement appeared in the *News Chronicle* announcing the establishment of the Left Book Club.

The original scheme was quite simple. Members would receive for 2s. 6d. (about 60c in 1936) a 'Left Book of the Month,' previously unpublished, often written specially for the Club, and always chosen from the book lists of Gollancz Ltd. Subscribers had to accept the monthly choice of the selection committee and would also be sent a copy of the Club's monthly periodical, *Left Book News* (later called *Left News*), characterized as 'something between a political magazine and a review of current "Left" literature'.[2] It usually contained a lengthy review by either Strachey or Laski of the Club's publications, an editorial by Gollancz, a summary of the Club's activities, and, in its first year, a regular monthly survey of the Soviet Union.

The Club's initial aim was to publish books that would appeal to the taste and pocketbook of a previously untapped left-wing audience. Gollancz was familiar with the obstacles publishers encountered when trying to gain a wide circulation for left books. Early in 1936, for example, when he sought a subscription from London booksellers for R. D. Charques and A. H. Ewen's book, *Profits and Politics in the Post-War World*, his London agent brought back 'ludicrously small orders' because, as Gollancz claimed, 'ninety-nine booksellers out of a hundred quietly boycotted socialism'.[3] This experience was the immediate stimulus for the establishment of the Club. Gollancz felt he could find a 'large number of people who would *undertake* to buy books provided they were published at a sufficiently low price.'

He was correct. The response to the Left Book Club advertisement was overwhelming. The three selectors felt 'we [would be] lucky to have 2500 members by the date of publication of the first choice, and gradually build up ... over a period of months to

---

2 *Left Book News*, May 1936.
3 Victor Gollancz, *More for Timothy* (London, 1953), p. 351.

5000'.[4] But after only one month, the Club's membership had passed 6000. By the end of the first year over 40,000 members had joined, and in June 1936, Gollancz was talking in terms of 100,000. This forecast was unduly optimistic, but, nevertheless, the Club's membership by April 1939 had reached 57,000. Its readership, moreover, was estimated at a quarter of a million people. At a time when not more than a few books each year sold 50,000 copies, the Left Book Club was able to publish every month a serious political book with a guaranteed circulation of over 50,000.

The Club's popularity, activities, and influence far exceeded the expectations of its founders. It quickly developed numerous supplementary activities and auxiliary organizations: discussion groups, week-end seminars, and political rallies were held, overseas groups, Russian language classes, and Left Book Club centres were organized. By April 1939 the local groups, created to discuss the monthly selections, numbered 1200, and the activities of the various affiliated organizations encompassed theatre, travel, photography, poetry, and music.

The Club was an immediate success because it was launched at a particularly auspicious time. It coincided with the triumph of the Popular Front in France and with the beginning of British interest in the Spanish Civil War. Moreover, extra-political groups, such as the Left Book Club, need a special political atmosphere to flourish, a climate where political debate and party activity have become atrophied. The political situation in the late nineteen-thirties was such that the existing voice of the progressive left, the Labour Party, had been stunned into relative inactivity by its 1931 knockdown; the Liberal Party was impotent; and very little outright political opposition to the National Government existed. The Left Book Club could and did provide an opportunity for rewarding political debate and meaningful political activity; it could and did offer a feasible political and economic alternative to the proposals put forward by the organized political parties. In short, it provided its members, in all but its name, with the excitements of a major political party.

The economic climate in 1936 also contributed to the Club's rapid success. The depression had passed its worst stage, and a scheme based on monthly contributions was workable, while the constant danger of economic crisis kept the enthusiasm of Club members at a high pitch.

[4] *Left Book News*, May 1936.

But the principal attraction was that the Club provided a vehicle of expression for the many people who were deeply concerned with the increasing threat of war and the growing menace of fascism. The Club's published aims were simply:

to help in the struggle *for* World Peace and a better social and economic order and *against* Fascism, by . . . increasing the knowledge of those who already see the importance of the struggle, and . . . adding to their number the very many who . . . hold aloof from the fight by reason of ignorance or apathy.[5]

Its goal was nothing less than the prevention of a second world war. Other considerations, economic decay, the establishment of socialism, were subordinated to this fight against war and fascism.

The Left Book Club was one of the first British organizations to mount a systematic attack on fascism. It canalized and mobilized anti-fascist opinion and, more significantly, it presented dramatic accounts of the danger and evils of fascist takeovers. The establishment of a Popular Front among left-progressive parties at home and a Peace Front among anti-fascist countries abroad became the cornerstone of Club policy. The Club was the most active and largest organized body in Britain working for a Popular Front. It forged a link, however tenuous, between supporters of the Labour and Liberal Parties, trade unions, the Socialist League, the ILP, and the Communist Party, and helped gather up the scattered efforts of left-wing activity for a Popular Front in the theatre, literature, and science.

Like all left-wing organizations in the Europe of the thirties, the Club became preoccupied with the struggle in Spain. It was a leading British supporter of the Republican cause. The defeat of Franco, Club members felt, would help to check fascism in Europe and lessen the threat of another world war. They urged the Labour Party to rescind its policy of non-intervention. Film shows, organized by the Club, acquainted Englishmen with the fierce war in Spain. Some local groups constructed motorcycle ambulances; others adopted Basque children. Women members organized 'knit-ins' for Spain, making clothes for the International Brigades. Club rallies collected large sums of money for 'the Cause,' and in 1938 a Left Book Club food ship for Spain was launched.

[5] Left Book Club *Brochure* (1936), p. 2.

Russia, as leader of the Peace Front, was viewed by Club members as a bulwark against fascism. Thus, Club policy stressed the necessity for closer cooperation between Russia and Britain and tried to break down prejudice against the Soviet Union, to explain its culture and government, and to familiarize people with Marxism. The Club organized tours to the Soviet Union and showings of the films of Eisenstein and Pudovkin. It published an account of Soviet politics by Pat Sloan, *Soviet Democracy*, and a description of Soviet life, *Comrades and Citizens*.

Its goals were broad, its methods simple. No particular political allegiance was required of its members and little doctrinal obedience was requested. It permitted its members to accept as little of the Club's creed as they desired and enabled them to mingle it with their old doctrines – pacifism, Marxism, Freudianism, even Swedenborgianism – with little intellectual effort. The comprehensive nature of the Club was reflected in its monthly book selections, which 'dealt with every aspect of the world about which it was possible to hold a Left opinion'.[6] The selection committee tried to maintain a balance between books on home affairs and on foreign affairs, between philosophical discourses or economic treatises and histories, chronicles, or political exposés. The books were designed to edify the faithful and to convert the indifferent. They were books 'requiring not the slightest knowledge of politics, economics or history for perfect understanding ... written in a most engaging style, and so persuasive as to be indeed unanswerable'.[7]

The committee attempted to satisfy 'the serious student's requirements on the one hand and those of the less politically advanced on the other'. To appeal to more popular tastes the Club occasionally published a novel or an autobiography.[8] Some of the selections may have been shallow, some no doubt were only glanced at, and others were never read,[9] but many were 'books of value and depth, likely not to cause momentary excitement so

---

[6] Robert Graves, Alan Hodge, *The Long Weekend* (London, 1940), p. 334.

[7] *Left News*, March 1938.

[8] Ibid. September 1937. André Malraux's *Days of Contempt* and Hillel Bernstein's *Choose a Bright Morning* were published as joint choices for August 1936. B. L. Coombes' autobiographical novel, *These Poor Hands*, was selected for June 1939. Stephen Spender's autobiographical fragment, *Forward From Liberalism*, was the January 1937 choice.

[9] Clement Attlee's *The Labour Party in Perspective* was so unpopular that thousands of copies lay unclaimed at the booksellers.

much as to make solid converts'.[10] As one reader put it (*Left News*, May, 1937):

When we have finished reading Palme Dutt's brilliant historical analysis, or Strachey's splendid, crystal-clear outline of the theory and practice of Socialism, all we can do is nod our heads and say, 'Yes comrades, you are right'.

Once the Club had amassed a substantial membership, it initiated numerous additional book schemes. Members could purchase each month a supplementary book, which was not an alternative choice to the compulsory monthly selection. Gollancz also offered the members a series of left-wing classics, including the Webbs' *Soviet Communism: A New Civilization*, without the original question mark; Emile Burns' 1000 page collection of the writing of Marx, Engels, Lenin, and Stalin; and the most influential book of the thirties, John Strachey's *The Coming Struggle for Power*. He issued cheap editions of books of special interest, like the symposium on *Christianity and Social Revolution* and Clifford Odets' *Waiting for Lefty*, and topical books on subjects of immediate importance, like Dudley Collard's *Soviet Justice and the Trial of Radek and Others*, and Koni Zilliacus' *The Road to War*. Gollancz even tried to establish a 'Left' Home University Library series, offering elementary textbooks on money, the Jewish question, the history of economic geography, and a short account of the Russian Revolution. In 1938 he started a Christian Book Club, under the direction of the Dean of Canterbury, Hewlett Johnson, as a subsidiary of the Left Book Club. But no books were ever issued and the idea was soon abandoned. Gollancz attempted to introduce teenagers into the Club organization through a Junior Left Book Club and even contemplated a Children's Left Book series and a Left Fiction Club. None of these three schemes materialized.

Although the Club's publications covered an enormously wide subject area, the majority dealt with three important and related topics: the threat of war, the danger of fascism, and the horrors of unemployment.

The monthly selections were of two kinds; propaganda tracts and factual analyses. The publications about the Spanish Civil War were typical of this balanced intellectual diet. *Spain in Revolt*, an

[10] G. D. H. Cole, Raymond Postgate, *The Common People* (2nd ed., London, 1946), p. 602.

early choice of the Club (December 1936), was written by two American communists and gave a biased Marxian analysis of the causes of the war. A year later Arthur Koestler's *Spanish Testament* was offered, and in June 1938, Frank Jellinek's *The Civil War in Spain* provided members with a historical account of the economic and social background of the war. By the outbreak of war in 1939 over two and a half million copies of its publications were in circulation. They provided its 57,000 members with 'an armoury from which a weapon could be selected for argument on any conceivable subject':[11] from the position of women in the USSR to life in an English prison; from a policy for British agriculture to the relationship between Freudianism and Marxism; from the evils of Hollywood to an account of the Paris Commune of 1871; from the life of Adolph Hitler to the benefits of artificial insemination.

The brochures distributed by the Club advertised that the selection committee of Gollancz, Strachey and Laski represented the three dominant shades of progressive opinion in Britain in the thirties. They formed a microcosm of a British Popular Front. Laski was a member of the Labour Party; Strachey was 'in broad sympathy with the aims of the Communist Party'; and Gollancz represented that ill-defined group of left-progressives who were 'interested in the spreading of all such knowledge and all such ideas as may safeguard peace, combat Fascism, and bring nearer the establishment of real Socialism'.[12]

But in reality this arrangement amounted to little more than a facade. Although Gollancz sent every book to Strachey and Laski for their opinion and the selection committee often lunched together, the Club was virtually run by one man – Victor Gollancz. He initiated most of the Club's additional activities and made all the major decisions on Club policy and expansion.

The extensive financial operations of the Club remain obscure. Gollancz never kept a separate balance sheet of Club expenses or profits. The money collected by the Club until 1939 seems to have been used for Club expansion, especially for the widespread advertising campaigns undertaken to increase membership, and for administrative expenses.

Gollancz refused to democratize the Club's decision-making apparatus. He resisted and eventually side-tracked the attempt by

---

11 Graves, *The Long Weekend*, p. 334.
12 *Left Book News*, May 1936.

local group leaders to influence Club policy and the choice of books. These local conveners tried to transform the Club into a loose federation of groups. They managed to hold two national conveners' conferences during which Club policy was discussed and criticized. At the 1937 conference a movement was initiated to loosen Gollancz's grip on the organization. A suggestion was made that 'it is . . . time to put the Groups on some more democratically organized national basis . . . through which members can express themselves'. A national council elected by the conveners and a written constitution were proposed.[13] Gollancz evaded both suggestions, and eventually the local leaders abandoned their attempt to temper his control.

Within a year of its establishment the Club was not only a book scheme, but a widespread movement with a network of local discussion groups. It was not until after they were founded in May 1936 that the Club became a truly mass movement. These groups served as a recruiting ground for new members, a meeting place for left-wing activists, and, in time, instruments of political propaganda. Their primary function, however, was to bring Club members together to discuss the monthly selections, international problems, or economic crises, and to formulate a common approach to the problems of war, fascism, unemployment, and peace.

John Lewis, national organizer, acted as liaison between the groups and the central Club organization. Through his efforts regional meetings of local representatives and annual conferences of local conveners were held, a *Handbook for Local Groups* was written, and printed 'aids for discussion' were circulated. Travelling organizers continually visited the groups. And Gollancz supervised the local group rallies even down to the wording on the posters and handbills.

The kind of political debate engaged in by local groups varied considerably. In the Home Counties the groups were largely social gatherings discussing the new selections over coffee and biscuits and 'enjoying the warm sense of shared feelings and common attitudes'. Many of the urban groups held meetings regularly, usually in a small café or bookshop, to discuss the chosen book, study its contents, make plans for a modest campaign for the Popular Front, and devise tactics for recruiting new members. Some group discus-

---

[13] 'Notes on Conveners' Conference', p. 6 (paper in possession of John Lewis).

sions were 'led by the few politically informed members of the audience, two or three Communists clashing with a Labour trade unionist about questions of ways and means, most of the others listening.'[14] A devastating picture of a typical group meeting is given by George Orwell in his novel *Coming Up For Air*.

The numerical strength of the groups varied greatly, ranging from five to six members in small provincial towns to 500 members in metropolitan areas like Manchester, Leeds, and Birmingham. Practically every London postal district had at least one active discussion group consisting of about fifteen to twenty participants. The degree of local support usually depended on the zeal of the local convener. This was particularly true of the University towns; Oxford, with a large left-wing population, was able to secure only fifty-three members; less radical and appreciably smaller Cambridge had a working group of 324.[15]

The groups were organized mainly on geographical lines. One critic imagined Gollancz seated at his desk with a map of England in front of him. Every time the telephone rang he stuck in a red flag – a new group for Blackpool, another for Manchester, and one for Stow-on-the-Wold.[16] If this map had existed, it would have looked one large mass of red flags, for within one year of the Club's founding over 500 local groups were operating and by May 1938 over 1000 discussion groups were serving 50,000 Club members. In 1938 an embryo international network was established. Groups were formed in Australia, South Africa, India, New Zealand, China, Canada, Norway, Belgium, France, Yugoslavia, and Ceylon. Although total membership in these foreign groups, composed mainly of British citizens living abroad, reached over 6000, their influence was negligible.

One striking development was the formation of vocational discussion groups. All kinds of organizations sprouted up, from accountants, busmen, taxi-drivers, commercial travellers, and railwaymen to scientists, architects, students, teachers, poets, journalists, musicians, lawyers, actors, and even cyclists.[17] The poets and writers groups included most of the influential members

---

14 Julian Symons, *The Thirties* (London, 1960), p. 107.

15 *Left Book News*, September 1936.

16 'Diary', *Time and Tide*, 22 January 1938.

17 The Musicians Group, led by Alan Bush and Arnold Goldsborough, had 100 members. Sybil Thorndike, Gerald Savory, and Michael Redgrave were members of the Actors Group.

of the left-wing literary establishment of the thirties: Randall Swingler, John Lehmann, C. Day Lewis, Rex Warner, Jack Lindsay, Alick West, Edgell Rickword, Arthur Calder-Marshall, Stephen Spender. Membership in the poets' group approached 200; its activities included poetry reading, mass recitations, and heated literary discussions. It tried to revive the broadsheet ballad, discuss the folk tradition in art, and devise declamatory verse for mass-meetings and revolutionary songs that could be sung in pubs. It even founded its own journal, *Poetry and the People*, which attempted to create a proletarian poetry movement among the English working class. While the magazine's influence was never great – its circulation reached only 1000 – it did gain the support of a considerable number of Bloomsbury 'Bolshies' and Mayfair 'Marxists'.

The scientists' group formed the most active of the special occupational groups, attracting over 300 people to its meetings and including among its leaders two of England's foremost scientists, Professors J. D. Bernal and J. B. S. Haldane. The most successful of the special groups was the Theatre Guild. It was established in April 1937 to express through the theatre the same interpretation of life and politics that Club publications expressed through the printed word. By September 1938 there were over 250 amateur Theatre Guild groups in existence, publishing left-wing drama, putting on topical skits at local political gatherings, and performing one-act plays. Under the leadership of its paid organizer, John Allen, and in cooperation with Unity Theatre, the leading amateur left-wing theatre in England, the Guild collected funds and contributed labour and materials to build a new home for left-wing theatre in London. Through its 250 groups it helped to develop an active left-wing provincial theatre movement. By February 1935, forty-five Theatre Guild groups had performed at least one play each. Audiences in Glasgow, Newcastle, Liverpool, Leeds, and Sheffield were introduced to the theatre of revolt through such productions as *Where's That Bomb*; Jack Lindsay's mass declamation, *On Guard for Spain!*; *Waiting for Lefty*; *Till The Day I Die*, and *Plant in the Sun*. The Guild published a monthly review of its local activities called *New Theatre*.

Although the great majority of the plays presented were of foreign origin, the Guild tried to start a grass roots dramatic movement by conducting classes in writing and acting. While little original material of merit came out of this venture and no play-wright of national stature emerged, the Guild made the first attempt to encourage English workers to develop their own revolutionary theatre. At the least it provided an excellent platform for socialist propaganda.

The Club did not neglect the social needs of its members. Over forty Club groups equipped their premises with coffee bars, rehearsal rooms, libraries, classrooms, and social halls. Many groups arranged tours to see socialism in practice. Members went to the Soviet Union, to the cooperative farms of Scandinavia, to the *Maisons du Peuple* of Belgium, and, with the avowed purpose of seeing Popular-Front France in action, to Paris, the Alps, and the Riviera. Dances and football matches were organized, in the belief that 'even games, songs, and recreation can, and indeed should, reflect an awakened Left-Wing attitude to things', and that 'walks, tennis, golf, and swimming are quite different when your companions are "comrades on the left"'.[18]

The members of the local groups represented a cross section of the country's social structure and a broad spectrum of political opinion. There were some working-class members, especially in South Yorkshire, South Wales, and the larger industrial centres. The Club tried to draw in more trade-union and working-class members and hired William Paul to act as trade union organizer. Gollancz also established an associate membership scheme for workers in which no financial contribution was necessary. The unemployed were likewise represented, occasionally banding together to purchase one membership. It was not uncommon, moreover, to learn of wealthy 'socialist' viscounts from Oxford 'folding the *Daily Worker* as their butlers pushed the Left Book Club books back onto the shelves'.[19] But the majority of members – according to John Lewis 75 per cent – were white collared workers, black-coated professionals, and newly-converted left intellectuals. The Club was predominantly a middle-class phenomenon. The social composition of the Essex group is a fair example of middle-class involvement in the Club. It consisted of 'a draughtsman, a doctor of physics, a printer, a bank clerk, a dental mechanic, a road mender, a school-teacher, a painter, [and] several clerks'.[20]

18 *Tribune*, 16 June, 7 July 1939.
19 Philip Toynbee, *Friends Apart* (London, 1954), p. 109.
20 John Lewis, 'Typical Groups' (unpublished).

Politically, the Club was composed of disgruntled liberals, professional communists, disillusioned labourites, and a large number of newcomers to the political arena. These latter were men and women without party allegiance, politically naïve and intellectually confused. They joined the Club because it enabled them to support popular radical causes without committing themselves to a party. For them the Club symbolized a new level of political consciousness, rather than an awakening of class consciousness. It represented an experiment in political education, converting 'thoughtless and apathetic men and women into eager, active and self-directing citizens'.

Prominent among the Club's supporters were the communist leaders Harry Pollitt and Palme Dutt; left-wing Labourites Sir Stafford Cripps and Ellen Wilkinson: Liberal Pacifists Richard Acland and Sir Norman Angell; Conservative Robert Boothby; the 'red' Dean of Canterbury Hewlett Johnson and even Lloyd George. The Club usually managed to include on its metropolitan speakers' platforms at least one Communist, one Liberal, one Labour MP, the 'red' Dean, and a left-wing intellectual. These gatherings became the physical embodiment of a British Popular Front, and occasionally Gollancz sent out his travelling circus of political celebrities to tour the country.

In its efforts to establish a Popular Front in Britain the Club sought to cultivate friendly relations with other left-wing bodies. In a period when the various labour organizations were attacking one another, the Club remained one of the few places where opposing elements in the labour movement could retain active contact. Labour Party members wrote some of the Club's selections, and Labour MPs were frequently headlined at its public rallies.

Although the Club tried to avoid official relations with any political party, it urged its members to join local Labour Parties, trade union branches and Co-operative Guilds. Members sometimes formed study circles within divisional Labour Parties. Gollancz hoped the Club would become a 'stronghold of truth', and that 'careful and patient thought' would lead to 'immediate and determined action by members in the organizations to which they belong'. In July 1937 the Club attempted to form a closer relationship with the Labour Party, which rejected the idea of a Popular Front. Largely on the initiative of Harold Laski, it offered the Labour Party executive the chance to present their policies on international and domestic affairs in two special issues of *Left News*. One issue was to coincide with the Trade Union Congress in September; the other with the Labour Party conference in October.

This offer was rejected by Hugh Dalton, Chairman of the National Executive of the Party, on the grounds that the Club 'is consistently critical of the present leadership of the Labour Party,' and that the books it published were 'in a too Left direction' – in particular, that they supported 'that United Front which the Labour Party rejects'.[21] In a letter to the *New Statesman and Nation* (28 August 1937), Dalton hinted that another reason for the rejection was that the Club was 'very sympathetic to Communism' and its 'books . . . show a heavy predominance of Communist and near-Communist authors'.

Dalton, however, did not completely shut the door on cooperation between the Club and the Labour Party. He presented an alternative plan under which *Left News* would 'give each month the same space to expositions of the "official" Labour view as it gives to John Strachey'. While Gollancz was willing to accept this suggestion he refused to agree to Dalton's other proposal that the book selection committee be 'so devised as to contain a number of members sympathetic to the views of "official" Labour'.[22] He felt that the addition of two or three Labour representatives to the selection committee would transform the Club into a semi-official Labour Party organization.

'Official' Labour came to view the Club as a potential threat and a political competitor. Herbert Morrison and Ernest Bevin attacked it in the press, claiming that it had 'become a political movement with substantial money behind it', and that its activities were 'in the direction of manipulation and controlling local Labour Parties'.[23] In March 1939 the Labour Party launched a competing book club, the Labour Book Service, and threatened to expel the whole body of Left Book Club members from the party by making 'membership of the Club incompatible with membership of the Labour Party.'[24]

Although relations between Henrietta Street and Transport

---

[21] *Left News*, August 1937.

[22] Ibid.

[23] Herbert Morrison, in *London News* (monthly publication of the London Labour Party), January 1939; Ernest Bevin, in *The Record* (journal of the Transport and General Workers Union), December 1938.

[24] *Left News*, April 1939.

House remained strained, the Club was able to ally itself successfully with those elements in the labour movement which supported a Popular Front. In September 1938 it made a formal arrangement with Sir Stafford Cripps' Popular-Front weekly, *Tribune*. Gollancz was elected to its editorial board and from 23 September 1938 each issue of *Tribune* contained a two-page section devoted to Left Book Club news. Club members often played a large part in their local labour movement, introducing middle-class people into the Labour Party, and revitalizing and in some cases initiating the establishment of local Labour Parties.[25] The Club even took credit for the joint Liberal-Labour by-election victory at Bridgewater in November 1938. It has also been claimed, perhaps justifiably, that the Club played 'a considerable part in making possible the Labour victory in 1945'.[26]

Although there was about the same amount of contact between the Club and the Labour Party as between the Club and the Communist Party, historical discussions about the Club have concentrated primarily on its relationship with the Communist Party.[27] It was scarcely necessary for the Communist Party to attempt to manipulate the Club or direct its operations; the Club's meetings and publications developed among its members a strong sympathy for communist policy. Like the Club, the party was dedicated to the fight against Franco and Hitler and to the formation of a Popular Front. In the circumstances of the thirties, joining the Communist Party seemed to many Club members the only available road to political action. Strachey expressed this attitude when he said, 'the Communist Party . . . embodies or groups round it almost all those extraordinary men and women who always form the living heart of a working-class movement'.[28]

In most people's minds the Left Book Club and the Communist Party were virtually indistinguishable. Gollancz's activities did little to discourage this identification. His picture appeared on a Communist Party handout with his comments on 'Why I Read

[25] For information on the relations between the Left Book Club and local Labour Parties, I am indebted to an unpublished report in the possession of John Lewis.

[26] John Strachey, *The Strangled Cry* (London, 1962), p. 220.

[27] See Symons, *op. cit.* pp. 99–110; and Neal Wood, *Communism and British Intellectuals* (London, 1959), pp. 60–3. Gollancz felt, however, in 1938, that too many local groups were coming under communist control. See *Left News*, November 1938, and *More for Timothy*, p. 357.

[28] *Left Book News*, September 1936.

the *Daily Worker*,' concluding that 'nothing is more important than an ever-increasing circulation for the *Daily Worker*'. In 1953 he admitted that for 'fifteen months' he was 'as close to the communists as one hair to another', adding, with the aid of hindsight, 'that for every minute of those months' he 'was billions of light years away from them'.[29] In the late thirties the light years seemed to have gone unnoticed while Club staff members often puzzled over the question whether 'V. G.' was a member of the Communist Party. Communist authors wrote some of the Club's most popular books. Communist leaders, especially Pollitt and Hannington, constantly appeared on Club platforms, lecturing audiences on the menace of fascist Germany and the magnificence of Soviet Russia. The Club entered into a special arrangement with Lawrence and Wishart, Communist Party publishers, whereby Club members could receive Lawrence and Wishart publications at reduced prices. The party also realized the value of the Club as a mass propaganda agency and gave full support to its activities. Some local discussion groups were completely under communist control and were often persuaded not to talk about the selected book at their meetings, but to chalk communist slogans on the streets. Thus, on many Englishmen's bookshelves the orange-covered volumes of the Club were placed comfortably alongside the 'solemn red-backed classics of the Marx-Engels-Lenin Institute, the mauve and bright yellow pamphlets by Pollitt and Palme Dutt', and near 'the Soviet posters of moonlit Yalta and sunlit tractors'.[30] On their own initiative, many Club members flocked to the Communist Party standard, and the Club became a market for new communist recruits.[31] The relationship between the Club and the Communist Party, however, was not always harmonious. Friction arose over the Club's publication of Orwell's *Road to Wigan Pier* and ex-communist Joseph Freeman's *American Testament*. But in general the Club gained from the Communist Party a devoted group of active members, a large number of writers, and a ready-made list of platform speakers, while the party, one of the smallest national communist organizations, secured from the Club a respectable, highly organized vehicle for its propaganda and recruiting.

---

[29] Gollancz, *More for Timothy*, p. 357.
[30] Toynbee, *Friends Apart*, p. 18.
[31] The Club can take some credit for the rapid increase in Communist Party membership, which rose from 6500 in 1935 to 16,000 in 1938.

While its enemies remained the same throughout the thirties, the Club varied its methods of attack. At first it concentrated on enlightening its own members, but in time these found it impossible to read and talk about current politics and yet do nothing about it. As Strachey foresaw, Club members were 'coming to the stage in which . . . what they want is not only to comprehend the world in various ways, but to change it'. Club leaders also felt, 'it is not enough to talk politics in small Groups with a restricted membership'. It was necessary 'to awaken sympathies in a very wide public'.[32] Gollancz recognized that in order to reach a mass adult audience, weapons besides books must be used, and large public rallies were organized. With his eye continually on the membership lists, Gollancz used these rallies to recruit new members. He gave the 'Club Speech', informing newcomers of the Club's activities and policies, and had small yellow recruiting leaflets placed on every seat. Time was set aside during each rally to permit those interested to fill them in.

Public meetings were also used to rally mass opinion on particular topics. At the time of Munich, Queen's Hall, London, was filled to capacity to hear a Left Book Club speaker urge his audience to 'Halt Hitler and Mussolini', to call for a general election, and to remember that 'Peace Depends on You'. Gollancz mobilized the full propaganda resources of the Club to try to force the Chamberlain Government to sign a three-power alliance of Russia, France, and England against possible fascist aggression. He urged members to organize public meetings, marches, and poster parades on the same theme, and on 29 June 1939, the Club held another public rally in Queen's Hall to urge the Government to sign the alliance.

Club rallies filled halls throughout England and Scotland. The Club's second annual rally in January 1938 at the Albert Hall was so successful that an extra hall had to be hired for the overflow. People were marched down to Queen's Hall and the speakers were shuttled between the two buildings by automobile. Attendance at the third and final national rally in April 1939 exceeded 10,000.

As the international situation worsened, the Club began to publish its own political leaflets and disseminate its own propaganda pamphlets. In February 1938 it published its first 'conversionist' booklet, the 'twopenny Strachey'. This 100 page pamphlet, en-

[32] *Left News*, October 1937.

titled *Why You Should Be a Socialist,* written by Strachey, was designed to serve as a 'Terse Guide to Such Questions as What causes unemployment ? What causes war ? What makes booms and slumps ? What is capitalism ? What is socialism ?' In a little over five months, Club members had sold 'twopenny Stracheys' to over three-quarters of a million people. The Strachey pamphlet was followed by a 'Twopenny Spain,' *The Truth About Spain*; the Dean of Canterbury's *Act Now*, published in March 1938, which sold over 100,000 copies by the end of April 1938; Professor Haldane's *How to be Safe From Air Raids* (November 1938); and Gollancz's own contribution, *Is Mr Chamberlain Saving Peace?* (1939).

The leaflets reached an even larger audience. In September 1938, a few days before the Munich crisis, the Club sold over two and a half million leaflets on the 'Hitler Menace'. In its largest mass effort, in November 1938, the Club, in cooperation with the Spanish Emergency Committee, circulated over ten million broadsheets protesting against a proposed Anglo-Italian agreement on Spain. In the spring of 1939 it distributed two million leaflets urging an alliance between 'France, Great Britain and Russia, with the assistance of smaller States, and the immense economic help of America' to halt the fascist threat. It was claimed that through its books, pamphlets, rallies, and leaflets, the Club had become 'an instrument of an unparalleled power for influencing the public mind'.[33]

Although the Club was not dissolved until 1948, it failed to maintain its influence beyond the outbreak of war. Indeed, it was severely weakened by the blow struck on 23 August 1939. The Nazi-Soviet Pact destroyed much of the appeal of the Club and undermined its authority. Its publications and actions now seemed, to many members, to have little relevance to the international situation. Underlying all its thinking had been the belief in the irreconcilable hostility between Soviet communism and German fascism. For three years members had been fed on a strict diet of anti-fascism and pro-communism. Russia symbolized all that was good, rational, and humane. Germany exemplified all that was evil, irrational, and inhumane. As Strachey put it, 'Amid the welter and chaos of the international situation, the position of one great power remains constant and clear. The speeches of the leaders of the

[33] *Tribune*, 31 March 1939.

Soviet Union do not change from appeasement to firmness and from firmness back to appeasement again overnight'.[34] After 23 August, these words had little meaning.

With the outbreak of war, many members felt that nothing more could be done. For them the Club had lost its *raison d'être*. Furthermore, a cleavage developed within the Club's membership over the question of the war. Gollancz and Laski spoke for those who believed that the war was primarily a war against fascism and should be supported. Strachey championed those who felt the war was an imperialist war, which might at any moment be turned against the Soviet Union.[35] Thus, internal dissension between a pro-Soviet, anti-war faction, and an anti-communist, pro-war faction prevented the Club from speaking with a single voice.

Resignations began flowing into Club headquarters. Middle-class progressives left because they were disillusioned with the Club's inability to present meaningful comments on the existing political situation. Marxian clichés, anti-fascist slogans, the myth of Soviet Russia, could no longer bear the weight of sustained criticism. Communists resigned because the Club began publishing anti-communist and anti-Russian books. Pollitt and Hannington severed relations with the Club early in 1940. John Lewis left in July 1940 over Club policy to the war and to the fall of France.

Technical problems contributed further to the Club's loss of membership. Booksellers no longer acted as reliable distributing agents. Local organizations broke down because people were constantly displaced, some going into the army, others becoming absorbed in war work. Large-scale rallies and meetings became impossible to arrange. Lines of communication between members, groups, and headquarters were dislocated. Moreover, it soon became evident that during wartime 'the number of men and women who will face the reading of a serious book regularly month by month, and will pay half-a-crown for it, is necessarily . . . small'.[36]

The outbreak of war started a new trend in the Club's choice of books and its editorials. Before the war most Club publications

[34] Ibid., 6 April 1939.
[35] Strachey later changed his view of the war. When the Germans opened their offensive in the Low Countries he found it 'indispensable to protest publicly against [the communist] line which continued, in the face of all the facts, to represent British and French Imperialism as the strongest reactionary force in the world today'. *Left News*, August 1940.
[36] *Left News*, April 1941.

presented clear and factual arguments aimed at intellectual conversion. It was assumed that established facts, set in a rational and logical argument, would lead to one true solution. Now the style changed: the new aim was to present conflicting facts and opinions. For example, the selections for November and December 1939, Leonard Woolf's *Barbarians at the Gate*[37] and the Dean of Canterbury's *The Soviet Sixth of the World*, were designed to give contrasting opinions about the Soviet Union. Similarly, the January and February issues of *Left News* presented an open debate between Laski and Strachey on the continuation of the war.

In May 1940 Palme Dutt's book on India was not treated to the customary review of a monthly selection, but was subjected to a long and sustained critique by Laski. His article was a rebuttal rather than a review.

By spring 1940 it was clear that the Club had come to resemble more a debating society than an experiment in political education. It became an 'open forum for the points of view of all writers who are genuinely concerned with human progress'. Discussions on Soviet Russia, China, Spain, and communism were replaced by debates on freedom of thought, toleration, justice, kindness, and mercy. Its early dedication to preserving peace, defeating fascism, and pursuing social justice became a commitment to the decisive defeat of Hitler. Its hopes for a Popular Front yielded to the belief that 'the Labour Party is the only possible spearhead for advance'. From a Club closely connected to communist party policy, it began to publish scathing anti-communist tracts.[38] Gollancz drew up a new prospectus and even contemplated changing the Club's name to 'The League of Victory and Peace'.

The Club managed, however, to survive the war, acting primarily as a home for the numerous socialist refugees living and writing in England.[39] But its popularity, its effectiveness, and its historical significance must be judged as a phenomenon of the

---

[37] The first attack on the Soviet Union published by the Club. Its selection set off a mass resignation campaign by Communist Party members. See *Left News*, January 1940.

[38] The most penetrating of these attacks, although not published under the Club's name, was a group of essays edited by Gollancz, *The Betrayal of the Left* (London, 1941), and Gollancz's own *Where Are You Going? An Open Letter to Communists* (London, 1940).

[39] One half of *Left News* was taken over by the 'International Socialist Forum', edited by Julius Braunthal.

thirties. It helped to modify the political outlook of a whole generation of English men and women. It sensitized them to questions of foreign affairs. Countries known only as names on travel posters became areas of intense political interest and personal concern. If the Club failed in its task to prevent war, its leaders could at least feel satisfied that 57,000 Englishmen knew why it happened, where it was taking place, and who was the enemy. Chamberlain's statement about far-away countries of which we know nothing certainly was not applicable to Left Book Club members and supporters.

The Club became the greatest single force in England for the dissemination of left-wing thought. It injected, especially through the works of Strachey, the first effective dose of Marxism into the English cultural blood stream. It became 'a landmark in the shaping of a self-conscious and more ideological "Left"', replacing 'the Fabian Society as the home of the intellectual *avant-garde*'.[40] It helped to popularize a new political vocabulary, especially such terms as full employment, socialized medicine, town planning, and social equality. Almost imperceptibly this new verbal consciousness helped to prepare Englishmen for the economic and social changes after the war.

The Club was not a unique phenomenon in English history, for it takes its place in a long line of extra-political organizations. In an age of mass literacy, it was the modern equivalent of Cobbett's Hampden Clubs, the London Corresponding Society, and the Chartists. But it differed from them in making its appeal not through oratory, local agitation, or national petitions, but primarily through the printed word.

Everything in the thirties tended to divide along Left-Right lines. Clergymen were Left or Right; intellectuals were either poetical prophets or political poets; literature was proletarian or bourgeois. The Book Clubs led the field. Following the pattern set by Gollancz's organization, a Labour, a Socialist, even a Right Book Club were established. As cartoonist Low visualized it, the clash between Right and Left in England was played out in a war of Book Clubs, where books became weapons and words ammunition. To this extent, A. J. P. Taylor is correct in seeing the Club as a

[40] David Thomson, *England in the Twentieth Century* (London, 1965), p. 162; R. H. S. Crossman, 'Towards a Philosophy of Socialism,' in R. H. S. Crossman, ed., *New Fabian Essays* (London, 1952), p. 5.

safety-valve, because reading became 'a substitute for action, not a prelude to it'; and Club members 'worked off their rebelliousness by plodding through yet another orange-covered volume'.[41] Yet it is difficult to see whether a more revolutionary movement could have developed in England in the thirties. Compared to the activities of the Left on the Continent, the work of the Left Book Club looks pallid. But in a country without a strong communist movement or a serious fascist threat, it seems the natural response.

Victor Gollancz must be awarded a significant place in left-wing history. His unfailing energy and organizational ability helped to

Cartoon by David Low, from the *Evening Standard*, 13 March, 1937

make the Club a great success. He was the ' "king-pin" of the cultural and political activities of the United Front, a demon of energy, capable, trustworthy, and possessed of so overwhelming a belief in the righteousness of his opinions as to bear a recognizable resemblance to the ancient Hebrew prophets'.[42] It was no easy achievement to persuade 57,000 people to read left books month by month; to organize 1,200 discussion circles which actively debated international and domestic questions; to develop interest in the films of the left, the theatre of the left, and in such social questions as unemployment, prisons, distressed areas; and to build up a following which filled the largest halls in England. The Club prided itself

[41] A. J. P. Taylor, 'Confusion on the Left', in John Raymond, ed., *The Baldwin Age* (London, 1960), p. 76.

[42] Fredric Warburg, *An Occupation For Gentlemen* (London, 1959), p. 222.

on fostering a new concept of political education. It was 'something more than a device for getting a 10s. 6d. book for half-a-crown; it [was] something more than obtaining ... interesting reading. It [was] a movement of *education*, undertaken in the hope that a devoted body of people will learn the truth in time, and proceed to act on the basis of the knowledge acquired'.[43] This suggested an exaggerated faith in the efficacy of reason, the power of public opinion, and the magic of rational argument.

To many of its members, the Club was much more than a book club. One day in the life of a dedicated member could conceivably consist of waking to find his Left Book Club monthly selection on his doorstep; attending a Left Book Club Russian language class; going to the local Left Book Club travel agency to arrange for a Left Book Club tour to the Soviet Union; spending the remainder of the morning selling Left Book Club publications in the town marketplace; attending a Left Book Club luncheon, organized by some local businessmen; then going to the Left Book Club Centre to play ping-pong and to relax reading left periodicals; selling Left Book Club pamphlets and leaflets for the remainder of the afternoon; in the evening attending a Left Book Club discussion meeting, followed by a Left Book Club film-showing on Spain and a one-act play performed by the local Left Book Club Theatre Guild group; chalking a few slogans on the way home; reading his *Left News* and then dozing off to sleep, secure in the knowledge that the Left Book Club was Not So Much a Book Club, More a Way of Life.

[43] *Left News*, December 1936, p. 167.

Laski Redivivus

Martin Peretz

It is now more than fifteen years since Harold J. Laski died, and it is almost as if whatever favourable words have been entered for him since have been in the defensive mood, slightly apologetic and with just the faintest traces of embarrassment. Such, in fact, was the case, one should add, even before his death, especially after his unsuccessful libel action. Moreover, 'there is no element of his work', as he himself rather sardonically wrote of Marx's, 'which has not been declared obsolete'.[1] And while one would not seek for Laski the voluminous attentions one naturally claims for Marx, it is surely reasonable to withdraw glib charges of obsolescence pending the kind of serious scholarly consideration which Laski has been denied and which, if only in virtue of his pre-eminent place in radical thought and in radical movements on four continents and over two generations, he should so easily command.

At the end even his friends felt obliged to justify, by way of their own personal caveats or his extra compensating qualities, what loyalties they felt for him. This was true for Beloff and for Strachey, himself no innocent when it came to egregious enthusiasms; true also for his London School of Economics students in their memorial publication, though perhaps it made more sense for them; true as well for Kingsley Martin who records, among other regrets, that Laski's brilliance and erudition 'did not in themselves compel affection'. What was true in England may be taken as only hinting at the fate suffered by his reputation in the United States, where Laski had become a totemic anathema to the always supercilious, already triumphant, if not yet quite vital centre. Max Lerner's 'lance for Laski',[2] moving and generous as it was, signalled the retreat of a wide milieu that a few years earlier would have been anxious to assert it had gone to school, literally and

[1] Harold J. Laski, *Marx and Today* (London, 1943), p. 3.
[2] See Max Lerner in *New York Post*, 27 March 1950, 30 March 1953, reprinted in Lerner, *The Unfinished Country* (New York, 1959), pp. 506–9.

metaphorically, willingly and by diffusion, to Laski and perhaps to him alone. He died in the same week that F. O. Matthiesen, the Harvard literary historian, jumped to his death from a Boston hotel room. The two events are a sheer coincidence, but they marked as well as any might – particularly if one recalls also the fatal seizure only days later of Léon Blum in France – the exhaustion of a hope and a temper. English socialism is, as Mr Crossman once told us, still 'bookless',[3] and, in partial consequence at least of this, his own ministerial efforts notwithstanding, also largely without vision and normative principle. The political and intellectual content of the American fifties is sufficiently well understood in the English-speaking world – better than America's most enthusiastic celebrants are wont to concede – not to require much characterization here. It may well be, however, that the grievances of Laski's ghost will be redressed there, where grass-roots discontent, academic engagement, and social inventiveness appear once again to be released, where on fronts domestic and foreign what Laski taught – about pluralism and federalism and the concrete economic determinisms of state policy – will appear relevant rather than archaic. It is of only mildly symptomatic interest, I suppose, that when the *New Statesman* put together a fiftieth anniversary collection, it found nothing of Laski's worth reprinting, though three of its long-time editor's contributions were redeemed from oblivion, including a rather insignificant piece on Buchman and the Oxford Group[4]; on the other hand, the almost simultaneous centenary anthology from *The Nation* (New York),[5] appropriately and with the regard due to one of its most distinguished associates, carried a Laski article on the history of the Labour Party, still provocative at this date.

In truth, of course, those who are most faithful to the letter of old bromides must ultimately find Laski doubly uncongenial: he was demonstrably wrong so often, and at the same time had the altogether disconcerting habit of changing his mind. If, then, it is not dogma one wants – though Laski decidedly was not without some penchant for that himself – but learning and a bit of wisdom, his twenty-odd books, to say nothing of many scores of essays and

[3] R. H. S. Crossman, *The Charm of Politics* (London, 1958), p. 139.

[4] Edward Hyams, ed., *New Statesmanship* (London, 1963).

[5] Henry M. Christman, ed., *One Hundred Years of The Nation* (New York, 1965), pp. 279–86.

tracts, are not likely to prove unrewarding. At the very minimum Laski, having at once, and over many years formulated, epitomized, and acted upon a whole constellation of values and beliefs, is a revealing chapter unto himself in the history of the era after the first world war.

In an even-tempered, albeit highly critical study of Laski's thought,[6] Herbert Deane, while assiduously noting continuities, delineates five more or less distinct stages in its development, the origins of at least two corresponding to particular historical circumstances (or alleged misreadings thereof), the others presumably more independent of such influence. The first three stages may be defined as pluralist, Fabian, and Marxian, respectively; the fourth as essentially of indeterminate 'popular-front' hue; the final one, covering the last five years of Laski's life, so confuses the author that he is content merely to recount where Laski is contradicted by events and where he contradicted himself. This inability to see that Laski's twilight period was one in which he was trying to bring his thought full circle in an honest reckoning with the real disappointments of the Soviet, American, and British socialist experiences alike, is shared by almost all who have had occasion to write about him. In large measure this is a function of the general acceptance of the quasi-official cold war ideology according to which: 1) Russia almost alone had undermined the peace and all but completely destroyed whatever meagre possibilities were open to it for internal liberalization, while (2) England and the United States were well on their way to having solved, gradually but certainly, the problems of quantity which had seemed so threatening after the 1929 crash and during the fascist ascendancy.[7] Indeed, little time passed before we were also being informed that problems of quality would likewise be resolved in short order. Laski, however, never owned to these particular simplifications; and he often quizzically noted how an intellectual generation that had become 'hooked' on ambiguity as antidote to its earlier addictions could become so oblivious to the moral difficulties of its new position. But this new position proved to be the great divide, and from that rigid perspective Laski clearly fell

---

[6] Herbert Deane, *The Political Ideas of Harold J. Laski* (New York, 1955).

[7] Many reviews of *The American Democracy* (1948) shrugged the book off as dated and irrelevant. The civil rights struggle and the fledgling war on poverty of more recent years show, however, just how time-bound such evaluations were.

on the other side. In the camp to which he was relegated, Laski was, one hastens to point out, equally ill at ease, and perhaps even more unwelcome. To have been thought a heretic, a dreamer, or a failure by the great sovereign systems of our time and by their academic pastorates may be, after all, in some final judgment, no mean encomium.

The perspective of east-west, communist-anti-communist conflict has coloured our understanding of more than the late Laski; of more even than his full twenty-year adherence to Marxism. It has caused us to isolate his early work from the rest, to idealize it, even as we are already too jaded to think that he himself did little else but idealize the real potential for authentic pluralist development towards freedom. On this score, it seems to me, Bernard Crick is wrong, writing in one of those end-of-the-decade premature obituaries-cum-exhortation for the Labour Party,[8] in calling the posthumous publication of Laski's uncompleted *The Dilemma of Our Times* 'a perhaps questionable act of friendship'. For it is there, rambling and discursive as the book is, and in several of his last articles, that Laski came to grips with his successively frustrated hopes. He had at last fully learned the lesson of great expectations which Dr Johnson had confided to Boswell. Most immediately it was Labour Britain that enveloped him in despair, and, as with the 1931 National Government, his sadness expressed itself as anger fixed largely on one man. In the late forties, of course, it was Ernest Bevin who became his *idée fixe*, an incarnation of vulgar anti-semitism, of sterile anti-communism as creed, of bureaucratic socialism without ideals. But it was obviously more than what he considered to be Bevin's malevolence that drove him to write about the future in futile and fatalistic terms. Kingsley Martin's biography has described in detail the turnings of Laski's mind in those years when he thought his party had renounced its internationalist socialist obligations and embraced almost entirely without reserve the alliance with Washington. His now famous letter to Justice Frankfurter, 'I now know why even victory left Lincoln with a sense that the dawn is not an awakening but mostly an opportunity to wait for the evils of the next night',[9] reflected a

---

[8] Bernard Crick, 'Socialist Literature in the 1950s', *The Political Quarterly* (London), July–September 1960, p. 361.

[9] Cited in Kingsley Martin, *Harold Laski* (New York, 1953), p. 241.

startling bleakness of mood. As is known, in February 1949 Laski quietly asked to have his name removed from the Labour Party National Executive's nomination lists. At times, however, he contemplated an even more precipitate course, perhaps a thunderous resignation or even, as he wrote to an American friend, to 'leave the party and fight it in every way I can . . . You can imagine what I feel after giving half my life to this party'.[10] This special dismay with Labour in turn indicated a deeper and all-pervasive disillusionment, the more ironic in that he was thought by so many to have wielded power over forces on which he had essentially no impact. Moreover, for all his posturings about proximity to the seats of the mighty, bitterness was added to irony, since he wanted no credit for a situation so different from his own imaginings. A socialist victory at the polls neither achieved what Laski yearned for nor made him the satanic eminence that Churchill had disastrously fabricated for the 1945 elections.

Having chosen successive *bêtes noires*, Laski, by a kind of historical symmetry, succeeded in becoming one himself, and not without reason. Thus, with the especial lucidity of the progressively insane, and indicative of the perceptions of the more cautious normal, Forrestal saw in Laski and his power a threat to the survival of capitalist ideology.[11] This 'mild obsession' of the first American Secretary of Defence, though based on a ludicrous over-estimation of Laski's real political significance, reflected a correct understanding of what his efforts were about: to undermine those received habits of thought which identify the operative patterns of the present with the principles of universal justice. While this read to Forrestal, predictably enough, as an apologia for communism, it lay at the bottom of all of Laski's writing and had emerged as its central core long before *Faith, Reason and Civilization* (1944) appeared to haunt the troubled nights of fearfully pursued men.

Arnold Hauser has written of the 'psychology of exposure' as the characteristic mode and theme of modern thought. The illumination of distorted consciousness has accordingly been the chosen task of historical materialism no less than of psychoanalysis. But the adepts of one method have been in the main hostile to practi-

[10] Laski to Max Lerner, 16 August 1948. The Lerner Collection, Yale College Library.

[11] See Arnold A. Rogow, *James Forrestal: A Study of Personality, Politics and Policy* (New York, 1963), pp. 145–8, and Walter Millis, ed., *The Forrestal Diaries* (New York, 1951), p. 80.

tioners of the other; and Laski on this score was no exception. In his 1926 Inaugural Lecture at the London School of Economics, for example, while conceding the light that psychology might shed on politics, going even so far as to amend Rousseau's aphorism to state that 'man . . . is born everywhere in chains, and becomes free only upon the grim conditions of self-knowledge', he nevertheless insists on the final inadequacy and inutility of the approach.[12] Significantly, then, his occasional references to Nietzsche were in the nature of asides while his allusions to Freud were flippant and derogatory.[13] This animus against the instinctivist orientation, even in its more modest formulations, revealed itself further in his pained ambivalence towards the work of the young Walter Lippman and of Lippman's mentor, Graham Wallas, whom Laski succeeded in the Chair of Political Science. Here, too, Laski is found to be on one more or less exclusive side of another great divide, though again not without dissociating himself on occasion from its dominant features. His first two books yield no substantive mention of Marx whatever, and he seemed to delight in giving regular vent to Justice Holmes' anti-Marxian spleen, from which, it should be clearly noted, he did not for a moment pause to dissent. In fact his 1922 Fabian essay on Marx, comfortably reissued in America by the meliorist League for Industrial Democracy a decade later, is a judicious but sharply critical effort, especially pointed in its remarks on economic monocausality and the theory of value.

All this notwithstanding, Laski was from the very first a socialist, which implied that he found the injustices of the world to be rooted largely in its economic relations. The state was the medium through which these relations were established and sustained. But the state also made supererogatory claims which the content of the lives of its citizens daily denied and belied. Yet legal theory and political doctrine – from Plato onwards and most relevantly in Bodin and Blackstone, in Austin and the idealists alike – had successfully justified the actual exercise of government authority by transcendental reference either to essential purpose or to the very nature of power itself, and sometimes to both. The state thus became a secular *unam sanctam,* in which the boundary of its sovereignty, the

[12] Laski, *The Danger of Being a Gentleman* (London, 1939), pp. 35–7.
[13] See Mark de Wolfe Howe, ed., *Holmes-Laski Letters* (Cambridge, Mass. 1953), pp. 120, 1206.

limits of its omnicompetence, was the expansive imagination of the legal mind. Nor had the *annus mirabilis* 1789 done much to change this situation, since a new and no more relenting sovereignty was in time fully to replace the old. Almost intact, and despite the rhetoric of the sovereignty of the individual, that theory of the state survived which omitted the shadow that fell between willing right and doing right, to say nothing of virtually ignoring the deeper question of knowing what is right in the first place. With juristic equality secured, the traditional argument about the use of power would seem to have been exhausted and all legitimate demands on the state met, or at least orderly and open and neutral processes developed whereby they could be met.

This congeries of ideas was the 'given' which Laski confronted in his earliest writings. His decision, however, was not to meet these notions on their own highly circumscribed terms, in which discussion would become more and more abstract and Jesuitical – or Talmudic – but to see what actually happened in the real world. That intellectual proclivity Laski shared with his aging friend Holmes. Now the Justice knew, for example, that his eminent predecessor John Marshall was wrong in asserting that 'courts are the mere instruments of law and can will nothing'. In realizing that the opposite was the case, moreover, he found himself embarked on a career that made him a forerunner of the sociological school. But Holmes was not as free from the ancient absolutes as he thought, and in consequence there was a tension between his judicial austerity and liberal constructionist views of the constitution on the one hand, and his experimental-social policy orientation on the other. This kind of ambiguity never puzzled Laski because he recognized that all political ideas have uses and that most of them, particularly when they are under fire from below, become the haven of motives that cannot allow the scrutiny of daylight.

'The hands and feet' (to use Hegel's metaphor) of theories of the state, Laski believed, were the protection and maintenance of privilege and of the exclusive control of sovereignty. The dimensions of these went beyond economic matters and, following Figgis and Barker, Laski focussed on dissident religious challenges to the long arm of temporal power. But surely his interest in the *Vindiciae Contra Tyrannos* and the rights of the Scottish Presbytery in the Disruption of 1843, as well as of the Catholic Church against both Gladstone and Bismarck, was a concern *à clef*, much as his elevation of Lamennais' stubborn conscience towards Rome was intended to evoke sympathy for the contingency of disobedience under different circumstances and towards different ends. The fuller contours of his scheme to persuade us that the sovereign state was discredited and the world plural were economic in character; and he assessed the inadequate performance of the state in terms of a socialized Benthamite calculus in which a growing and ever more self-consciously cohesive part of the population felt itself taken insufficiently into account in the distribution of society's multiple bounties.

There is, we might say, an escalation in the intensity of complaint in the early Laski. Thus, writing in 1917, he asserts, 'A state may in theory exist to secure the highest life for its members. But when we come to the analysis of the hard facts it becomes painfully apparent that the good actually maintained is that of a certain section, not the community as a whole'.[14] A year later he reports, 'We were simply forced to the realization that majority rule could not be the last word on our problems. So long as political power was divorced from economic power the jury of the nation was in reality packed'. Or 'the state . . . is in reality the reflection of what a dominant group or class in a community believes to be political good . . . for the most part defined in economic terms'.[15] He would soon be creating the theoretical scaffolding for a new philosophy of the state directed towards a new purpose. The present 'instruments with which we work . . . do not suit a temper in which the development of initiative in the humble man is the main effort of the time . . . [This] is in a direction which challenges the legal rights established by prescription in the name of an equality for which our institutions are unsuited'.[16]

The essence of this analysis of the crisis in political thought and institutions survived all of the changes in Laski's thinking, though when, as Crane Brinton once wrote, he was less 'under the influence of Acton and Maitland than of Marx and Lenin', a certain stridency entered into his indictment of liberalism. In any event, these shifts manifested themselves on the programmatic level. But even some of the major premises of the analysis are not much strained by the mechanics that were to resolve the problems he

[14] Laski, *Studies on the Problem of Sovereignty* (New Haven, 1917), p. 11.
[15] Laski, *Authority in the Modern State* (New Haven, 1918), pp. 113, 81.
[16] Laski, *Foundations of Sovereignty* (New Haven, 1921), p. 29.

posed. For while much of his appeal in argument was to natural rights and personal ethics, his individualism was neither anomic nor atomic in character. Moreover the doctrines of corporate personality and social solidarity emerged early as the crucial categories of group polyarchism. At the same time the pluralist state was still a normative proposition, though the struggles of government with church and union suggested its impending fulfilment. Indeed, the sovereignty which he viewed as incompatible with the evidence of its own obsolescence was never something he dismissed as sheer *res ficta et picta*; he knew full well its operative coercive strengths.

The retreat from pluralist government was admitted, it appears, more in sorrow than in desire. It was in keeping with the original perception of the centrality of economic power and the expanding sense that only a direct assault on its political expressions would relax the grip of capital on the valve giving access to Locke's commodious life. What Laski was in effect conceding was that even the accelerating drift towards pluralism could be deflected by the very forces that had so long possessed sovereignty as their own. Nor was the increasing harshness of his response to this situation altogether at variance with the guidelines reluctantly set by liberalism to meet demands that it extend its promise from the political to the social and economic spheres. If vested economic privilege fed on the deprivations of the many, if it sustained itself at the cost of the democratic principle, it would have to be the object of social surgery. Much can be made of the fact that when Laski turned from diagnosis to prognosis, he too had to seek the shelter of something akin to sovereignty. But his critics are left in that peculiarly uncomfortable position of arguing that Laski's emphasis on the primacy of economic matters in politics reflected a materialist malaise, while they themselves, to protect their own economic interests, would tolerate almost anything in preference to a candid recognition of that primacy. He was fond of quoting Machiavelli to the effect that men would sooner forgive the murder of their relatives than the theft of their property; and he found little in the post-war world to disprove this view. It should not be thought, however, that he was untroubled by the fate of his pluralist values in socialist circumstances: embattled as he was, Laski did not have the unfurrowed brow George Sand is said to have credited to Herbert Spencer. On the contrary, he pondered these quandaries till the end of his life and resisted the temptation, now the fashion in political sociology, to describe those systems as pluralist which make concessions to the bottom and important decisions at the top. Presumably if one lowers the stakes, it is easier to win.

Nineteen thirty-one was Laski's trauma, and in truth he never quite got over it. The scene is being revised, MacDonald's backbone has been refurbished, and he has even had some revenge on his tormentors. Mr A. J. P. Taylor, for example, has given his verdict on the episode. Laski, he tells us, 'worked up the legend that the constitution had been manipulated against Labour during the crisis of 1931 and drew from this the conclusion that socialism could not be introduced with the existing machinery of parliamentary government'.[17] Now that is not exactly what Laski concluded; but if Sir Patrick Hastings could persuade a special jury that it was, presumably there is no reason why an author of a volume in the *Oxford History of England* could not persuade himself of the same. If, however, one is old-fashioned enough to respect fine distinctions, one should point out that Laski's writings on democratic institutions were conditional. He did not foreclose options. Nor was it with relish that he contemplated the joint impact of the economic crisis and the rising tides of fascism and socialism.

Yet, granting that there was something apocalyptic in the thrust of Laski's argument at the time, it is not at all certain that his loss of confidence in capitalist democracy was unjustified. His speculative hypotheses on the relationship of socialism to traditional political forms in England have not been adequately or even minimally tested. The war, after all, as Professor Titmuss has shown, intruded on to the partisan arena to create by force of circumstances a nascent neo-socialism and ease the pains of what might come after. Despite this, as no one would deny, socialism has never really been attempted, and not only because Labour failed in socialist will. What reasons there might have been for a failure of socialist nerve in 1945 Laski had adumbrated in the thirties, and these were made only the more impelling by the war-exhaustion of the economy and by the international situation. Is it not possible that the entrenched reaction of extra-parliamentary

[17] A. J. P. Taylor, *English History: 1914–1945* (Oxford, 1965), p. 348. The most extensive criticism of Laski on this score is in Reginald Bassett, *Nineteen Thirty-One: Political Crisis* (London, 1958), pp. 361–5, 393–407.

bodies which Laski above all feared never developed because no complete and systematic assault on the profit system was undertaken that would have occasioned it?

'All philosophies of history', a wise historian has written, 'are revelations of true history'. There is no reason why Laski's should be exempt from this rule. But the point here is not only that he reflected reality and thus in turn may even have helped to shape it, as well as its later refractions. More significantly, he gave us an extended historical Baedeker to the vicissitudes and prospects of democratic government. And while the particular events of August and September 1931 assumed for him in the ensuing years greater proportions than from a distance and after so much now seems warranted, the crisis he was then describing in such detail had already been tentatively sketched in *The Grammar of Politics* (1925). During the spring before the establishment of the National Government, in informal talks at Yale and lectures at the University of North Carolina, Laski argued that the success of parliamentary democracy derived from two principal causes.

The period of its consolidation was one of continuous and remarkable economic expansion; it became associated, accordingly, in men's minds with outstanding material progress. The standard of life increased for every class; and most of the important questions which were debated – the franchise, education, public health, the regulation of women's and children's labour, the place of churches in the state – admitted of a fairly simple solution. More important, perhaps, was the fact that the two main parties in Parliament were agreed about the fundamentals of political action. After the triumph of free trade, there was hardly a measure carried to the statute book by one government which could not equally have been put there by its rivals.[18]

These prerequisites, Laski argued, had now vanished, and there was no lack of corroboration in events of the strain on parliamentarism and liberal theory which he saw as the consequence. Rather than being indifferent to the fate of parliamentary institutions, he was anxious – because he perceived value and wisdom in the forms – lest they founder together with the limited social purposes for which they had originally been fashioned.

It is from this perspective that we may understand, for example, his antagonism to MacDonald's National Government or even his

[18] The Weil Lectures at the University of North Carolina were reprinted as Laski, *Democracy in Crisis* (Chapel Hill, 1935); see p. 33.

mixed response to the coalition under Churchill. For, as he wrote in his summing up on constitutional government,

Mr Ramsay MacDonald's conception of the ideal Parliament as a Council of State in which the Opposition co-operates with the government for the common good – seems to me to come near to opening the door to the one-party state; and the nearer we approach, even by consent, to that condition, the more likely we are to destroy the essential virtues of Parliamentary democracy, which rests above all upon the full freedom of constitutional opposition.[19]

Though it may be that his fixation on MacDonald led him into hyperbole, what really weighed on Laski were the practical political implications of the crisis. True, in an otherwise perfunctory business letter to O. G. Villard, he could not resist at least one jab at the 'defects of essential character in MacDonald'. But, writing to the same correspondent some months later, while he still thinks MacDonald's singular achievement to have been blocking 'a peaceful transition to socialism in this country', it is his fear that 'the Tories are demanding a stronger second chamber as insurance against socialism'[20] which reactivates his old distrust of traditional institutions and their hostility to radical change. It is for developments such as this and for allowing the king to compromise his formal neutrality, let alone undermine the party system, that Laski heaps ignominy on Labour's former leader. 'It is not, I think, unreasonable to term Mr Ramsay MacDonald's emergence as Prime Minister of the National Government a Palace Revolution.'[21]

Coke's monarch as 'dignified hieroglyphic' was for Laski at once a constitutional principle and a safeguard against the crown's always latent tendency to obstruct the democratic will; and if that implied that the king would have had to sign his own death warrant provided it was voted by the Commons, this was the meaning and price of 1688. He had long argued for the clarification of the boundaries of monarchical power, most notably on the issue of the right of dissolution, and he viewed as inadmissible the emergence of new royal prerogatives relating to the fate of governments.

[19] Laski, *Reflections on the Constitution* (Manchester, 1951), p. 71.
[20] Laski to O. G. Villard, 1 December 1931, 12 March 1932. The Houghton Library, Harvard University.
[21] Laski, *Parliamentary Government in England* (New York, 1938), p. 340. See also Laski, *The Crisis and the Constitution: 1931 and After* (London, 1932), pp. 31–6.

Essentially his argument was a formal one, but he thought it wise to illuminate by elementary sociological data the origins and real biases of men of power. Here, it should be said, Laski's seminal study of British cabinets from Addington to Baldwin is, as Guttsman's useful book points out, the very first of the genre.[22]

Thus, committed as he was to the institutions of democracy, of choice and opposition, and wary as he was of 'democracies of the general will', he nevertheless believed that 'no political system has the privilege of immortality'.[23] When American federalism seemed to him to flaunt the will of the *demos* and to apotheosize the irrationality of political rule he did not hesitate to call it obsolescent; and, pausing for a moment over obstacles to the enforcement of civil rights and civil liberties, or over issues Laski scarcely imagined, such as the administration of conscription, who can dismiss his concern as a crochet ? Or is the fetishism of structure more appropriate to theory than the mediation between ends and means ?

The American frame of reference elucidates just how undogmatic Laski was. Franklin Roosevelt's New Deal was not designed to create the new society that Laski hoped for. But where he saw a liberal creatively seeking to transcend the limitations of liberalism he there, after great initial scepticism, saw merit. He was not beyond asking, in accusing tones, in his famous debate with Don K. Price on the parliamentary and presidential systems, why

a progressive Democrat, like President Roosevelt, was led to acquiesce in policies which could have no other result than the overthrow of the nascent Spanish democracy in the interest of that Franco whose status as a puppet of Hitler and Mussolini was clear even when the President helped to pave his way to Madrid . . .[24]

And in Laski's bold ideas, forced now into a wholly experimental cast, Roosevelt, it appears, was much interested. There are on deposit at Hyde Park several not very characteristic notes in

---

[22] Laski. 'The Personnel of the British Cabinet, 1801–1924', *Studies in Law and Politics* (London, 1932), pp. 181–201; W. L. Guttsman, *The British Political Elite* (London, 1963), p. 16n.

[23] Laski, 'The Obsolescence of Federalism', *The New Republic*, 3 May 1939, p. 369.

[24] Laski, 'The Parliamentary and Presidential Systems', *Public Administration Review*, Autumn 1944, pp. 347–59.

F.D.R.'s hand instructing some member of his staff to set up meetings for him with Laski.[25] This was a relationship which Laski obviously treasured and he did not compromise it, as he had others, by indiscretion or embroidery.[26]

Laski told the Americans where he thought they were going wrong. And he did the same to the Russians. Even in those rather embarrassing writings over which the epic of Stalingrad so awesomely presides, he would not let up. Felix Frankfurter used to say that what the later Laski was all about was 'Marxism plus habeas corpus'. But habeas corpus was shorthand for all the demands which Laski would extract from any society, including the Soviet, before he thought it fulfilled the rudimentary requirements of providing the good life for its citizens. All the same he did not adopt a consistent anti-communist posture which he thought, in the contemporary configurations of politics, would almost invariably be manipulated towards inhumane and counter-historical ends. Where he did not believe this was the cost, as within the ranks of the Labour Party, he argued that

for socialists of democratic outlook, the unity demanded by the Communist Party is incompatible with the major purposes for which the Labour Party was brought into being. It would be foolish indeed if . . . the Labour Party . . . should substitute for its own philosophy an outlook which is built upon distrust of the common people and denial of their right to experiment with the institutions of freedom.[27]

Nor is this an anomaly. Laski was not afflicted by that sin of pride which so often makes Westerners think that coincidence with their own institutions and ideals is the criterion of justice and utility by which to judge the rest of the world.

Neither anomalous nor antediluvian! In fact, from the perspective of the sixties, Laski appears to be quite modern – and this is not intended as a denigration. The wide stirrings among the young, in America no less than in Europe, of anti-anti-communism, to the lament of intellectuals for whom anti-communism has been their

---

[25] This is on the authority of Professor Paul Freund of the Harvard Law School. See also James MacGregor Burns, *Roosevelt: The Lion and the Fox* (New York, 1956), p. 204.

[26] See, on this, the very sensitive *New Yorker* review by Edmund Wilson of the Holmes-Laski letters, reprinted in Wilson, *The Bit Between My Teeth* (New York, 1965).

[27] Laski, *The Secret Battalion* (London, 1946), p. 30.

stock-in-trade and habit for a generation, is reminiscent of radical currents among the intelligentsia between the wars. But these new radicals are not like Bourbons with their notorious learning difficulties. They are ideologically indentured to no centre of power, and if they idealize or romanticize at all it is the dispossessed who engage their unabashed affections. Their philosophy is still a pastiche but it evokes the best of Laski. They talk of counter-communities, and are, in Mississippi and at Aldermaston, perhaps the first since Laski in the twenties seriously to question the traditional doctrine of political obligation. They are already beginning to see that merely because a law prohibits a march or a strike, it cannot prevent it, and they are drawing corollaries which Laski himself once drew. If they were to read Laski now they would also find that his perceptions about the tenuous social peace in the western democracies are akin to their own. He too had given warning that a war of the hungry, in revolt and weary of their suffering, would break out and challenge both the ideology and strength of the sated nations. And if they cared to find a point of common understanding with those who had mobilized the power of colour and of misery they would discover that Laski animated the intellectuals of the underdeveloped world as almost no one else has done. They could read in his pages a sober faulting of aestheticism and solipsistic personalism which would strike a chord in their own rebellion against the ennui of their most immediate memories. A Harvard student, just returned from what is portentously called a 'freedom summer' in the south, burst out, after a long disquisition by his teacher on the guarantees of liberty under the division and separation of powers, that 'the constitution is a lie'. In anger and overstatement, not quite lucidly, what he was saying is that a vast gap exists between 'the state in theory and practice'.

Leopold Schwarzschild and the *Neue Tage-Buch*

Hans-Albert Walter

On 1 July 1933, barely three months after he had escaped from Germany, Leopold Schwarzschild brought out in Paris the first number of the weekly *Das Neue Tage-Buch* (The New Diary). Just as the *Neue Weltbühne* (The New International Scene, published first in Prague, then in Paris, 1933–9) continued the traditions of Ossietzky's and Jacobsohn's Berlin weekly, so Schwarzschild set out to carry on those of the former *Tagebuch*. This highbrow weekly appeared until 1933 in Berlin, first under the editorship of Stefan Grossmann and then under that of Schwarzschild himself. While the *Weltbühne* was indubitably the more important of the two before 1933, the *Neue Tage-Buch* became under Schwarzschild's guidance far and away the best of all German emigré publications.

Schwarzschild was in no way prepared for life in exile. After Chancellor Papen's unconstitutional take-over of Prussia in 1932, he had moved his offices and residence to Munich, believing that the dividing walls of German particularism would provide adequate protection against 'further departures from strict legality'. An astute enough precaution against the encroachments of a Papen-like regime, but of course utterly ineffective against the sort of terror Hitler was going to unleash. Elisabeth Castonier, until 1933 herself a *Tagebuch* contributor, described this 'naive dodge' as a 'repression of an underlying sense of impending doom'.[1] Be that as it may, the episode certainly highlights the delusion common even among highly perceptive democrats that their sworn enemies would deal with them according to the customary procedural rules.

For a brief interval after Hitler's accession to power, the paper continued unmolested. But when, on 9 March 1933, Bavaria was brought to heel (*gleichgeschaltet*), the *Tagebuch* was immediately banned and its editors had to flee the country.

[1] Elisabeth Castonier, *Stürmisch bis heiter* (Munich, 1964), p. 204.

The weekly's speedy reappearance in exile was entirely due to the exertions and munificence of Mr J. C. S. Warendorf, a wealthy Dutch lawyer. He was in Rome when Hitler became·chancellor, and the comparatively mild terror of the fascist blackshirts helped him to gauge what was happening further north. When a few weeks later an English acquaintance mentioned Schwarzschild's difficulties, Warendorf decided on a salvage operation enabling the *Tagebuch* to be published outside Germany. He and Schwarzschild formed the *Société Néerlandaise d'Editions* with a share capital of 200,000 French francs (approximately £4,000), subscribed entirely by Warendorf, an amount he later increased by an additional loan. It was he who had the periodical installed in the exclusive Rue du Faubourg St Honoré, opposite the British Embassy.[2] Motivated by a feeling of political solidarity and human fellowship, Warendorf's unstinting generosity demonstrated what democratic dedication coupled to a sense of civic responsibility could achieve.

At first the weekly carried on with an almost unchanged panel of contributors, among them such well-known political analysts as Konrad Heiden and Rudolf Olden and essayists of the calibre of Ludwig Marcuse and Joseph Roth. Later the *Neue Tage-Buch* provided a forum for luminaries even more illustrious; Heinrich and Thomas Mann, Alfred Döblin, Arnold Zweig, Ernst Toller, Lion Feuchtwanger, Siegmund Freud wrote for it. So did distinguished foreign commentators like Ilya Ehrenburg, Wickham Steed, Harold Nicolson, Pertinax, and Wladimir d'Ormesson. The articles regularly contributed from 1933 onwards by Winston Churchill did perhaps most to mould the paper's characteristic political physiognomy. Still a voice in the wilderness in his own country and an outsider in his party, Churchill had been one of nazidom's earliest and most implacable foes.

On sale everywhere in the countries of Europe with a free press after July 1933, the *Neue Tage-Buch* deliberately avoided any commitment to a specific programme. But its first editorial still rings out today like a proclamation of its purpose and objectives.

It seems hardly necessary to provide this publication with an introduction or a programme. Two points may be briefly made: the special

---

[2] Personal communication to the writer by Mr Warendorf, during a conversation in Amsterdam in 1963.

circumstances under which a German journal is being published in an alien environment justify their mention. Since we shall be compelled to report on ·German affairs, indeed since it will be one of our main tasks to do so frequently and in minute detail, we want here to state and explicitly acknowledge – because our present condition painfully impresses this fact on our consciousness – that the unhappy country beyond the Rhine remains our homeland. Impossible ever to sever the innumerable ties that consciously and unconsciously link us through our own experience and the accumulated heritage of generations to our country; impossible to tear out the roots that bind us to German society, its culture and its language. It is precisely because we feel our responsibility towards the best traditions of our fatherland, and have remained loyal to them that we must now expose the motives and deeds of the thugs who are on the verge of obliterating, desecrating, and poisoning whatever was once noble and beautiful in Germany. Love for Germany must nowadays assume the guise of implacable hatred of those who have enslaved it. This is the first point we want to make. The second consists in what one might call a pious hope. Emigration, the process of uprooting oneself, can have two results: it can blur one's vision or add to it. It can infuse such hatred and bitterness into people as to blind them completely. On the other hand, the greater distance it inevitably imposes on places and events, in terms both of time and space, can make for a deeper understanding, a more objective and detached insight into the essence of things. The history of emigration knows of both alternatives. It is our earnest hope that we may ultimately come to exemplify the latter.[3]

The *Neue Tage-Buch* did not aim at mass appeal; facts were analysed rather than reported and the paper assumed that current events as well as the context within which they occurred were known to its readers. Insisting on such exacting standards, it virtually selected its own readership. Though exiled, it still addressed itself to an opinion-forming and decision-making elite, which in view of the special circumstances of its publication could not consist entirely of the weekly's own compatriots.

The emphasis on political and economic developments greatly restricted the space available for the arts and literature. These limitations, however, made for reviews so intelligently selective and concise as to provide today's reader with an unfailing guide to the truly representative works of the period. Roughly three-quarters of

[3] *Neue Tage-Buch* (hereafter, NTB), 1 July 1933, p. 3.

its thirty pages dealt with political and economic topics; the rest was given over to articles of general interest, literary reviews, and such regular features as the glossary entitled 'miniatures' and the highly informative news column 'Outside the Reichskulturkammer'.

In one respect, however, the former *Tage-Buch* style had to conform to the requirements imposed by the conditions of exile. Before it could be analysed in the usual manner, news from the Third Reich had first to be made to yield the information the nazis tried to conceal. Cutting through the web of deliberate official deceptions and half-truths required an all-embracing expertise able to illuminate, assess, and correlate intricate inter-relationships, and familiarity with the crucial factors in the highly complex structure, of, for example, the economy or the monetary system, against which the veracity of official information could be checked. Particular attention was paid to Germany's secret rearmament and to the economic and financial policies that made it possible. The weekly's greatest journalistic triumph was the discovery of the near-fraudulent circulation of 'Mefo' treasury bills which paid for the clandestine arms. The way in which Haniel and Hans Hermes managed, by careful analysis of official German figures and information published in the business section of the daily press, to disclose Schacht's financial manipulation, qualifies as one of journalism's classic exploits. It would go beyond the scope of this article to retrace the intricate procedures and elaborate cross-checks employed to substantiate Schwarzschild's findings – they took almost a year to complete. Finally, in September 1935, the painstakingly collected evidence yielded incontestable proof, based, as the article explained, 'on official figures, subjected only to a novel method of evaluation'.[4] The entire, highly technical investigation rested on official data concerning the circulation of treasury bills, the income from stamp duties, and divergences between these sets of figures. The importance of the exposure and the consternation it caused became obvious when within a week of its appearance, the German government introduced legislation prohibiting the publication of such vital data. It was possible to score such a scoop because Schwarzschild combined an unusually imaginative analytical

---

[4] Ibid., 31 August 1935, p. 829. The account of the investigation opened in the issue for 21 July 1934, and was continued at intervals, the final article appearing on 6 September 1935.

intelligence with exceptionally wide and solidly based knowledge. Company reports, balance sheets, import and export statistics, promotion lists from the army gazette, in short every scrap of public and private information from nazi Germany was carefully scrutinized. Sometimes seemingly unimportant snippets of news would contain intelligence of great significance.

The *Neue Tage-Buch* was read by the chancelleries and the general staffs of Europe; it counted among its subscribers diplomats, high-ranking officers, industrial and financial leaders; it was frequently quoted by the international press, and its articles and commentaries were debated in the Parliaments of Britain, France, and Holland.

Looking back across the distance of thirty years and in the light of evidence now available, it is of course easy to show how often the paper went wrong. Yet set against the difficulties of gathering news in exile, and compared with the delusions and misinterpretations of other emigré papers – for example on the effectiveness of refugee resistance or the impending overthrow of the Hitler regime – the *Neue Tage-Buch* strikes a note of exemplary realism. It erred neither in its appreciation of the general situation nor in its judgment on immediate fact; it did, however, misjudge occasionally some of the most inscrutable factors in a dictatorship; the power structure, and personal rivalries between various leaders, as well as frictions between contending organizations such as the army and the party, or between party factions. Liable to be mistaken on such detail, Schwarzschild was, nevertheless, more often than not right in his overall conclusions. For he had intuitively grasped Hitler's essentially expansionist aims, and it was its tireless and consistent exposure of these which earned the *Neue Tage-Buch* its lasting fame, pre-eminence, and international reputation.

Nowhere else between 1933 and 1939 were warnings against Germany's war preparations more frequent and urgent, and more discerningly documented than in the *Neue Tage-Buch*. Time and again the western democracies were shown what to make of nazi protestations of peaceful intent; official assurances were constantly compared with the relevant passages in *Mein Kampf*; the incontestable economic evidence of the sustained armament drive was continuously scrutinized; and Schwarzschild untiringly demonstrated to his readers everywhere the futility and folly of appeasement. Half-jokingly but aptly, they nicknamed him Cassandra.

Through him the other, the civilized Germany, denounced its monstrous alternative. This record allowed the *Neue Tage-Buch* to share the proud self-awareness which induced Thomas Mann to proclaim: 'Where I am is Germany'. Schwarzschild – a Jewish German rather than a German Jew – hated nazidom so relentlessly because, as Klaus Mann noted with undisguised admiration, it simply outraged his innate patriotism.

For all that, little notice was taken of the *Neue Tage-Buch's* exhortations. Inertia, lack of imagination, preoccupation with internal problems, the social upheavals of the economic crisis, all these were issues that seemed more immediate and pressing than insubstantial prophecies of future doom. Schwarzschild noted the stupidities of the appeasing years with a sort of frenzied bitterness; week in week out he recorded them, commented upon them, inveighed against them, and, forgetting none, entered them each on the debit side of history. His articles often reflected the fury of the unheeded prophet, the wrathful desperation of a man who, to keep his sanity, had to shrug it all off in fits of derisive laughter. The European Left – and here lay the irony of the situation – which should have been his most understanding and reliable ally, slowly turned into his most obstinate adversary.

We have to get used to the paradox that the social-democrats and certain ageing radicals in some of the most important countries are actually aiding and abetting Hitler. This of course is not their intention. But it is their policy all the same. For insofar as they insist on equating peace with disarmament, they are playing Hitler's game. The 'disarmament of the rest' which they demand, amounts *ipso facto* to the 'rearmament of Germany', which they oppose. The labour parties might have learned from the fate of their German comrades that with Hitler, brute force, naked and undisguised, has entered upon the scene. But with what other than force can you counter force? Failure to grasp this fact and trust in the persuasiveness of moral arguments destroyed Germany's democracy and her labour movement. What a spectacle to see labour parties of other countries now proposing policies which, if successful, would inevitably repeat on a global scale what had previously happened in Germany.[5]

This was written in November 1933, and similar charges were to be repeated again and again in the years to come. The paper had to fight a war on two fronts: on one against Hitler, and on the other

[5] NTB, 4 November 1933, p. 444.

against misguided democratic attitudes. It was endlessly and furiously attacked by 'dedicated' liberals, but gave as good as it received. Schwarzschild's tone grew increasingly contemptuous as with the passage of time the blind obstinacy of his opponents became more and more apparent. Once challenged, he fought back ruthlessly, often holding his adversaries up to undying ridicule with one of his telling quips. When, in spring 1939, after the occupation of Prague, Western opinion finally awoke to the truth he had preached for years, it was already too late. In one of his most moving and eloquent articles, Schwarzschild, drawing the moral from these wasted years, wrote:

This did it. After six years, this finally did it. The sinister documentary of violence, robbery, and murder during the ides of this March, rammed the lesson home. A country which, because it was a credit to civilization, had already been assaulted and crippled, was finally to perish in the process. An honest, hard-working, trusting nation has now to pay the price and to endure the long night of bondage. But this has opened their eyes! They now know what they are up against. They now know what to expect. At long last it is understood, acknowledged, and accepted. No more attempts to prevaricate, construe, twist, contradict, and indulge in fantasies. It has at long last been recognized: these men are out to subjugate everything and everybody. To exercise power, to rule, is their one and only objective.

For six years we have tried to get this message across. For six years people either pretended not to notice, or managed to repress any glimmer of understanding. Bah, they said, this is none of our business ... If he touches us we will rap him over the knuckles good and hard ... We're not afraid, we won't let him spoil our fun. When the monster was already strong we warned them again. How come, they said, what gave you this idea? ... It is absurd, improbable, unproved and unprovable. You are prejudiced, that's all. Didn't he explicitly assure us? ... Well then. Didn't he sign this agreement? ... Well then. All of a sudden he made a startling and alarming move. Ah, they said, obviously an exception when seen in proper perspective. Ah, they continued, when something similar happened again, an isolated incident, not really typical. And the next time they said it was nothing more serious than acting out a sort of inner compulsion. Any loophole offering escape from reality would be seized upon. This is now over and done with. Yes, notwithstanding the lessons of scepticism learned over the years, this period is now over and done with. That much can be asserted.[6]

[6] NTB, 25 March 1939, p. 207.

A bitter triumph to have been proved right by such catastrophes. Actually, and although Schwarzschild himself may not always have been aware of it, he had already gone beyond merely resisting Hitler and repudiating nazi philosophy. He was evolving a new concept of humanism, a new insight into the meaning of exile which added to the self-knowledge of the expatriates. Gone was the optimistic acceptance of progress, the lofty humanitarianism of the well-intentioned; gone too was the axiomatic belief in the superiority of moral and intellectual forces. The 'new humanist' was no longer the smiling sage of the Erasmic tradition, nor was he either the uncommitted onlooker who retired to the heights until the waters of the deep had receded or the dedicated pacifist, who for the sake of peace was ready to sacrifice himself and all he stood for. The new humanism as Schwarzschild perceived and practised it (without, however, making much use of the term, or explicitly defining it) was infinitely more active, forward-looking and militant than it had ever been in the days of Weimar. It was also completely free of any doctrinal or party affiliation.

The latter point is of importance and accounts for the difficulty in defining the *Neue Tage-Buch's* exact political position. By nature not a contemplative man, writing was for Schwarzschild a deliberately chosen substitute for action. This gave his work its brilliance and its compelling sense of urgency. Moreover, he had the rare gift of expressing with seeming ease, concisely and clearly, what he felt and wanted to say. His striking analytical power operated on causal and linear rather than on dialectical lines, so that, even if incorrect on some minor details, the structure of his thought and reasoning remained cogent and unassailable.

Schwarzschild would certainly have objected to being called a liberal. In exile, left-wing pacifist opponents repeatedly referred to him as a 'man of the left'. He never contradicted them, although increasingly aware of the irrelevance of such classifications. A liberal camp follower in his younger days, he quickly changed his views when he became professionally acquainted with the results of *laissez-faire* economics. The clash between private gain and social need soon persuaded him to equate liberalism with 'Manchester', to him a derisive term, signifying the buccaneering exploitation of the many for the benefit of the few. The down-to-earth, no-nonsense Schwarzschild, rather than the economic theoretician, became more and more convinced of the urgent need for a complete overhaul of the economic system. In this respect he had completely outgrown his bourgeois background. On the other hand his middle-class upbringing had bequeathed him an outspoken independence of spirit which compelled him to subject every issue to close rational analysis rather than to trust his instinct and spontaneous reactions. Such dispassionate detachment presupposed a pioneering mind, untrammelled by considerations of expediency and totally oblivious of conventional patterns of thought and behaviour. Schwarzschild was an outspoken pragmatist, and although much of his strength lay in this rigorously practical approach it could on occasion mislead him. He was indubitably on slippery ground when in his eagerness to strengthen the anti-Hitler forces he supported the near-nazi regimes of Dollfuss and Mussolini. The Spanish civil war demonstrated the danger of being swayed by considerations of short-term expediency, just as the Moscow trials shocked him into a realization of the basic difference between totalitarianism and democracy. He had, however, never allowed his pragmatic approach to override moral scruples, and he unfailingly backed departures that promised to promote the cause of human progress. He was one of the first to welcome Roosevelt's New Deal at a time when such unconditional support was still quite rare:

The first attempt at capitalist planning, this first testing of steering mechanisms, devised for the time being to overcome the present crisis, but ultimately to be used for the prevention of other crises, will in all probability be looked upon in years to come as one of those colossal landmarks that here and there dominate the landscapes of history. No one before him has dared to interfere as radically and as decisively with the workings of the capitalist machinery. Inasmuch as the changes he introduced were rooted in the concept of a socially responsible and responsive economy and tended to restrain the freebooting approach of private enterprise, he may well be called a socialist. It is one of the more grotesque ironies of history that the presidency of Roosevelt should coincide with the emergence of the German Führer who, assuming the garb and guise of a socialist revolutionary, yet manages to stifle all change and to cling like grim death to the most ancient of the old reactionary orders, vociferously and shamelessly denouncing any departure from established procedures.[7]

[7] NTB, 22 July 1933, p. 89.

Given his approach to the structural problems of modern society, it can hardly be surprising that Schwarzschild was greatly impressed by the Soviet Union and the vast promise of its social experiment. Louis Fischer had been the periodical's Russian correspondent since long before 1933, a choice that speaks for itself; but its own attitude, as expressed in editorials on the various five-year plans, was equally enthusiastic, and there can be little doubt that Schwarzschild's admiration was sincere and independent of the Soviet Union's usefulness as an ally against Hitler. He regarded the dictatorship of the proletariat as a transitional phase, and the restrictions on individual liberty, odious as they were to him, as indispensable though strictly temporary expedients. Since, among the mushrooming European totalitarianisms, he accepted the Russian as the only progressive one holding out some hope for mankind, he felt that in this particular instance the ends justified the means.

Schwarzschild's independence of any party line or doctrine, the strange blend of his middle-class upbringing, revolutionary fervour, and personal approach to socialism, inevitably brings the word 'humanist' to mind. This, in the circumstances of exile and in the political context of his day, implied, in practical terms, support for some kind of comprehensive, undoctrinaire popular-front coalition. From 1935 onward he campaigned for a united front among all anti-Hitler refugees. When the 'popular front' finally emerged, he whole-heartedly backed it and played a leading part in its councils. But he was soon disillusioned and shocked by the failure of the various parties to sink their differences and to agree on a common policy. 'It would have been better to have started from scratch, without parties obsessed by the imagined necessity to maintain their petty identity.'[8]

His subsequent lone-wolf approach to politics, his complete aloofness from party groupings even among his fellow exiles, dates from this chastening experience which, of course, included knowledge of and contact with the exiled German Communist Party. Yet even familiarity with its tortuous tactics hardly explains why Schwarzschild should have turned into one of the most rabid communist baiters among the German expatriates. Ludwig Marcuse, a

---

[8] NTB, 26 December 1936, p. 1231. The break with the popular front came only after the first Moscow trial.

close collaborator and friend of Schwarzschild, calls him a premature McCarthy among the German refugees.[9] What had happened? Like Arthur Koestler and Willi Münzenburg, Schwarzschild was deeply outraged by the Moscow show trials.

The tragedy of this trial is not even that of the victims. What is tragic is the way it is being conducted and that it should have taken place at all. To state this in public is the prerogative and indeed the duty of those who have consistently advocated a coalition with Russia, and have openly acknowledged their admiration for the Soviet Union's progressive approach to social and economic issues. Just as they were busily refuting the false alternative of 'western civilization on the one hand, and bolshevism on the other', so assiduously spread to subvert the undecided nations, they suffered the mortification of being confronted with a spectacle of such sinister barbarity as to reinforce the very prejudices they were trying to demolish.[10]

The particular application of these general conclusions to his own political conduct Schwarzschild summed up as follows:

Those who oppose to the totalitarian ideology the concepts of democratic government and the rule of law would undermine their own position if they were to acquiesce in any act of dictatorial arbitrariness. They could then be reproached with condemning it in some countries while condoning it in others.[11]

In spite of its studiously moderate tone, the article in which this appeared marked a turning point, the rethinking of accepted ideas, a disenchanted new departure. But why did Schwarzschild keep on returning to the same subject whether it was topical or not? Is it really too far-fetched to suggest that something akin to disappointed love, perhaps an only half-acknowledged, deeply emotional commitment, compelled him almost obsessively to regurgitate the same issue time and time again?[12] This would account for the savage editorials which followed this first onslaught. The crude and excessive violence of later articles was his reaction to the slanders German emigré communists had published about him in a Prague paper. These purported to prove on the strength of forged documents that the *Neue Tage-Buch* was subservient to Goebbels. Schwarzschild's inability to treat the matter with the contempt it

[9] Ludwig Marcuse, *Mein 20. Jahrhundert* (Munich, 1960), p. 204.
[10] NTB, 29 August 1936, p. 826.
[11] Ibid., p. 828.
[12] The persistence of the obsession can be seen in his biography of Karl Marx, entitled *The Red Prussian*, published in New York in 1947.

deserved, and to be satisfied with having unmasked and made fools of the clumsy forgers, reveals a serious flaw in his character. Unaccountably, and to the detriment of the paper, he treated these absurd imputations as a reflection on his journalistic integrity. Unrequited love and personal resentment combined to generate an insensate, almost paranoiac hatred of communism, the Soviet Union, and all communists. His comments on the twentieth anniversary of the Russian revolution were shameful and at the same time ludicrously at variance with his normal standards of excellence. Blinded by hate, he resorted to the wildest accusations and his articles soon vied with the Moscow trials in the sheer grotesqueness of their charges. Where his pet hate was concerned, this most painstaking journalist, who would never print a news item unless it was properly verified, unscrupulously manipulated facts, substituting venomous invective for rational argument. One such article published soon after the outbreak of war proved particularly vicious. It anonymously tarred the membership of the *Schutzverband Deutscher Schriftsteller im Exil* (Association of exiled German writers) with the communist brush, casting doubt on the democratic reliability of men who had for years contributed to the paper. These allegations had serious and sometimes fatal consequences, for they debarred those libelled from obtaining visas to oversea countries, especially to the United States. After the fall of France this was often tantamount to a death sentence. The writers never forgave Schwarzschild this infamy and shunned him for the rest of his days. The entire unedifying episode revealed an unsuspected and grave weakness in his personality.

As Schwarzschild had a journalist's nose for what was in the air, the *Neue Tage-Buch* often initiated discussions which were then taken up by a larger and occasionally world-wide public. One such topic, which the *Neue Tage-Buch* first debated in spring 1939, when war was imminent, was the post-war treatment of a defeated Germany. It sparked off an animated discussion not only among German exiles but also between such widely different papers as the *Populaire* of the French socialists and *Das Schwarze Korps* of Hitler's SS.

The brilliantly prophetic *Neue Tage-Buch* editorial on the subject correctly anticipated the collapse of all authority (the simultaneous destruction of the economic potential could not be foreseen); the annihilation and corruption of cadres which could form an alternative administration (forgetting perhaps too glibly the political concentration camp prisoners); the totalitarian – read communist – danger of a power vacuum; the impossibility of continuing, as if nothing had happened, where the Republic had left off in 1933. Analysing the presumed German situation at the 'zero hour of defeat', Schwarzschild concluded this exercise in abstract computation as follows:

It would probably be best if after the collapse of Nazi power in the finally defeated Germany a way could be found to prevent the country from once more assuming the ambiguous position which her demons and her genius, her fortune and her misfortune, have apparently conspired to mark out for her. One wonders, therefore, whether for some considerable time to come the victors should not deploy their administrative and military personnel as teachers in government. This would allow the victors to introduce rational considerations into the question of governmental succession which, without such intervention, would have to be left to the workings of blind chance. Before handing over to new men and institutions, they could slowly re-educate the country in the arts of government and citizenship, and step by step wean the Germans from those aggressive and self-destructive habits acquired over centuries of misdirected effort.[13]

Here Schwarzschild had the courage to bring into the open a problem which German exiles of all political denominations, from Konrad Heiden to Prince Löwenstein and the communist Hermann Budzislawski, indignantly and patriotically refused to face. Their ingrained 'national pride' invariably clouded their judgment and sense of reality. They were all, of course, spokesmen of 'the other Germany', and hoped to assume power as representatives of the bourgeoisie, the Roman Catholics, or the proletariat. Their party bias perhaps even more than their Teuton patriotism prevented them from grasping the full implications of the problem. On the other hand it is surprising that the hard-bitten Schwarzschild, familiar as he was from his fight against the follies of appeasement with the amazing staying power of the irrational, should have set such store by the slow, steady process of education. For anyone who actually witnessed the workings and the failure of 're-education', the hope that reason will ever be a guide to national attitudes turned to despair.

[13] NTB, 15 July 1939, p. 685.

Had the controversy over Germany's future continued, it would have run the entire gamut of illusions, fantasies, hopes, and insights that exercised the mind of the German expatriate. But war intervened before the last contribution could be published. The German emigré press was one of the first casualties in the countries that fought Hitler. In this emergency, Schwarzschild and Warendorf's foresight in registering the *Neue Tage-Buch* as a Dutch company, paid off. As a 'neutral' publication, the paper was not banned. Its last number, pre-dated 11 May 1940, appeared on the very day when Hitler unleashed his 'Blitzkrieg in the West', and when Winston Churchill, Schwarzschild's most distinguished contributor, became Prime Minister. Seldom in the history of journalism has a paper gone down in such a blaze of vindicated predictions.

Schwarzschild escaped to the United States and died in Italy in 1950.

Austro-Marxism: A Reappraisal

Norbert Leser

Although generally associated with the emerging Austrian Republic, Austro-Marxism was actually rooted in and formed by the conditions prevailing in the pre-1914 days of the Austro-Hungarian empire. Indeed, only under the aegis of the last Habsburgs were its most forceful and eminent exponents still agreed on the principles and application of Marxist thought. Later, when confronted with a world war, and then under the Republic, when faced with the strains and inevitable compromises of decision-making, the group lost its former cohesion and members began to go their own separate ways.

Among those who put Austro-Marxism on the map and maintained its reputation for decades, Otto Bauer, whose epoch-making *Die Nationalitätenfrage und die Sozialdemokratie* appeared in 1907, is perhaps the best-known figure. Other members of this brilliant circle were Karl Renner, later Austrian Chancellor, an authority on government, constitutional law, administration, and similar subjects; Rudolf Hilferding, later Minister of Finance in the Weimar Republic, whose *Das Finanzkapital* reappraised and extended Marxian economic thought; Max Adler, a truly original interpreter of Marxian dialectics, whose sadly neglected writings deserve a revival; and Julius Deutsch, later Defence Minister and organizer of the socialist defence league, the *Republikanischer Schutzbund*. He contributed a fundamental study of the Austrian trade union movement and a number of sociological and military monographs to the socialist literature of the day.

The meeting of such exceptionally talented minds gave Austro-Marxism its specific edge and flavour. It became an historically identifiable entity with the founding in 1903 of the Fabian-type society *Zukunft*. The impulses generated there exerted a lasting and widening influence on the entire structure and performance of

Austrian socialism. One of the first acts of the group was the establishment of a workers' college, the first of its kind in Austria and the nucleus from which, in time, the entire system of Austrian socialist education was to spring. From 1904 the *Marx-Studien* were published, in which members of this circle presented most of their major works for public discussion. Three years later the journal *Der Kampf* was launched. It remained for the duration of the party's existence its official theoretical organ, and true to its mast-head, carried on underground after the party was banned in 1934.

The party itself emerged as a political organization only after Victor Adler at the Hainfeld congress of 1888–9 had managed to persuade hitherto contending factions to accept a common plat-form. Before his intervention internecine dissensions had rendered any united action impossible. The programme finally accepted re-affirmed the fundamental concepts of orthodox Marxism and re-mained in force without major alterations until 1926. The glaring failure of the course of economic development to bear out the Marxian prognostications inevitably led to demands for a re-appraisal of the theoretical approach. Such agitation, although it had little in common with Eduard Bernstein's more formidable revisionism, was strenuously resisted by Adler, not so much on ideological grounds, for he was anything but a doctrinaire Marxist, but rather for fear of provoking dissensions which might once more endanger party unity. Adler nevertheless supported some modifica-tions of the Hainfeld programme at the 1901 congress.

Marxism, if it was to live up to its reputation as a valid interpre-tation of social phenomena, had to furnish answers to the urgent problems of the society in which it operated. In the case of pre-1914 Austria this meant, among other things, suggesting solutions to the problems created by an autocratically ruled multi-national state. Austrian socialists, like all others, were primarily concerned with the emancipation of the working class, but their day-to-day political work compelled them to acknowledge the overwhelming importance of the nationality issue within the context of the Habs-burg empire. To the bulk of the population these questions were at least as real and of equal immediate concern as the tactics of the class war. Moreover, being the only supra-national party, the social-democrats were the one political organization prepared to think out solutions to a problem threatening to tear the whole state apart. Indeed, during the Party Congress of 1899 in Brünn and elsewhere, they proposed a number of reforms which, had they been accepted by the establishment, might have saved the multi-national concept.

Karl Renner in particular believed in its validity and published under pseudonyms pamphlets like *Staat und Nation* (1899), and *Der Kampf der österreichischen Nationen um den Staat* (1902), in which, like the Czech historian Palacky, he argued that Austria-Hungary served regional requirements so perfectly that it would have to be invented were it not already in existence. While advocating radical administrative reforms guaranteeing national as well as individual equality within the state, Renner denounced the over-heated nationalism and the fashionable insistence on national sovereignty as a historical anachronism. Otto Bauer shared most of these views, although a marked difference of emphasis allowed him to regard the Habsburg empire merely as a convenient point of departure rather than the final consummation of a sociological process.

In Austria as elsewhere 1914 saw the abandonment of the time-honoured socialist doctrine of the international solidarity of the working classes. However, as the war dragged on, the ferocious blood-letting of the increasingly self-defeating and inconclusive struggle caused party intellectuals to re-examine their position, and led during the Zimmerwald and Kienthal congresses in neutral Switzerland to the emergence of a militantly pacifist Left. This new group opposed the ruling party majorities, and in the case of Germany produced a split in the Social-Democratic Party, followed by the establishment of the 'Independents' as a separate party. Renner particularly was accused of the sin of 'social-patriotism', and his writings on war problems, published in 1917 under the title *Marxismus, Krieg und Internationale*, were cited as characteristic examples of the betrayal of socialist principles. His efforts to maintain Austria's territorial integrity and multi-national structure were also harshly criticized by the new group. Countering his views in the *Nationalitätenprogramm der Linke*, published by *Kampf* in 1918, they formally acknowledged each nation's right to self-determination and independence. Although the document did not propose the dissolution of the Austrian empire *expressis verbis*, its demand for the convening of a nationality congress practically implied it. Renner considered the measures advocated by the party's left wing

– and borne out by the actual course of events – as intrinsically retrograde. He stubbornly refused to draw the practical conclusions from irrefutable portents, although by an irony of fate it was he who, after the fall of the Habsburg monarchy, was destined to become the Republic's first Chancellor. But before this particular juncture was reached, Renner had consistently backed the party leadership's support for the war effort, holding that conquest and the exercise of force could also lead to such civilizing power constellations as those represented by the Roman Empire and the British Commonwealth. So long as actual international interdependence was not given formal shape in agreed codes of international behaviour and law, even a world war, he argued, by producing new and more comprehensive power structures, could do the work of history and should, therefore, not be condemned as wholly evil.[1] Hence, for the duration of the war, Renner was in favour of a *Burgfrieden*, an internal armistice during which the class war was to be suspended and the proletariat was actually to support the war effort on the understanding that it was to share in the eventual rewards of victory. Exertions to stop the war, such as on an international scale the left wing were demanding of the workers, presupposed, according to Renner, a simultaneity and compatibility of international economic developments which failed to correspond to the facts of the situation. He in turn accused the Zimmerwald congress of having disregarded actual realities; for the duration of the conflict Austria's survival was the most immediate concern; the self-sacrifice demanded by the left, far from leading to a socialist victory, would allow contending imperialism, and probably the imperialism of the Tsars, to stay the course and win. Renner believed as fervently in internationalism as the men of the left; all his life he had supported endeavours to create the organizational framework within which an international code with power to prevent war could function. But at this particular juncture he regarded the initiatives of the left as repeating the historic error into which the anarchists had fallen when they argued that individual action could relieve them of the responsibility to take over and administer the state. It remains arguable whether, from a Marxist point of view, Renner's assessment did not make better sense than that of the left, which so conveniently failed to face realities.

[1] Karl Renner, *Marxismus, Krieg und Internationale* (Stuttgart, 1917), p. 167 ff.

Be that as it may, the dissensions within the Zimmerwald inter-national already foreshadowed those cleavages in the socialist movement which were to dominate the decades to come.[2] While the entire Zimmerwald congress was united in its repudiation of 'social-patriotism' and the various party leaderships supporting the war, its right wing, to which Friedrich Adler and the other left-wing Austro-Marxists belonged, dissociated itself from the bol-sheviks who, under Lenin's leadership, had begun to use the con-gress as a slipway for the launching of a communist international. At Kienthal, the right wing – owing to Lenin's tactics already in a minority – were branded as Kautskyist and consequently rejected. From the International Socialist Commission set up at Kienthal emerged, after the October revolution, the Third International under Moscow's leadership, while the socialist parties agreed at the 1919 Berne congress to continue the Second International.

The Austrian party, now dominated by its left wing, disagreed with both factions. It was unwilling to join the Third International and to abide by the 21 points which had been made a condition of membership at the Comintern's second congress, and it felt unable to countenance the 'social-patriotism' of the socialists. At an inter-national socialist conference held in Vienna in 1921, the Austrians promoted the formation of the *Arbeitsgemeinschaft sozialistischer Parteien*, for which Karl Radek coined the irreverent appellation Two-and-a-half International. Although its ranks were swollen by the Independent Socialists who had broken away from the majority parties of Germany and Switzerland, the International did not prove viable. At its Hamburg congress in 1923 the dissenters de-cided to rejoin the Socialist International. The early demise of the movement epitomizes the failure of Austro-Marxism – which, according to Otto Bauer, 'had always striven to adopt a middle course between reformism and Bolshevism'[3] – to act as a pace-setter and to exert a permanently synthesizing influence on the polarized elements of Marxist thought. Looking back, the fate of this short-lived effort to defend an intermediary position seems to presage Austro-Marxism's inability, even on its home ground, to hold its own between the upper and nether doctrinal millstones.

Austro-Marxism's ambiguous position on the state and the

2. cf. Jules Humbert-Droz, *Der Krieg und die Internationale – Die Konferenzen von Zimmerwald und Kienthal* (Vienna, 1964).

3 Otto Bauer, 'Nach dem Parteitag', in *Der Kampf*, December 1927, p. 549.

exercise of power was to prove its main stumbling block and the cause of its final undoing. The dilemma confronting the party had already been reflected in its attitude to the war effort. The 1917 Declaration of the Left (*Erklärung der Linken*) stated clearly: 'Only by adhering to the concept of the class struggle can social-democracy discharge its historical task. The party must not allow itself to sink to the level of a charitable organization solely preoccupied with the attainment of slight improvements in the living conditions of certain groups of workers'.[4] Similarly Renner was told: 'Reformism is bound to lead to ministerialism. We reject all permanent co-operation with the bourgeoisie. We stick to the time-honoured socialist practice of refusing to contribute either a man or a brass farthing for the preservation of the capitalist state'.[5] Renner, on the other hand, pointed out that the conquest of state power was socialism's ultimate objective. Long before the congress was convened, he had explained in a number of papers how the trend towards state capitalism inherent in the war economy might provide the labour movement with a useful jumping off base. Analysing the social conditions of his own day, he concluded: 'Capitalist society as Marx knew, experienced, and described it, no longer exists', and peering into the future, he prophesied: 'The state will become the key to socialism'.[6] He regarded working-class support for the war effort as a token of its realization that the attainment of state power was within its reach, and refused to accept the Marxist all-or-nothing approach to power. He told the left wing at the 1917 congress: 'The state controls our processes of work and now dominates our entire existence. In these circumstances the working class cannot indulge in policies concerned only with abstract principles, irrespective of their actual relevance within the context of the state in which it lives. This is what my reformism amounts to'.[7] Renner was not without backing. Wilhelm Ellenbogen, one of the most amiable and gifted of Austria's social-democrats, took up the cudgels on his behalf. He summarized the problem that confronted this conference and which was to assume increasing importance as time went on. 'For twenty years (he said) we have lacked the courage to define our attitude to the state unequivocally. We denounce it as the root of all evil, often castigate it as neither viable nor fit to

[4] *Protokoll der Verhandlungen des Parteitages 1917*, p 115.
[5] Ibid., p. 116.
[6] Renner, *Marxismus, Krieg und Internationale*, pp. 9, 28.
[7] *Protokoll der Verhandlungen des Parteitages 1917*, p. 122.

live in, and having incessantly inveighed against it, we merrily proceed to work for its preservation. In the words of Victor Adler, we "denounce it as a dunghill; since, however, this is where we have to stay, we try to install ourselves properly on it". These are contradictions and Renner's efforts to resolve them are laudable. Although his recommendations may not meet with our wholehearted approval, his endeavour to face the problem should not give rise to totally irresponsible and extravagant attacks'.[8]

The emergence and subsequent consolidation of the Austrian Republic – it was proclaimed a day after Victor Adler's death on 12 November 1918 – rested right from the beginning on a working agreement between the bourgeois christian-socials and the working-class social-democrats. In the specific conditions facing a defeated, disillusioned, and impoverished Austria, only such a broadly-based coalition held out any hope of avoiding civil strife and of revitalizing the material and spiritual resources needed to rebuild the country. Moreover, a show of national unanimity was deemed a great asset in dealing with the victors and in impressing on them the overwhelming popular desire for fusion with the German Republic, demonstrated by the resolution of the Provisional National Convention. In these circumstances the social-democrats could not willingly dissociate themselves from the newly created republic. They rightly regarded it as the fruit and outcome of their political labours, as the symbol of a new social order which, shorn of outdated privilege and class prerogatives, readily acknowledged the dignity, standing, and achievements of the working class. Propelled by the dynamics of its newly won importance and authority, the party could not but consider the state as an ally in the battle for the realization of its socialist demands. Thus it found itself once more trying to preserve its own identity 'poised between reformism and bolshevism'.

The confrontation with bolshevik theory was no longer an exercise in Marxian interpretation, but a matter of immediate practical consequence. A substantial number of workers and demobilized soldiers were clamouring for the establishment of a proletarian dictatorship along Russian lines, and for a workers' republic on the Hungarian and Bavarian model. The socialist leaders not only resisted the temptation to use the power that was

[8] Ibid., p. 148.

momentarily theirs to further these objectives, but on the contrary exerted their considerable authority over the workers to steer them clear of violence. It was the important but unenviable task of Ministers Deutsch (Defence) and Eldersch (Interior) to quell a series of communist uprisings, the last of which was put down on Easter day 1919. The socialist leaders, in any event opposed to violence, realized moreover that attempts to bring about the dictatorship of the proletariat by a putsch, would inevitably induce the Entente and the agricultural hinterland to close its stranglehold on the capital, thus paving the way for a punitive white counter-terror.

The two years of socialist support for the coalition brought the working class substantial material and political benefits going considerably beyond the social and economic demands formulated in the Hainfeld programme. Among the most notable achievements were the introduction of the eight hour day, paid holidays for workers, the banning or drastic reduction of child labour and night work for women, new enlightened regulations concerning outworkers, the extension of the scope and authority of the factory inspectorate, as well as the passing of fundamental social legislation establishing a comprehensive system of health and unemployment insurance.[9] These enlightened and progressive enactments will always evoke the name of Ferdinand Hanusch, the minister of social welfare, who fathered them. Moreover, by creating such institutions as works councils and chambers of labour, intended to rank with agricultural committees and chambers of commerce, he greatly advanced the social standing, self-esteem, and morale of the working class.

These substantial benefits notwithstanding, social-democratic participation in a bourgeois government – according to Marx merely an instrument for the oppression of one class by another – constituted an anomaly that needed justification. As a theoretician and also because he had initiated these policies, Otto Bauer, once the party had left the government and resumed its traditional role in opposition, felt called upon to account for these historical irregularities and to square them with Marxist theory. In his *Die österreichische Revolution*, an excellent and vivid account of these eventful years published in 1923, he cites Engels in support of his

[9] cf. Maria Szecsi, 'Ferdinand Hanusch', in Norbert Leser, ed., *Werk und Widerhall – Grosse Gestalten des österreichischen Sozialismus* (Vienna, 1964), p. 178 ff.

unimpeachable orthodoxy. From the latter's *Origins of the State, the Family and Private Property*, Bauer quotes a passage on the eventuality of 'the embattled classes having reached a state of equilibrium'. When power was thus evenly matched, Engels argued, the state ceased to be an instrument of class rule and assumed the role of mediator, until external influences upset the balance and made it once more revert to its original role.[10] Bauer contended that such a balance had obtained in Austria after the short period of proletarian supremacy. The country, he argued, had been a genuine people's republic from the autumn of 1919 to the autumn of 1922, from the time, that is, of the re-emergence of the bourgeoisie to the ratification of the Geneva Protocols. Bauer regarded Seipel's efforts to ward off the currency crisis with large injections of foreign loans as the bourgeoisie's attempt to regain the controlling positions it had lost immediately after the war. He called the day of the signing of the Geneva protocols, 4 October 1922, 'Seipel's revenge for 12 November 1918'.[11]

Although the social-democrats failed to persuade the nation that the economic crisis could best be overcome by the imposition of capital levies and the expropriation of indigenous capitalists, they did manage to prevent the planned boycott of Parliament over the issue of how foreign aid was to be administered. The battle over the ways and means of resolving the crisis glaringly revealed the fundamental differences between the two camps. The Austrian bourgeoisie never ceased to disparage the 'ill begotten' republic which had replaced the ancient and once glittering monarchy. The middle classes especially found it difficult to accept on equal or any other terms what they described as 'social rubble', the men and women who had come to the top during the period of socialist participation in the government and the social legislation they had carried through. To this day the twelfth of November 1918, the republic's birth day, far from being commemorated as a unifying national symbol, remains one of those ambivalent, emotionally charged turning points still capable of reviving smouldering resentments.

The misgivings generated by the Austrian revolution are the more surprising since, for all the substantial administrative ar d

---

[10] Otto Bauer, *Die österreichische Revolution* (re-issue, Vienna, 1965), p. 257 ff.
[11] Ibid, p. 285.

constitutional changes it wrought, it certainly did not transform the established order. Notwithstanding its social reforms, it did not interfere with property relationships or control over the means of production. Repeated social-democratic attempts to bring certain key sections of the economy under public ownership were successfully resisted by the christian-socials. Once the party of the lower middle class, these had long since become the party of vested interests, of property and high finance. The failure in 1919 to nationalize the *Österreichische Alpine-Montangesellschaft*, Austria's most important industrial corporation, was destined to seal the fate of the republic. For it was from within this vast industrial empire, which the state had been unable to subdue, that the christian-socials launched their para-military *Heimwehr* in their final assault on the republic. When it became clear that attempts to restore the monarchy were doomed, the Austrian middle classes, adamant in their hostility towards the republic, began to flirt with fascism in their efforts to move beyond the exercise of purely economic power.

The nationalization laws of 30 May 1919 had, in view of the christian-social and *Grossdeutsche* opposition, remained mere declarations of intent without practical consequence. The same fate befell the entire body of legislation designed to bring the public utilities, vast tracts of forest land, and the largest feudal estates into public ownership. Its actual impact was negligible. In pursuance of the act of 27 July 1919 a number of state-owned corporations like the *Österreichische Heilmittelstelle* (Austrian Pharmaceutical Supplies) and *Österreichische Werke*, incorporating the former army arsenals, were set up. This, however, hardly affected the social structure; and since nothing was done to modify the actual control over the means of production, Otto Bauer's claim to have created a people's republic did not go unchallenged. Both the party's right and left wings were critical; the right emphasized that Bauer had already abandoned orthodox theory, especially the doctrine of power equilibrium, to which he himself subscribed.

In his *Sozialismus und Staat* (1920), Professor Hans Kelsen, the still living architect of Austria's constitution, analysed Marxian thought on the exercise of state power. He found it wanting and contended it was bound to fail as a guide to practical action when confronted with the exigencies of actual situations. This view, he argued, was borne out by Bauer's inability to vindicate his policies in terms of Marxist doctrine: Bauer had based his argument on a misinterpretation of Engels' words; these implied that the state's detached neutrality in the period of equilibrium was illusory. Had not Bauer, in his eagerness to accord post-war Austria the standing of a people's republic, overstressed the significance of purely formal aspects while playing down the importance of the underlying economic realities ?[12] Kelsen tried to convince the vigorously dissenting Bauer that he had already invalidated Marx's dogma of the exploiting state if he conceded that even in a single instance and under exceptional circumstances the state could use its power for purposes other than legalized exploitation. Kelsen believed, as he explained in his *Reine Rechtslehre*, his theory of 'Uncommitted Legality', that the state at a certain stage of its development had become an inherently neutral piece of social machinery, ready to serve whatever purpose it was put to.[13] He did not deny the role the capitalist state had played as an instrument of legally sanctioned oppression, but he repudiated the notion that this was its only function or reflected its essential properties. The state could easily accommodate a socialist society; indeed its coercive powers might well prove useful when it came to implementing and enforcing the party's policies.

While on the right Kelsen had dwelt on Bauer's inconsistencies in an effort to convince him that he had already advanced beyond Marx, Otto Leichter criticized him from the left. He denounced Bauer's theory of equilibrium as an artificial contrivance specially designed to meet a particular set of political circumstances. Summing up his doubts on the general validity of Bauer's interpretation, he observed: 'Equilibrium in the class struggle can perhaps be best defined as a state of affairs in which, for the time being, neither class dares to engage the other in combat . . . It is a passing and accidental situation and does not warrant a new system of elaborate theories regarding the class struggle or the function of the state at a given moment in time'.[14]

Bauer's attitude to the state and to his continued participation in a coalition government was, of course, not exclusively motivated by Marxian theory. Nevertheless its impact should not be under-

---

[12] Hans Kelsen, *Marx oder Lassalle – Wandlungen in der politischen Theorie des Marxismus* (Leipzig, 1924), p. 285.

[13] Hans Kelsen, *Reine Rechtslehre*, 2nd ed. (Vienna, 1960), p. 283 ff.

[14] Otto Leichter, 'Zum Problem der sozialen Gleichgewichtszustände', in *Der Kampf*, May 1924, p. 184.

estimated, and statements describing 'opposition as the proletariat's natural attitude to the bourgeois state even in its republican guise'[15] must obviously have influenced his decisions. On the other hand, he was not the man to ignore practical considerations or the susceptibilities of the rank and file, and nothing describes his respect for the masses he was called to lead better than his dictum: 'Infinitely better to err with the masses than to be proved right in opposition to them'. Fears that a further extension of the coalition might induce the masses to transfer their allegiance to the communists were justified. In these circumstances it is not surprising that a minor disagreement in 1920 over the appointment and status of political advisers in the army was seized upon as a heaven-sent opportunity by both sides to terminate a coalition which they had come to regard as unnatural. In taking this decision Otto Bauer was backed not only by Marxian theory but also by the majority of a working class now increasingly disenchanted with operating the machinery of a bourgeois government. In the light of subsequent events and with the benefit of hindsight, as one looks today on a situation almost exactly reversed, one wonders whether working-class clamour in the twenties to dissolve the coalition, compared with its contemporary insistence on sustaining it, does not reflect rather the leadership's skill in manipulating opinion than any assertion of the collective will. Among the prominent social-democratic politicians, Karl Renner never ceased to deplore the grave and fateful error of having surrendered the machinery of government to the bourgeosie.[16]

The price the social-democrats paid for maintaining doctrinal purity and party unity was indeed high. While all key positions in the army, the police, and the ministries were reoccupied by the stalwarts and trusted agents of the resurgent bourgeoisie, the workers just managed to hold on to their stronghold in Vienna, the traditional bastion of social-democratic power, and the control over the country's railwaymen. These were the only positions of real strength they still commanded, apart from such influence as they could exert through parliamentary pressure or the threat of extra-parliamentary action. How little all this amounted to when con-

[15] *Protokoll der Verhandlungen des Parteitages der Sozialdemokratischen Arbeiterpartei Deutsch–Österreichs* (Vienna, 1920), p. 143.

[16] *Österreich von der Ersten zur Zweiten Republik*, II. Band des Nachlasses (Vienna, 1953), p. 42.

fronted with the smoothly organized and ruthlessly deployed power of the state, was dramatically highlighted by the abortive uprising of 15 July 1927, an unmistakable turning point in the history of the first Austrian republic. Incensed by the acquittal of members of a right-wing soldiers' league responsible for the killing of several workers, angry crowds sacked the Ministry of Justice and rioted in the streets. Eighty-five people were killed and more than a thousand injured, the government never lost effective control, and was able to proceed ruthlessly against the rioters, over whom their own *Schutzbund* officers and political leaders had temporarily lost control. After 15 July 1927 there was no turning back from the road leading inexorably to civil war and the tragedy of February 1934. Renner's frantic and repeated efforts to resuscitate the coalition failed as lamentably as Julius Deutsch's attempts to prevent the outbreak of civil strife by demanding the disbandment of the rival para-military party formations. The *Heimwehr*, now riding the crest of the wave, was sufficiently powerful to spurn offers of a compromise peace.

There is no doubt that the bourgeoisie, by trying to exclude the social-democrats from all participation in the government, must bear the overwhelming responsibility for the developments culminating in civil war. Nevertheless Austro-Marxism also contributed to its own undoing, at least to the extent of providing the *Heimwehr* gratuitously with the sort of wild and violent statements which right-wing extremists would successfully employ to frighten the undecided and the gullible into active partisanship. Seipel and the christian-social leadership cannot, of course, claim to have been deceived by this propaganda or to have taken socialist threats at their face value. They must have known from their own experience, at the very latest by 15 July 1927, that the social-democratic leadership – actuated by a genuine sense of responsibility and an equally genuine lack of revolutionary zeal – was not only unwilling to resort to violence, but on the contrary could always and under any circumstances be relied upon to curb its followers and to avoid any show of force. Even when on 15 March 1933 the legally elected representatives of the people were forcibly prevented from entering their parliament, and Dollfuss' violation of the constitution became starkly evident, the socialist leaders still shrank back from calling for armed resistance or organizing a general strike.

It was Austro-Marxism's tragedy neither to have heeded

Renner's plea for unequivocal acceptance of parliamentary democracy, nor to have forgone the pleasures of barnstorming revolutionary rhetoric and of supplementing it with dedicated action. The heated controversy between Bauer and Max Adler in the twenties touched on precisely such questions as the correct Marxist approach to the constitutional and the revolutionary alternatives, or the advisability of retaining revolution in the party programme as the final objective and with it the use of inflammatory terminology irrelevant both to prevailing conditions or to any situation in the foreseeable future. The 'messianic outlook', as Renner called it, far from being dead, still preoccupied the leaders as well as the rank and file, to such an extent as to cloud their assessment of political realities. In this way social-democratic propaganda, by continually emphasizing the transitoriness and disparaging the institutions of the republic – which in fact it did its utmost to uphold – allowed the middle classes to distort and misinterpret much of what it had to say on the subject of democracy and dictatorship. One of Austro-Marxism's classic statements, the Linz programme of 1926, proclaimed: 'The social-democratic workers' party will govern in strict accordance with the rules of the democratic state, scrupulously observing all the safeguards entrenched in its constitution. However, should the bourgeoisie by boycotting the economy, instigating insurrections, or by conspiring with foreign counter-revolutionary forces, attempt to obstruct the social change which the labour movement in assuming power is pledged to carry out, then social-democracy will be forced to employ dictatorial means to break such resistance'.[17] The purely defensive planning for a clearly hypothetical contingency nevertheless provided the bourgeoisie with welcome evidence of their opponents' dictatorial ambitions. Such deliberate misinterpretation was time and again given the appearance of verisimilitude by tub-thumping party hacks who used exalted revolutionary phraseology to compensate for their loss of real power.

Even Max Adler – ever since he published in 1922 his *Die Staatsauffassung des Marxismus* the acknowledged guardian of orthodoxy and the movement's defender against revisionist corruption – insisted on having a paragraph dealing with the 'dictatorship of the proletariat' inserted in the Linz programme. To Bauer's

---

[17] *Die österreichische Sozialdemokratie im Spiegel ihrer Programme* (Vienna, 1964), p. 43.

objection that since the Russian Revolution[18] the term dictatorship had assumed an ominous meaning, Adler replied by enlarging on the fallacies of 'democratism', a new creed which exposed the masses to the perils of bourgeois thinking. He went on to an adamant defence of the orthodox point of view, long since relinquished even by such purists as Kautsky, that only a 'social-democratic' class-less society deserves the name of democracy. As an instrument of class rule, the bourgeois version of this institution could not really lay claim to this appellation. Only the final establishment of the dictatorship of the proletariat, Adler insisted, could, by substituting majority for minority rule, effect the hoped for transition to an ultimately classless communist society. Bauer, although opposed to Adler's rigid formalism, was ideologically not all that far removed from his position. What the latter described as the 'illusions of demo-cratism' the former castigated as a substitute creed for 'vulgar petty-bourgeois democrats, who preferred democracy to socialism'.[19]

Moreover the entire theory of Bauer's brand of socialism as well as its tactics was shot through with, and to a certain extent handi-capped by, his belief in the inevitability of the historical processes and their almost automatic unfolding. Events, he held, could be influenced by individual action only in certain periods and in special circumstances; by and large their evolution would prove impermeable to outside intervention. This is not to dispute that the decline and ultimate collapse of the Austrian republic and the Austro-Marxist experiment did not have a certain air of tragic inevitability about it. Nevertheless repeated references to the un-alterable laws of history tended to promote an all too submissive surrender to the inescapable logic of events, rather than to en-courage the single-minded determination needed to retrieve a desperate situation. This overpowering sense of impotence seems to have moved Bauer to remark in 1930, when the process of iso-lating the Austrian working class was already well advanced, that 'the proletarian revolution which had demolished the monarchy was but a phase in an historical process culminating in the estab-lishment of a bourgeois republic'.[20] Historical determinism, like its religious counterpart, the belief in predestination, fosters

[18] *Protokoll des sozialdemokratischen Parteitages 1926*, pp. 269 ff., 286 ff.
[19] Otto Bauer, 'Die Zukunft der russischen Sozialdemokratie,' in *Der Kampf*, December 1931, p. 518.
[20] 'Die Bourgeois-Republik in Österreich', in *Der Kampf*, May 1930, p. 194.

gravely pessimistic attitudes as well as confident and positive ones. In stressing the futility of trying to tamper with the mechanics of history, they paralyse the will to act; and many of Bauer's comments of these later years reveal his bitter though clear-sighted acceptance of the inevitable. In 1927, for instance, he informed his right and left wing critics that 'the re-emergence of the repressive machinery of bourgeois government had been implicit in all European developments since 1919'.[21]

Whether resolution rather than resignation could either have halted or reversed the general trend towards restoration, is difficult to say. History's alternatives remain forever speculative. However, faced with a comparable situation, those who have inherited that dilemma today must be allowed to penetrate beyond the fatuities of apportioning blame or providing self-righteous justifications, and to ascertain the typical and the recurrent features in a bygone situation. The lessons of history can be learned, if at all, only if by renouncing value judgments and the comfort of being wise after the event, the fundamental and exemplary as well as the misguided responses to a particular political situation are fully analysed and their relevance to the present correctly assessed.

Even where Austro-Marxism erred, whether in its theoretical assessment or its practical approach, it still was always preoccupied with worthwhile issues, issues which, divested of their evanescent features, remain enduringly relevant. Attempts to resolve the conflict, to heal the breach between democratic socialism and communism, and to discover an alternative to the dichotomy between reformism and bolshevism, remain commendable even if in strictly Marxian terms these aims can never be attained. Any accommodation between social-democracy and bolshevism could not, it seems, be the result of an inherent convergence, but would depend rather on evolutionary changes within the Soviet sphere. These, by involving the transmutation of quantity into quality, would modify the entire character of the movement, an obviously slow and gradual process and one that might never take place; on the other hand – the spirit bloweth where it listeth – it could not be entirely ruled out. Hence communist developments ought to be studied dispassionately, and the investigator should be swayed neither by exaggerated expectations nor by the desire to arrive hastily at final judgments.

[21] 'Kritiker links und rechts', ibid., October 1927, p. 444.

Though the Austro-Marxist analysis of bolshevism has not proved superior to other interpretations, it did nevertheless give greater sharpness and depth to our insight into the socio-political forces at work in Russia. The Austro-Marxists believed that a political movement based on socialist tradition should offer the masses something more inspiring than gradual material improvements; it ought to excite the imagination and kindle a fire that would illuminate and transfigure the drabness of their condition. Austro-Marxism deserves our gratitude for having opposed its own moral concepts and considerations to the pursuit of exclusively utilitarian policies, and for having striven to educate people towards the image of what Max Adler called 'New Men'.[22] This aspect of socialism was not to be abandoned, even though all its other basic assumptions might have become untenable. For although Austro-Marxism, like its Marxist progenitor, failed to interpret and modify reality in a single, all-embracing system, it nevertheless injected impulses and made contributions which, surviving their transitory historical context, constitute, in Hegelian terms, the elements of a new situation. In its specific Marxist and Austrian manifestation Austro-Marxism is dead, but its underlying objectives are timeless and will continue to exert a formative influence.

[22] Max Adler, *Neue Menschen* (Berlin, 1924).

'Mot Dag' and the Norwegian Left

Jens A. Christophersen

Of the left-wing intelligentsia in Norway in the inter-war period it can be said for a start that they presented a new as well as a familiar phenomenon in Norwegian intellectual life. It was new by virtue of being socialist, a rare thing in Norwegian academic circles up to the end of the first world war; on the other hand, its radicalism can also be seen as part of an established trend in Norwegian politics and literature. A good deal of Norwegian writing in the nineteenth century bore a radical character, and major authors played an active part in politics, probably to a greater extent than in most other countries. But the radical romanticism of a Byron or a Pushkin was of little importance among the left wing of the inter-war years; like other countries, Norway also had its radical romantics, such as Wergeland and Björnson; but this idealistic and national trend had few followers in Norway at the time, although Nordahl Grieg clearly belongs in this tradition. For the intellectual socialists, however, that romanticism belonged to a world quite different from their own. The times were hard and unsentimental, and, on the surface at least, there was little place for feeling. Ibsen, but not Björnson, can with fairly good reason be reckoned among their spiritual fathers, although the size of the inheritance should not be exaggerated. Ibsen was not a socialist. On the other hand, it is hardly convincing to present him as an anarchist, as Plekhanov did. If a brief characterization can be allowed in this case, Ibsen can more correctly be regarded as an uncompromising individualist, not very different perhaps from Doctor Stockmann, one of his own literary creations.

From one point of view there are, without doubt, marked differences between Ibsen's individualism and collective socialism; but in relation to the radical intellectuals there are also important common characteristics: a profound realism, a typically intellectual approach, a deep emphasis on form and style, and a strikingly negative attitude towards sentimentality of any kind. It should be noted that Gunnar Heiberg and Helge Krog, the dramatists who continued the Ibsen tradition, played an important part among the left. In 1919, the aged Heiberg made the central speech at a mass meeting protesting against the Western blockade of Russia; and in that way he was more than a symbolic link between Ibsen and the young intellectuals. Throughout the inter-war period, Helge Krog played a significant role, both as essayist and dramatist. In 1936 he was almost alone in defending Trotsky during the latter's enforced isolation in Norway.

Of another world-famous Norwegian author, Knut Hamsun, it can be said without hesitation that he had no influence whatever on the left wing. Hamsun was always on the other side of the fence. It is true that clearly anti-capitalist tendencies can often be discerned in his writings, but it was from a romantic attachment to pre-capitalist and patriarchal society that Hamsun came to despise commercialism and industrialism. In this respect there is a fairly high degree of similarity between his views and the conservative anti-capitalism which can be seen in Fichte, Carlyle, Nietzsche, and also in Ruskin. Hamsun's ideas are not very original; what made him a great writer was the magic way in which these ideas were presented. It was by no means a mere accident that made Hamsun an outstanding defender of national-socialism, probably the only eminent author in the world to take this position – although it must also be said that Hamsun never adhered to any kind of anti-semitism.

Initially, Norwegian radical socialism was not the work of intellectuals. In contrast to several other European countries, especially Germany and Russia, social radicalism in Norway was mainly a trend within the trade unions. At the head of this movement stood a young house-painter, Martin Tranmæl, a man of quite unusual gifts, and without doubt the most significant figure in Norwegian socialism. A strict teetotaller and moralist, he was at the same time a brilliant speaker, a very able journalist, and a great organizer; above all an indefatigable agitator. Without any higher education, he was probably never familiar with the more abstract problems of socialist theory. Somewhat similar to that of Keir Hardie, Tranmael's socialism was mainly ethical. Two prolonged visits to the United States at the beginning of the century brought him in close contact with the new radicalism in American trade unions. Here he witnessed a kind of class struggle much more tough and spontaneous than what he had seen in Norway, and these experiences undoubtedly had a great influence on his general outlook on the labour movement. After his return to Norway in 1905 he immediately started an intense socialist agitation, and, most typically, that absence of class solidarity which characterized the so-called strikebreakers aroused his anger and contempt. In 1912 his name spread all over the country after he had proposed that the strikers should conceal dynamite in the mines in order to deter strike-breakers. From 1911 he led his own faction within the trade unions as well as within the Labour Party, and it was mainly this faction that was able to win control of the whole party at its congress in 1918, and which in the following year established contact with Moscow.

By and large, as has been said, radical socialism was a rare phenomenon among the Norwegian intelligentsia up to the end of the 1914–1918 war, in spite of the fact that Edvard Bull, Kyrre Grepp (chairman of the party from 1918 to his death in 1922), and Emil Stang (its vice-chairman and later Chief Justice of the Supreme Court), were intellectuals. From that time, however, and especially from 1919, one can note a new and strongly radical trend in academic circles and especially among students. It was in 1919 that the mass meeting protesting against the blockade of the new regime in Russia was held, a meeting led by the chairman of the Students Association. About the same time a highly critical attitude towards the Versailles peace settlement began to take shape. During the war there had been very few pro-Germans in Norway. On the other hand, very few were opposed to neutrality (although during the years of unrestricted submarine warfare most people had been very anti-German). Now this attitude gave way in part to a deep distrust of the Versailles *Diktat*, and as usual the reaction was most marked among academic people and especially among the younger ones. The strongest evidence of this new trend was the refusal of the Students Association, after a very intense debate, to send representatives to the reunion celebration in Strasbourg, to which they had been invited by the French students association. For many, it was as if their sense of justice had been offended by the behaviour of the Entente, and the presentation of Versailles as proof of democracy and civilization was regarded as mere hypocrisy. It was Versailles that drew a poet of the calibre of Arnulf

Överland out of his ivory tower and made him a literary protagonist for Germany (though he became a most uncompromising opponent of Hitler, and still later also of Stalin). And Överland was not alone.

In themselves these attitudes did not necessarily imply a belief in radical socialism. But as a result of what many of the younger students had experienced during the war, and especially of their disgust at the behaviour of the *nouveaux riches*, anti-capitalist attitudes took a firm hold. During the war more than two thousand Norwegian sailors had lost their lives at sea, a fairly large number for a small country which had not taken part in any war for more than a century. At the same time, industry, and shipping especially, had brought great wealth to a number of people sitting safe on shore. At no other period has Norwegian social life been so markedly characterized by a group of *nouveaux riches* spending their easily earned money in an ostentatious and provocative way. The contrast between vulgar luxury on the one hand and the risks the sailors faced from German submarines on the other, increased unrest. Although it is hardly possible to speak of any generally held political theory at that time, there was a blend of attitudes, moods, and ideas coalescing into feelings of unrest. And now, just as Tranmæl had earlier organized the discontented workers, another man, Erling Falk, was able to organize the discontented intellectuals.

When Falk returned to Norway in 1918 after eleven years in the United States, he was no learned Marxist. During his stay in America he had been in contact with the Industrial Workers of the World, but, unlike Tranmæl, he had also seen American industry from the employers' point of view. Even as a pronounced revolutionary he was to retain a certain respect for efficient leadership in big business, in contrast to his unalloyed contempt for the petty bourgeoisie. When seen in relation to the influence he was soon to acquire as undisputed leader in a most intellectual group, his lack of Marxist reading may appear as an anachronism. But he had something which more than compensated for this possible drawback; he had a typically intellectual grasp of every problem, and without ever becoming lost in vague theorizing, he was a master in debate; better still, he had those special qualities which make a man a natural leader. The frequently misused expression 'charismatic leadership' is justified in reference to Erling Falk.

Norway was by no means alone in possessing academic radicals in the early twenties. What was unusual, however, was the strict and disciplined type of organization which was created. This organization, *Mot Dag*, or *Towards Day* (a somewhat inadequate English translation), was to endure until 1936; during that time, and also partly after the dissolution of the group, *Mot Dag* was to mould political life in the Norwegian academic world. The group emerged from the circle around the periodical of the same name, of which the first number appeared in September 1921, and represented probably the best-written political periodical in Norway. Its contents were often malicious, but always with a strong emphasis on form and style. Its main weapons were irony, wit, and learning. It never sank to that kind of vulgar and repetitive demagogy so often characteristic of *Pravda* or *L'Humanité*.

The influence of the group was of course felt mainly within intellectual circles, but it was not limited to them. In a few cases this group, and especially Erling Falk, played a significant part in Norwegian politics in general. Broadly speaking it can be said that while the Labour Party's road to Moscow was not built by intellectuals, the way out of Moscow was paved in large part by the work of radical intellectuals. In 1919, when Norwegian socialists had their first contact with Moscow, no one in Norway knew about Lenin's theory of the party as the enlightened vanguard of the whole class, the special theory worked out in *What is to be done?* in 1902. This ignorance was by no means limited to Norway. As late as 1911, the learned Robert Michels made no mention of Lenin in his famous book on *Political Parties*, although he possessed a very detailed knowledge of different socialist parties, and in spite of the fact that probably nobody but Lenin could have illustrated so well Michels' theory about the iron law of oligarchy. What the Norwegians saw in the Russian Revolution was primarily two things: a people in revolt, and the emergence of the new regime by elected Soviets. This view was not entirely unrealistic at that time. Contrary to all later Soviet versions, the October Revolution hardly substantiated Lenin's theory of the party as the vanguard: many people fought in the streets without any membership cards, and while a newcomer to the party such as Trotsky played a most decisive part in the revolution, perhaps the most decisive role played by any single individual, Lenin's closest colleagues, Zinoviev and Kamenev, stood for a while outside the revolutionary tempest. It was not until later, and especially after the tenth congress in 1921, that the centralized one-party system became the dominating factor in political life. And it was in relation to questions concerning organization and the influence of the Comintern over the national parties that Russian and Norwegian socialism differed.

It is not possible to present here a detailed review of the various issues in Russian-Norwegian relations during the years 1921-23. The Russians clearly regarded the Norwegian question as important. Prominent communists like Bukharin and Radek were sent to Norwegian party congresses, and some concessions were made to keep the Norwegian Labour Party within the fold. Later Tranmæl and Falk were to become bitter antagonists, but during these years they stood on the same platform. In spite of great differences, both had a profound belief in the workers as a class, and also in the influence of the rank and file. The Kristiania draft of 1922 is one of the classic documents in the history of the Norwegian labour movement; mainly worked out by Falk, it contains what both men held to be the political essentials. Characteristically enough, it started with the statement that the emancipation of the working class must be achieved by the workers themselves, without directly referring to Marx in 1864. It was also emphasized that the right to take decisions of central importance belonged to the members, and that leaders must be under permanent control.

Seen from a general and comparative point of view, these Norwegian attitudes may be classified as 'unconscious Luxemburgism'. Nobody in Norway knew what Rosa Luxemburg had written about the Russian Revolution in her prison cell in Breslau in the autumn of 1918, but a fairly high degree of similarity without doubt exists. To be less abstract and probably also more correct, the draft can be regarded as a blend of Norwegian democratic traditions with a popular kind of American pragmatism, and above all with a typical American distrust of bureaucracy in general, and in this case of the Comintern bureaucracy in particular. Thus American influences can be traced in the Norwegian Labour Party's move into Comintern, as well as in its move out of it.

It was in this connection that Falk, a newcomer to the party, played an important role. Comintern correctly regarded Erling Falk and *Mot Dag* as a resistance centre. And Bukharin's final formula in 1922 was that the Norwegian party had to choose between good relations either with Comintern or with Erling Falk. This was not a question of radicalism versus reformism, but of two very different kinds of radicalism. In summer 1923 Falk was the chairman of a party delegation which was sent to Moscow to present the Norwegian view. Tranmæl himself was one of the four members of the delegation. In the history of the Comintern Falk, speaking American with a Chicago accent, was probably the only man who treated Zinoviev, Bukharin, and Radek as his equals, entirely without the reverence towards Russian leaders already common among foreign communists, and completely forgetting the maxim that while all communists are equals, some are more equal than others. For the Russian leaders such conduct was unheard of. Zinoviev stated in the summer of 1923 that only Lord Curzon had behaved with such arrogance, and Radek is alleged to have said in Oslo in December 1922 that Falk should be thrown into the grave with his bones broken.

In retrospect it is fairly easy to see that Tranmæl and Comintern could not in the long run work together. Sooner or later a break had to come. It cannot be taken for granted, however, that even Tranmæl would have been able to take with him the bulk of the party after the split in 1923. That he did so was at least in part due to Erling Falk and *Mot Dag*; certainly their role was not without significance.

What has been said here puts the emphasis on *Mot Dag* in its earlier period. Later this group was to play an important part in Norwegian intellectual life, but hardly in relation to Norwegian politics in general. Collaboration between Falk and Tranmæl, which had been of decisive importance during the Comintern time, was soon replaced by bitter antagonism. In 1925 the group was collectively expelled from the Labour Party. Formally, differences over anti-militarist tactics were the reason for the exclusion, but it is more probable that Tranmæl as well as Falk were in the long run unable to accept anybody's leadership save their own. It may not be unduly malicious to add that although both of them had revolted against Zinoviev and Comintern and its centralized leadership, both were out to establish undisputed leadership within their organizations. As regards *Mot Dag* it is amazing that Falk succeeded in keeping the group together until 1929, even after a brief second spell with the Comintern during Bukharin's right-wing period. From 1929, with the onset of the Great Depression, the group found a new *raison d'être* in extensive studies in Marxism. Then, but only then, did this Marxist group become really acquainted with Marx's writings. Falk himself translated *Das Kapital*, rendering the original into readable and fluent Norwegian. The most outstanding achievement, however, was without doubt the production by this fairly small group of a *Worker's Encyclopedia* in six large volumes (1932–36), each of about five hundred pages. This *Encyclopedia* is the only one, outside the Soviet Union, which was based on Marxism, and the only one in the world not to be scrapped by the authorities later on. The work represents a monument of intellectual capacity and learning, in spite of some dogmatic extravagances. Even today it is useful and readable, irrespective of the political opinion of the reader.

As regards another aspect, *Mot Dag* without doubt played a fairly important role in the struggle against fascism. On the whole fascism was weak in Norway. Quisling's party won 2·2 per cent of the votes in 1933 and only 1·8 per cent in 1936, and it would have had no chance at all in Norwegian politics had it not been for the German occupation. During its initial years, however, this party and related groups were not without a certain following among younger students; here *Mot Dag* obviously was a dominant influence in preventing fascism from gaining many adherents in academic circles.

Yet in spite of its pro-Soviet attitude, *Mot Dag* never displayed that uncritical admiration for Moscow which could be found among certain intellectuals and semi-intellectuals in most countries, especially during the Great Depression in the West and the first five-year plan in Russia. *Mot Dag* still regarded the Soviet leaders as equals, and the strong intellectualism of the group evidently debarred the 'ideological balalaika' not uncommon among people with a smaller endowment of *reservatio mentalis* in relation to the Soviets. Extremely few of this group were later to join the communists; nor did the Communist Party win many recruits among academic people.

It is equally significant, that, probably on account of this *reservatio mentalis*, hardly any member of *Mot Dag* was later to become infected with that extreme anti-communism often to be found among ex-believers; Arnulf Överland was an exception.

These factors are important, but even more so is the relation of *Mot Dag* to the large Norwegian Labour Party. Their ambitious aim of dominating the party, and thereby the greater part of Norwegian society, was a complete failure. The leaders of the Labour Party were recruited from the working class, a feature still characteristic of the party today. After a transitional period extending over some years, this party can with good reason be classified as an ordinary social-democratic party after the early thirties. After its electoral victory in 1933, it became the governing party in 1935, and remained in power for almost thirty years. In 1936 *Mot Dag* was collectively accepted into the mother-party, but Falk himself had to remain outside up to his death in 1940. It was the Labour Party which absorbed *Mot Dag*, not *vice versa*. But the mere fact that this influential group held together for so many years in itself represents a unique phenomenon, at any rate in Norway. This academic group had been of central importance in 1922 and 1923, when the party was faced with international problems of magnitude, when the main question was to remain independent of Comintern and Zinoviev. In 1936 the situation was quite different. The new governing party needed skilled administrators and they were not averse to recruiting these from *Mot Dag*. But *Mot Dag* was allowed to return only on these terms. The group could not assume political leadership or dominate ideologically.

These matters were of concern almost entirely in domestic Norwegian politics. In two cases, however, Norwegian politics and Norwegian debates in the thirties touched upon central world events. In the one case, concerning Ossietzky, Norway, or more correctly the Norwegian Nobel Committee, stood firm against a foreign totalitarian dictatorship, whereas in the other, concerning Trotsky, Norway yielded to foreign totalitarian pressure.

When in 1936 the Nobel Committee of the Norwegian Storting awarded the Peace Prize for 1935 to Carl von Ossietzky, it was after a most intense public debate. The country was by no means united behind this award. Many people considered it an affront to Germany to give this prize to a man in a German concentration camp. The famous author Knut Hamsun attacked Ossietzky with unbridled vehemence, and he was supported by a large part of the conservative press. In this debate left-wing authors such as Helge Krog, Överland, Sigurd Hoel, and Nordahl Grieg played prominent parts, although it must also be remembered that a conservative and a Catholic, Sigrid Undset, signed the protest against Hamsun. Of the authors mentioned here, Helge Krog, Överland, and Sigurd Hoel had for a long time been in close contact with *Mot Dag*. They were probably a little too independent directly to accept Falk's leadership, but all three were deeply influenced by him, not only in their political thought, but even in relation to their literary style. To Överland, Falk was the most powerful man he had ever met.

When the award to Ossietzky was announced there was bitter resentment in Germany, and Hitler even issued a decree forbidding Germans to accept any Nobel Prize in the future. The Swedish explorer Sven Hedin proposed that Norway should be deprived of the right to award this prize. Of those with entirely different views André Gide congratulated not only Ossietzky, but also the courageous Nobel Committee, and similar opinions were also expressed by Thomas and Heinrich Mann; the award, said the latter, is 'our first victory'. Among Norwegians, Nordahl Grieg stated: 'That afternoon in November when the newspapers brought the message that the Peace Prize had been awarded to Ossietzky was a happy occasion. Something noble-minded and fine had happened . . . It was a manifestation of justice from our people which had gone out over the world . . . Next day we read the "national" newspapers. They felt solidarity with a very small part of Norway, with a few square meters of Norwegian soil only: Drammensveien 74, the German Embassy.'

The treatment of Trotsky offers a marked contrast. When Trotsky was given political asylum in Norway in 1935, this did not initially bring the country into international difficulties, although the conservatives at home protested against the presence of this 'sanguinary monster' on Norwegian soil. But a new situation arose during the first Moscow Trial. Shortly after Zinoviev and Kamenev had been brought before the court and became objects of the most fantastic accusations, Trotsky was interned and ordered not to make any public comments on events in foreign countries. In Moscow Vyshinsky was 'proving' that Trotsky was a terrorist agent of the Gestapo. Later it was often asked whether or not this internment and this isolation of Trotsky took place in response to Soviet pressure. Trygve Lie, then Minister of Justice and later the first Secretary General of the United Nations, definitely denied that the internment of Trotsky was a result of Soviet demands. It can also be shown that, whereas Trotsky was interned on 26 August 1936, the first *written* communication from the Soviet Embassy arrived three days later. It is, however, most probable that there had been one or more oral communications earlier. Koht, then Minister of Foreign Affairs, who was away from Oslo at that time, stated later that the difficulty in establishing the exact date when the Soviet Ambassador first asked Norway to deny Trotsky asylum arises from the fact that this was done in an oral communication, of which no record seems to exist. This certainly suggests an oral request from the Kremlin; indeed, it is difficult to think of any other factor that can explain the sudden change in the behaviour of the Norwegian government towards Trotsky.

Ossietzky was defended from several quarters; Trotsky was almost alone. With only slight exaggeration it might even be said that there existed a sort of united front stretching from Vyshinsky to Norwegian conservative circles and even to the Norwegian Labour Government. The earlier hero of October 1917 was now an 'Enemy of the People', an expression frequently used by Vyshinsky, but which had been coined by Ibsen in 1882, and was then the laudatory designation of Doctor Stockmann, the uncompromising individualist who never capitulated. Like the original Enemy of the People, Trotsky became the object of the joint hatred of the conservatives and especially of his earlier radical friends when he tried to disclose the truth about the poisoned source of their wealth. Isaac Deutscher draws an analogy not very flattering to Norway. 'We are now in Ibsen's country once again . . . The drama and the stage are essentially the same; and so are the family traits of the actors, especially of the sons and the grandsons of Ibsen's pseudo-radicals'. In this case, too, a small handful of independent individuals stood up for the Enemy of the People, and it is noteworthy that it was Helge Krog, the dramatist who continued the Ibsen tradition, who campaigned in Trotsky's defence with brilliance and fire. Krog's intention was not to prove the political correctness of Trotskyism, but to unveil systematically the many half-truths, evasions, and spurious justifications of the Norwegian Government. In Norwegian political literature these articles stand out as a monument to intellectual integrity and the sense of justice. But at the time they did not create any widespread protest movement (although Trotsky's stay in Norway may even today lie on the political conscience of some people there). In retrospect it seems strange that members of *Mot Dag*, the earlier revolutionaries, kept quiet at the only time when one who was indisputably a revolutionary needed support in their own country. But at that time *Mot Dag* was well on the way to absorption in the governing party, a party which on this issue would not have tolerated dissent.

In December 1936 Trotsky was sent to Mexico under the surveillance of a police officer who later was to become Quisling's infamous Chief of Police. In his last talk with the Minister of Justice, Trotsky repeated his earlier prophecy: 'In three to five years . . . you will all be emigrés'. In contrast to several of Trotsky's other predictions, this one actually came true. After less than four years the same government had to flee from Norway before the nazi invasion.

This survey of the Norwegian left-wing intelligentsia would be incomplete without a few additional remarks on Nordahl Grieg. It is doubtful whether Grieg should be included in the left wing. While radical authors such as Överland, Sigurd Hoel, and Helge Krog were in close contact with *Mot Dag* and received lasting impressions from Erling Falk, Nordahl Grieg was never in touch as a student with this Marxist group. His heroes were not Marx, Lenin, or Freud, but eminent non-socialists such as Nansen and Kipling. He was also very patriotic, at a time when patriotism was by no means fashionable among radicals. He was a great romantic, never afraid of using grand and lofty words. As in the works of the Danish author and Lutheran clergyman Kai Munk, an anti-intellectual strain can be seen in his dramas. Very different from Helge Krog, he had little in common with Ibsen and nothing in common with Anatole France. It was his two years stay in the Soviet Union, and this stay only, which made him a convinced socialist, and also a staunch Stalinist.

In contrast to the scepticism prevalent among Western intellectuals, a habit of mind which he despised, Nordahl Grieg in 1932 was submerged in a wave of unqualified enthusiasm for Russia, for the *Aufbaudynamik* of the young Russian state and the Russian theatre; Meyerhold and Boris Pilnyak (both purged by Stalin) became his friends. Intellectual arguments, for or against, were irrelevant and beside the point. His communism was the result of a revelation, perhaps not very different from that of St Paul on the road to Damascus. To a greater degree than any other Norwegian author, Nordahl Grieg can be taken as an illustration of Eric

Hoffer's thesis in *The True Believer*. Among Norwegian writers he was the only one to defend the Moscow Trials, whereas Överland, Sigurd Hoel, and Helge Krog publicly declared the trials to be nothing but judicial murders. Not that, looking further afield, Grieg was alone. Many famous authors and writers, such as Theodore Dreiser, Romain Rolland, Lion Feuchtwanger, Sidney Webb, and perhaps one can add the name of Malraux, held similar opinions. In any case, it would be wrong to present Grieg as a crude Stalinist. What he said in connection with the Ossietzky award is fairly representative of his many political writings. There is an enduring and profound humanist undertone in his dramas and poems, and a genuine identification with the weak and the oppressed. If his picture of Stalin's Russia had been true, few people would have had reason to disagree with him. Unfortunately, it was far from true. It is perhaps typical, for other countries as well as for Norway, that the romantics went in when the intellectuals were on the way out.

Although it is outside the frame of this article, it should be added that Nordahl Grieg did not hesitate for a moment when Germany invaded Norway in April 1940. His identification with his own country could never be questioned. (In this he differed from the Norwegian communists who were faithful to the Moscow line which followed from the Stalin-Ribbentrop pact.) More prominently than any other Norwegian author, he was in the forefront of events, first during the eight weeks of fighting in Norway, later in London during the blitz, and then in convoys in the Atlantic. Through the BBC his voice and his poems reached thousands of Norwegian homes. He was killed when the British bomber in which he was flying was shot down over Berlin in December 1943.

In retrospect it may appear somewhat paradoxical that the only important Scandinavian authors who lost their lives during the war, Nordahl Grieg of Norway and Kai Munk of Denmark, had both been admirers of dictatorships, Nordahl Grieg of Stalin, and Kai Munk of the fascist dictators. One was killed over Berlin, the other murdered by the Gestapo in 1944. It is easy to discern the political naiveté in their pre-war writings. As typical romantics, logic and analysis were never their strong points. But it has also to be remembered that when the real test actually came, these men – the descendants of Byron as we might call them – had inner resources and an inner strength not always to be found among Voltaire's pupils.

REFERENCES

In addition to general works such as Borkenau's *The Communist International* (1939) and G. D. H. Cole, *Communism and Social Democracy* (1958), the reader is referred to *Trade Union Movement in Norway* (1955), published by the Norwegian Trade Union Centre, and Edvard Bull, 'Die Entwicklung der Arbeiterbewegung in den drei skandinavischen Ländern 1914–1920', in *Archiv fur die Geschichte des Socialismus und der Arbeiterbewegung*, 1922, pp. 329–61. In the Norwegian language the chief work is *Det norske arbeiderpartis historie I–II* ed. by Halvdan Koht, (1939), covering the years up to 1924. On *Mot Dag*, see Trygve Bull, *Mot Dag og Erling Falk* (1955), and Andre Bjerke, 'Erling Falk og hans menn', in *Vitenskapen og livet*, 1958, pp. 130–51. On Ossietzky, see Arne Stai, *Norsk kultur- og moraldebatt i 1930 arene* (1954), pp. 75–92, and August Schou, *The Peace Prize* (1962), pp. 604–8. Quotation from Nordahl Grieg, *Veien frem* (1947), p. 89. On Trotsky's stay in Norway, see Isaac Deutscher, *The Prophet Outcast, Trotsky 1929–40* (1963), pp. 292–8, 324–55 (my review of this work in *Historisk Tidsskrift* (1964), pp. 319–24), Helge Krog, *Meninger* (1944), pp. 214–64. On Nordahl Grieg, see Kjolv Egeland, *Nordahl Grieg* (1953), Harald Grieg, *Nordahl min bror* (1963), and Gerd Grieg, *Nordahl Grieg – slik jeg kjente ham* (1958). See also Plekhanov, 'Henrik Ibsen', *Neue Zeit* (1907), no. 3.

Radical Writers in Hungary

Paul Ignotus

To belong to the Left in Hungary, after the victory of the 1919 counter-revolution, entailed the dual liability of being treated like a cad, or at least as incurably adolescent, for demanding social change, and of being despised, at best pitied, as incurably old-fashioned. It was to have the worst of two worlds: to look moth-eaten and yet not look virtuous.

To this was added mental discomfort, a mood of bewilderment and disenchantment, often of remorse. The White authoritarian regime had been preceded by ten months in which all leftist world-redeemers, from the Wilsonian to the Leninist, had tried their hand at governing Hungary and had failed. Their failure could be excused. Wilsonians could plead that they had come too late; Leninists that they had come too early. Indeed, when, in October 1918, Hungary joined the Entente powers and prepared to fraternize with neighbouring Slavs and Rumanians, its place on the dissecting table had already been marked out by the victors; and when, in March 1919, it plunged into a Soviet experiment in the half-articulate hope of recovering St Stephen's crown, communists were more taken by surprise than anybody else. It was possible to demonstrate that the tragic avalanche of those ten months was but the continuation of the one unleashed in 1914 amidst the cheers of the Junkers, Prussian and Hungarian alike. Much could be said to prove how unjustified the self-righteousness of the reactionaries was; but not enough to relieve the Left of its feelings of frustration and guilt.

The greatest boon to the authoritarian Right, with its military and para-military caste, was the Treaty of Trianon. Under it more than three million Hungarians were – *sub titule* self-determination – compelled to live under non-Hungarian rule. This gave the extreme nationalists a strong hand. Trianon was not, and could not be, accepted as reasonable by any Hungarian: but as to ways of getting it revised, opinions were divided and sub-divided. The Left hoped for rapprochement with the neighbouring countries, with a view to future federation, as had been more or less clearly urged by pre-revolutionary radicals. Official Hungarian policy, whatever its variations, concentrated on estranging Hungarians from all or some of their neighbours (most consistently from the Czechs).

White Hungary was set up in reaction to communism but used anti-communist slogans to hit liberal institutions and traditions as well. It came to restore capital, including capital of pre-capitalist character, such as the entailed latifundia; it helped the big banks and manufacturing concerns to raise profits, partly by protecting them against working-class pressure; but it was no less conspicuous for curbing free enterprise and subordinating it to the needs of a swollen and privileged government and county bureaucracy, interlinked with the military. It boasted of its counter-revolutionary roots, but as the late historian, Bela Ivanyi,[1] pointed out, the counter-revolution it cherished meant different things when exemplified by its most scholarly theoretician, the historian Gyula Szekfu, or its most dynamic pamphleteer, the novelist Dezso Szabo; whereas Szekfu campaigned to discredit *all* revolutions, Szabo had a new revolution in mind, one running counter to both the previous 'bourgeois' (1918) and 'proletarian' (March 1919) revolutions but no less a revolution than either. This distinction is correct; yet the two trends converged on two major issues: anti-semitism, and hostility to Budapest, that city being regarded as the leading spirit of the liberal era which opened in the 1830s.

Anti-semitism in the years under review had many varieties, religious and racial, extreme and moderate, aristocratic and plebeian, feudalist and *communisant*, pro- and anti-Christian, pro- and anti-German; the varieties conceived by Jews (and/or ex-Jews) also played a part. It was not rich Jews alone, and certainly not conservatives only, who showed sympathetic understanding for a selective anti-semitism: there were many who thought that a peasant revolution, akin to Dezso Szabo's vision, might redeem the Hungarian nation, including its Jews, if they gave up the 'Budapest spirit'.

White authoritarian rule, in a word, combined a great number of complementary and, seemingly at least, conflicting tendencies.

[1] Reviewing an anthology of essays on Hungary between the two world wars in *Szemle* (Review) (Brussels), no. 4, 1963, pp. 69–73.

There were many to denounce some of its outstanding anomalies – the abuses under the open vote, for instance, manifest on innumerable occasions, or the distress of the rural proletariat, of the 'three million beggars';[2] here we shall concentrate on the few who faced these anomalies and opposed the forces behind them as an interdependent whole. Seven authors seem particularly suitable for exemplifying the role and fate of that small band of intellectual resisters. Four of them (Zoltan Szasz, Bela Zsolt, Geza K. Havas, Zoltan Gaspar) are rarely mentioned today, either in Hungary or in the non-Hungarian and refugee literature dealing with Hungary. Two (Lajos Nagy and, particularly, Attila Jozsef) have survived in public memory but with their faces posthumously doctored. Only one of them is alive and, at almost 80, still a vigorous controversialist in Hungary (Lajos Kassak).

In pre-revolutionary Hungary, the left intelligentsia had as it were two flagships: the radical, largely sociological monthly *Huszadik szazad* (Twentieth Century), and the literary and artistic magazine, non-party but with a marked preference for non-conformity, *Nyugat* (West). Much could be salvaged of their wreckage after the hurricane of 1918–19, but not their old dynamism. The two had had a common source of inspiration in the leading poet of that epoch, Endre Ady, a visionary in his art, most often reproached for incomprehensibility by his contemporaries, but an unmistakable Radical in politics. He died before the 'Dictatorship of the Proletariat' was proclaimed; and when the Whites took over, he was vehemently denigrated by some of them, and falsified and expropriated by others. *Nyugat*, whose pugnaciously liberal editor-in-chief, Hugo Ignotus, had entered a sort of self-imposed exile, gradually paled into political colourlessness; in the thirties, having been taken over by the virtuoso of Hungarian verse, Mihaly Babits, it retained its standing as the highest authority on literature but no longer acted as a ferment in Hungarian life. *Twentieth Century*, on the other hand (its editor, Professor Oscar Jaszi, in an exile that was not self-imposed), had to stop publication: yet a 'tolerated but unlicensed' periodical – a speciality of that authoritarian regime with its many carefully preserved loopholes[3] –

---

2 Originally the title of a book by the able publicist of the extreme Right, Gyorgy Olah.

3 Throughout most of the period, a Government permit was required to run either a newspaper or a periodical; but serial publications bearing the same title,

Szazadunk (Our Century), went on professing its doctrines, with Professor Rusztem Vambery as its editor-in-chief and *spiritus rector*. Vambery was a brave, witty, and knowledgeable man, and an eloquent lawyer. A god-son of the then King of England,[4] he knew his arrest would cause a stir in the West, and though subsequent British governments ignored him when he advised them against the Horthy regime, he made ample use of his exceptional position. His journal was honest, scholarly, often entertaining, and still struck even its adherents as somewhat stale. In short, of the two leftist literary flagships *West* was no longer leftist, and *Twentieth Century* (renamed *Our Century*) was no longer a flagship.

Two other left-wing intellectual magazines surviving from the pre-revolutionary years deserve attention. The first was the theoretical monthly of the Social-Democratic Party, *Szocializmus*, which, edited by Illes Monus (killed by the Nazis in 1944), often served as a platform for intellectual discussion, although its party allegiance, while enhancing its importance, also imposed restrictions.

The second was a less orthodox venture and should be identified by its founder-editor rather than its title. Lajos Kassak, poet, novelist, essayist, and later non-figurative painter, was a textbook character devised by fate to combine and embody everything revolutionary. Coming from a poor working-class family of Slovak origin, he could scarcely spell correctly when he entered highbrow literary life. During the 1914–18 war he became a contributor to *Nyugat*, but it was taken for granted from the outset by the editors as well as by himself that he would have to create his own platform. He was avant-garde in art, bohemian in dress, unwilling to compromise with proletarian taste, but in politics unequivocally dedicated to the international proletarian cause, that is, as he saw it, to anti-militarism and socialism. Even at that time, when hardly anybody knew what bolshevism was about, he got involved in the sort of controversies that can, with some hindsight, be interpreted as the rebellion of the humanist-communist against the *apparat*.

From the White Terror, Kassak fled to Vienna, but when order was restored – counter-revolution consolidated – returned to

if not appearing more than ten times a year, were tolerated although banned from news-stands, denied lower postage rates, and, in general, deprived of the facilities granted to periodicals proper.

[4] He was the son of the orientalist, Armin Vambery, friend of Edward VII. Armin Vambery was born a Jew and, when converted, became the god-son of Edward; his son, Rusztem, that of King George V.

Budapest. In and outside Hungary, he launched experimental magazines of which *Ma* (Today) made the most lasting impact. His first venture in non-experimental writing was the first – and excellent – volume of his autobiography, *Egy ember elete* (Life of a Man, 1927).

Communists attacked him as an opportunist and a renegade. People less versed in the niceties of extreme-left fratricidal arguments placed him politically halfway between social-democracy and communism; he was as much a red rag to some comparatively moderate conservatives as he was to faithful Muscovites. He was no doubt despotic and quarrelsome, but his steadfastness in matters of principle and his stimulating influence on the young cannot be denied. Jozsef Revai, the 'Hungarian Zhdanov'; Jozsef Lengyel, the 'Hungarian Solzhenitsyn'; the exceptionally sensitive aesthete, Andor Nemeth, who may be remembered by the English reader from Koestler's autobiography; Tibor Dery and Gyula Illyes, possibly the most important authors in Hungary today, and, for a brief space, the poet Attila Jozsef – all had their *Ma* periods, though Kassak would not recall them all with pride. The liberalized communist regime today has come round to recognizing his merits.

Two of the old-guard *Nyugat* authors stood out in the early twenties for their moral and intellectual courage: Zoltan Szasz and Lajos Nagy. Hungarian literary historians would be surprised to find their names so closely linked, and so would they themselves. Though on quite friendly terms, as they met in the cafés that served as the natural habitat of a Hungarian man of letters, they did not seem to be particularly interested in each other. Yet they were alike even physically: broad shoulders slackened by sedentary habits; baldish, broadly-curved foreheads; skin like parchment impregnated with tobacco smoke. Both had a way of talking with aphoristic terseness and graceful tactlessness. They shared an inability to lie.

But, once compared, the contrasts between them seem quite dramatic. Zoltan Szasz, offspring of Transylvanian squires and Calvinist bishops, was a *raisonneur* of Voltairean wit and approach, controversial and uncompromisingly middle-of-the-road. In the radical camp to which he belonged, most intellectuals had a weak spot for Marxism; its ideas were 'after all, progressive'. To Szasz it was just humbug. Under Bela Kun, he attacked the dictatorial government at a meeting in the journalists' club. He was arrested and might have been killed had it not been for the respect felt for him by the communist Chief Inquisitor who – unlike his successors under Stalinism – still had some of the Dostoevsky touch and invited him to an ideological discussion. Under the Whites, Szasz was no less outspoken in his protests and went so far as to write openly for a Hungarian refugee publication in Vienna.[5] Again he was imprisoned. After his release he lived in proud misery; he could never recover his previous standing as *magister elegantiarum*.

Lajos Nagy, born out of wedlock of a peasant mother, had always lived in wretched poverty, whether in country or town. As a writer of naturalist short stories and satirical sketches – his proper domain – he protested against the world he lived in by revealing it. Under the White Terror, however, his fury drove him further; first, in defence of the Jews. At his own expense (he had begged the money from friends, since no publisher would risk such a venture at that time) he published the booklet, *Talalkozasom az anti-szemitizmussal* (My Encounter with Anti-Semitism) in 1922, with skits on the Jew-baiters of the day, including the military. It was printed in 1,200 copies, and has been out of print since; Jews bought it up, in charitable haste, and with a view to having it disappear. It was too provocative, too outspoken.

Not that Nagy was a Quixotic character or a 'do-gooder'. He was selfish, crudely and honestly so, advertising his powerful appetite for steaks and women and his need for cash to buy them. What he could not stand was empty words, and it was the anger they aroused in him that turned him, materialist though he was, into a crusading idealist, his hopes focussed on a proletarian world revolution. He is said to have joined the illegal Communist Party, and was certainly in touch with it. In 1934, after diplomatic relations had been established between Budapest and Moscow, Lajos Nagy was allowed to accept an invitation from the Soviet Writers Union to visit their country. What he published on his return was a cold shower for his comrades. He did not say he was disappointed; he just made a wry face over the undrinkable coffee, and retailed the conversation between the Russian lady comrade and maid comrade who aired their views on 'Europe'.

There was something else the communists could not stomach:

_____
[5] *Jovo* (Future), daily of the moderate emigrés, edited by the Liberal Martom Lovaszy, and the Social-Democrat, Erno Garami, and sponsored by Baron Louis Hatvany.

his obsession with sex. He was under psycho-analytical treatment – in itself proof of a heretical attitude. In his books on village conditions he attributed the troubles of the peasantry largely to neuroses. Dearth of food, of clothes, of sex – they were equally killing, and anyone who denied this was a liar.

After the communists took over, he feared their vengeance and tried to conform. But he was not a gifted liar; his autobiography, written shortly before his death (1954), could not be so emasculated as not to betray his feelings.

Both Szasz and Nagy were outspoken philo-semites, in a way that Jews themselves would find irritating. Their ideas did not fit the clichés accepted in defence of Jewry in the White – or for that matter, the coming Stalinist – era. Szasz thought that Jewry contained an elite comparatively larger than any other ethnic category and that their main fault was not to behave accordingly but, once out of the ghetto, to ape the parochial gentry or take refuge in working-class postures instead. Nagy had scathing skits on some Jewish types; 'but', he cried, 'what's the good of lying? If it weren't for Jews, a Hungarian writer could never enter a Hungarian gentleman's home except as a valet or a tutor, as I did when coaching the idiot son of a count . . .'

This was not the sort of praise many Jews liked to hear. They wanted to be mistaken for members of the old nobility rather than be distinguished from them as more intelligent, that is, more dangerous. Szasz and Nagy shared the same fate. Though coming from the countryside, there was nothing folksy about them; for all their differences in background and outlook, they were both urban middle-class in style and behaviour. The half articulate idea of White Hungary was that it was bad enough for a Jew to be like that; for a gentile it was treacherous.

The man who, more than anyone else in the twenties, brought some dynamism into the radical intelligentsia, was Bela Zsolt. Zsolt, back from the trenches with severe wounds and in the mood typical of a harassed and prematurely-aged generation, started as a poet under Ady's and Babits' influence, and was acclaimed as their younger equal. This was, no doubt, rash, though no more undiscriminating than the complete oblivion into which his poetry has fallen today. The limitations of his art were those set by its strength: brilliance, elan, over-richness. Tongue in cheek, he accepted the verdict of an age inclined to free verse and buried his lyre to concentrate on prose (he once remarked about a fellow novelist, 'The trouble with him is he has no sense of rhythm, and nowadays without that, you can only write poetry'). His prose did have rhythm and his novels sometimes strike the reader as unfinished masterpieces. In them, and also in his plays, he mirrored Hungarian middle-class life. He was a Jew (though not of Budapest, where most of his stories are placed), as were his most competently dissected characters. As the essayist Aladar Komlos pointed out,[6] he was as merciless in representing the Jewish middle-classes in belles-lettres as he was uncompromising in standing up for them in journalism.

He acquired tremendous popularity as a leader writer on the staff of the dailies of the liberal bourgeoisie. A recurring feature of the liberal papers was the protest against anti-Jewish discriminatory measures of which the *numerus clausus*, open in the universities and *de facto* in Government appointments, was most conspicuous. Zsolt's feat was to combine such protests with the perpetuation of the radical demands of the 1918 revolution. Of these the most important had never in so many words been dropped by moderate opinion: universal suffrage and secret ballot; democratic local government; fairer distribution of land; fairer wages; social services. The demands were repeated and repeated; Zsolt put his finger on the spots where their fulfilment was blocked, sparing neither persons nor groups.

In 1929, under the Bethlen regime with its liberal loopholes, Zsolt succeeded in editing a weekly, *A Toll* (The Pen), in this spirit. He turned it into the intellectual centre for all the radical anti-Whites, from the gentlemanly democrat, Zoltan Szasz, to the revolutionary socialist – or rather anarchist at that time – Attila Jozsef. It lasted for some months; then the Ministry of the Interior clamped down on it, and *The Pen* was reduced to a 'tolerated', slim, irregularly published journal; but as a symbolic meeting-place of intellectuals it survived for many years although no longer under Zsolt's leadership. Its commentator, second in charm only to Zsolt himself, used to be the *feuilletonist* and novelist, Sandor Marai, who, however, in the middle thirties, parted company with everything smacking of 'leftism'.

[6] 'Elfelejtett arcok' (Forgotten Faces), *Elet es Irodalom* (Life and Literature), weekly, Budapest, 28 August 1965.

In the late thirties, with Hitler's shadow threatening, liberal journalism disintegrated, many of its outstanding writers seeking refuge on the Right, and the capitalist press itself seeking refuge under the protection of diehard reactionaries, the sort of gentry whose main objection to Hitler was his humble origin. Thereafter Zsolt had little opportunity to dissect the shibboleths accepted by the quasi-liberal press; but on the few occasions when, in a 'tolerated but unlicensed' journal, he did get a chance of doing so, he was at his best. His satire *Ars scribendi or Aretino on the Questions of Topical Journalism* (1936), in which a sound and experienced press-mercenary explains to a zealous newcomer how to blow hot and cold, and satisfy at one and the same time readers, advertisers, and the magistrates, should be studied by everybody interested in the give-and-take arrangements and corresponding phraseologies that dominated the Hungarian scene in those years; unfortunately, each paragraph would require special explanatory notes for the non-Hungarian reader of today to understand its implications.

A feature of *The Pen*, dating from Zsolt's editorship, was its bitter fight with the weekly, run by the member of Parliament Endre Bajcsy-Zsilinszky, *Eloors* (Vanguard). Bajcsy-Zsilinszky had started his career as a fanatic of squirearchic paternalism and militarism. In 1911 he took part in killing a peasant leader in his home town, for which subsequently he was toasted at smart banquets. In the early twenties he helped to found the Racialist Party in Parliament (together with Gyula Gombos, later Prime Minister, and Tibor Eckhardt, later the leader of the Smallholders Party). Then came a period of doubt: he discovered that many of the peasants were in distress and that some of the Jews were human. He drew some new conclusions whilst still upholding his cherished myth of Hungarian racial purity,[7] and the moral superiority of the Village over the City. He founded the National Radical Party. Zsolt and his circle, speaking up for denigrated Budapest, found this a most confused pattern of ideas: the two groups disliked each other intensely.

The postscript to this controversy came in the thirties and forties. Hitler's success drove most people towards the extreme right, but not Bajcsy-Zsilinszky. His journal was re-named *Szabadsag*

---

[7] His surname was Zsilinszky, doubtless of Slav origin; but to demonstrate his 'Hungarian blood', he added his mother's surname, Bajcsy, with its genuine Magyar ring.

(Freedom). He himself grew into a symbolic figure of national resistance. He fought racialist legislation, made common cause with the Radicals of 1918, the deputies Rezso Rupert and Vince Nagy, and with their leading publicist, Bela Zsolt. It was he who saved Zsolt's life in the war by getting him out of a labour battalion where he had been at the mercy of officers and nco's who specialized in torture. When, in March 1944, the Germans occupied Hungary, Bajcsy-Zsilinszky received them in his home with a gun. Some months later he was executed. He was one of the few genuine romantics: above all, a patriot.

The part played by communists in the ideological war on the Horthy regime was not so predominant as either Admiral Horthy (and the guardians of his heritage) or the communists would have us believe. For one thing, their refusal to admit basic differences between one non-communist regime and another made them uninterested in the peculiarities of the regime existing in Hungary. Until the summer of 1935, when the Popular Front was launched, they had shown no sympathy for non-communist left-wingers, and more hatred for social-democrats, Trotskyists, and their own disenchanted followers than for either the diehard conservatives or the subversive racialist Right. They could not, in a word, be allies of either the liberal or the socialist opposition. After 1935, on the other hand, when the green light to fraternize with non-communists was switched on, it was their lack of selectiveness that kept them apart from a non-repentant and fastidious Left. Some – not all – gave the impression of using the recently authorized formulas simply as means to curry favour with the established authorities. In the fight for freedom and social equality they were more often a nuisance than a help.

This is not to deny their sacrifices and their merits. Barring the final 'Brown' period of the White regime, when Jews were indiscriminately exterminated if caught, whatever their political allegiance, there is no doubt that no definable category of people was more persecuted than the communists; it was from them that the greatest toll was taken by the Whites. They ran, and knew they ran, the grimmest risks. But as to the achievements in art, literature, and scholarship to their credit, these were demonstrably due to their deviations from the party line rather than to their adherence to it. There was Andor Gabor, writer of amusing cabaret skits and satirist of the pre-revolutionary years, a typical (and graceful) specimen of 'superficial bourgeois culture'. In the early twenties he was in Vienna as a communist refugee, writing amusing, venomous articles and topical verses against Horthy and his officers. Then he moved to the Soviet Union; the most one can say about him since is that he managed to survive. Of those who had once been associated with Kassak, Jozsef Revai survived as a leader; Jozsef Lengyel survived as an inmate of Soviet prisons and labour camps[8]; the poet Aladar Komjat died whilst engaged in illegal political activities in the West; and another poet, probably the best in combining the grimace of *dada* with the passion of a socialist revolutionary, Sandor Barta, died at the hands of the Stalinists in the Soviet Union.

In Paris, Gyorgy Boloni, the once left-liberal writer who gradually stiffened into rigid communism, was one of the few refugees who even from abroad could get some response at home, but the work with which he achieved this, his book on Endre Ady who had been his intimate friend, and his articles on post-impressionist painters, also his friends (as well as, later, his biography of Mihaly Tancsics, the first Hungarian socialist), were more in the spirit of *Nyugat* radicalism than Marxist-Leninist doctrine.

Two old-guard *Nyugat* authors, the poet Bela Balazs and the philosopher George Lukacs, arrived as communist refugees from the White Terror in Weimar Germany. Intellectuals in Hungary were interested to learn that Balazs, now concentrated on film aesthetics, was making quite an impact on the *Kulturbolschewisten*, and that Lukacs, with his *Geschichte und Klassenbewusstsein*, exasperated doctrinaire communists.

The young *Kulturbolschewist*, Gyula Hay, started his career as a writer for the Weimar German stage and entered the Hungarian scene only much later.

Tibor Dery, after long years in Vienna, Berlin, and Paris, settled in Budapest. He was known to be a communist sympathizer, and in October 1938 was sentenced to two months imprisonment on the charge of glorifying the Soviet Union by translating Gide's *Retour de l'URSS*, a book which, it will be remembered, was decried as a pack of Trotskyist-reactionary calumnies by the Kremlin and its international following. In the knowledge of his later role and fate,

---

[8] Cf. Paul Ignotus, 'The Return of Jozsef Lengyel', *Encounter*, May 1965.

it may seem like wisdom after the event to point to the hetero-doxies in his past; but these are facts. His was certainly not a very orthodox path in communism.

The communist underground ran a number of 'tolerated but not licensed' periodicals; most memorable were two successive socio-logical journals, *Tarsadalmi Szemle* (Social Review) and *Gondolat* (*Thought*), and the literary *100 per cent* with avant-garde leanings. Everybody knew whose mouthpiece they really were, and the political police used them as signposts. But then, short of risking that, how could one do anything? Of their editors, one whose per-sonality commanded respect in broader circles was Dr Jozsef Madzsar, successful dental surgeon, prominent figure of the liberal middle classes, pushed by his uncompromising defiance of the Horthyites into capitulation to the Stalinists. He fled to the Soviet Union; on his arrival he published an article saying he was now in the freest country on earth; shortly thereafter he was liquidated.

If communism itself did not serve as a rallying point for left intellectuals, the indignation at the way communists were per-secuted often did. Bela Bartok, for instance, earned the admiration of his audience when he stood up for his old partner Bela Balazs, the librettist of his *Prince Bluebeard's Castle*, then a refugee, by refusing the offer of the State Opera to perform it with another text.

A significant and in a way symbolic protest was a manifesto against capital punishment for political crimes issued on 26 July 1932, at a time when two underground communists, Sallai and Furst, had been arrested and were awaiting trial under summary jurisdiction. Three days later, on the 29th, the death sentence on the two was passed and immediately executed. Subsequently, six persons stood in the dock: Lajos Szimonidesz, Protestant theo-logian and rationalist historian of the *Our Century* group; Mrs Eugenia Meller-Miskolczy, a feminist humanitarian; the painter, Robert Bereny; Bela Zsolt; Gyula Illyes; and the poet Attila Jozsef. Three of them had never been involved with communism; Bereny and Illyes had had slight connections many years earlier. Attila Jozsef was at the time the only communist amongst them; he had drafted the manifesto (with Szimonidesz's and, secretly, Madzsar's assistance). Some two years later Attila Jozsef was expelled from the party, denounced as a fascist by Hungarian writers in Moscow, and treated accordingly by their comrades in

Budapest. Today he is venerated as a communist saint throughout Hungary.

Attila (hardly anyone in Hungary would identify him by his surname only) was the son of an itinerant worker and a charwoman, orphaned as a child at the end of the first world war. His life was one of privations and adventures. He worked as an usher in cinemas and then as a cabin boy on a Danube steamer. He was a quick learner, and got sympathy and help from a well-to-do and intelligent lawyer who married, successively, his two sisters. He was destined by both his rather disorderly family background and his temperament to live on the fringe of the middle classes, the no-man's land between all classes. He matriculated and read Philosophy and Languages at the University of Szeged (now named after him), but his poems were thought to be unpatriotic, blasphemous, and subversive (although not scandalous enough to win large sales), and advance in academic life was ruled out. Moreover, although he was determined to work regularly and accurately, he was disabled by recurring fits of restlessness and melancholia; he committed suicide at the age of 32, shipwrecked by metaphysical uncertainties.

His was a non-conformist spirit *par excellence*; typically of an age dominated by a belief in subordination, it was not the young but some of his elders in the *Nyugat* old guard who first recognized his talent. He was an obsessed searcher for truth; much as he suffered from the sight (and, quite frequently, from the experience) of squalor and misery, it was less these than a drive towards a vision of balance and justice which turned him into a revolutionary. In his opposition to the regime he was steadfast; but in his youth he tried all possible variants of socialist, populist, and anarchist theories to get to the bottom of social problems. By the beginning of the thirties he had become a communist, an illegal 'party worker'. In January 1932 he turned up as the editor of a newcomer amongst the 'tolerated but not licensed' magazines, *Valosag* (Reality), with another young 'party worker', the schoolmaster François Fejto, as his associate; it was discontinued after its first number.

Attila Jozsef's break with communism was an involved process, but his two main heresies were unmistakable: interest in psychoanalysis; and, as he saw Hitler's threat coming, the idea of a liberal-socialist alliance. He tried to stop the attacks on social-democrats: 'It would be desirable for workers to recognize before fascist terrorists knock it into their heads with clubs, that to support one another's actions is more important than the observance of an ideal party discipline'.[9] When his comrades reproached him for lack of discipline, he went further in questioning their wisdom, which earned him the label 'fascist'.

No sooner had this anathema been pronounced than the Popular Front was adopted by the Comintern. Attila then turned 'Trotsky-ist',[10] refusing to support the efforts being made to bring about an understanding between the Government of General Gombos and the writers agitating for social reforms either under racialist or (this was the novelty) under leftist colours.

The swirl of ideas drifting over the scene was immensely confused. Paranoia had started shaping history (and was to continue to do so until Stalin's death). Common sense had become a rarity. No one displayed it more powerfully than did the poet Attila; his analyses of current popular slogans displayed an uncanny perspicacity. He felt that he had to make a clean sweep and discard all versions of 'the new tale of a fascist communism', by which he meant both Stalinism and the leftist-sounding excuses found for one or another right-wing authoritarian trend. He renounced communism and joined the social-democrats, though on his own terms; his main effort at that time was to arrive at a 'synthesis of Marxism and Freudism'.[11] He set forth the view that class rule established by violence was incompatible with any sensible socialist philosophy, including the Marxian. Even more sharply he rejected the populist idea that democratic reform could be brought about by an accommodation with a Gombos-style right-wing government.[12] (The saddest part of the latter controversy was his estrangement from his old friend Illyes, a populist who, perhaps precisely on account of his more intimate ties with Attila and other left-wingers, felt more deeply hurt by such attacks than the rest.)

Early in 1936 a new 'tolerated but unlicensed' periodical was launched, the literary magazine, *Szep Szo*. This may be translated, literally, as 'Beautiful Word', or more freely, as 'Argument' (in idiomatic Hungarian, to achieve something by 'beautiful words' does mean to achieve it by the strength of argument and not by

[9] *Uj Harcos* (New Fighter), May 1933.
[10] He did not join them but accepted many of their views (cf. Arthur Koestler, Poetic Interlude', *Invisible Writing*, 1954).
[11] Cf. his essay, 'Hegel, Marx, Freud', *Szep Szo*, Jan.–Feb. 1938.
[12] Cf. his essays in *Szocializmus*, November 1934, May 1935.

violence). The title was suggested by Attila Jozsef, one of its founder-editors; the other editor – standing for 'left liberalism' – was the present writer. The associate editor was, from the outset, Fejto, who, like Attila, had ceased to be a communist while still professing a variety of Marxism; its leading literary critic was Andor Nemeth. On the conservative wing of the set-up there was the orientalist, Baron Bertalan Hatvany, who, politically, would describe himself as a Tory Democrat, and the most elegant Hungarian stylist of those years, Andras Hevesi.[13] The honorary subeditor was the young orientalist and archaeologist, Tibor Horvath, until the Museum authorities by whom he was employed clamped down on him for this subversive activity.

Szep Szo set out to challenge authoritarianism as a whole; mainly right-wing authoritarianism, which in its moderate version was ruling Hungary, and in its extreme version was heading for victory. Dynamism seemed the privilege of the nazis; even their opponents thought them the pace-setters of the twentieth century, particularly in matters of social reform. Communists disagreed with this view but tacitly agreed with them in regarding freedom as a value of the past. This was the 'new tale' Attila Jozsef challenged; no moral order, and certainly no socialist one, he argued, could be created without freedom of opinion. '*Szep Szo* is not only our means but our end as well', he wrote. 'We are aiming at a society in which argument decides.'[14]

Attila Jozsef (like Ady some twenty or twenty-five years before) was outspoken in his advocacy of friendship with Hungary's neighbouring nations, mainly in defence against German militarism. He translated Czech, Slovak, and Rumanian poetry, and encouraged the literary-minded and music-loving Czechoslovak press attaché in Budapest, Anton Straka, in his endeavours to bring about understanding between the two countries, at least in the field of culture. As a result of these efforts, *Szep Szo* organized a lecture tour in Czechoslovakia in October 1937; for which the Hungarian Government and the nazi press, with *Uj Magyarsag* in the front line, accused them of treason. Attila, knocked out by his disease, was unable to travel, but some of his poems were recited

[13] There is a good (though not wholly accurate) portrait of him in the memoirs of Simone de Beauvoir, who had known him since his youth when he read philology at the Sorbonne. He died in battle, as a volunteer in the French army, in 1940.

[14] *Szep Szo*, April 1936.

and quoted again and again in addresses to left-wing and moderate (that is, non-nazi) Hungarian minority audiences. By the end of that year he was dead. On 20 January 1938, an Attila Jozsef memorial meeting held by the *Szep Szo* circle was interrupted by nazi demonstrators, who turned out to have no idea against whom they were demonstrating; some of them had not even read the leaflets they distributed.

The Anschluss was the end of it all. The pressure to turn Hungary into a German colony became unmistakable, and resistance to it, even on the part of intellectuals, had become a matter less of intellectual insight than of decency, patriotism, and courage. When recording anti-nazi statements made under the swelling (and occasionally ebbing) Brown Terror from March 1938 to April 1945, there is hardly any other yardstick applicable to them than that of bravery; words had ceased to mean what they were supposed to mean, and a piece of writing presented as a discussion of ideas could be understood only as indicating the extent to which the writer was prepared to rely on a German or an Allied victory. The outcry against Jews was to some extent an exception; quite a few did mean it, mainly when it came to sharing the loot, irrespective of the outcome of the war. But other terms such as 'the New Order in Europe' or 'right-wing *Weltanschauung*' simply stood for 'the Germans have the arms, and that's that'; whereas 'national independence', 'constitution', 'Christian morality', 'humanism', and, particularly towards the end of the period, 'peace', were euphemisms for the coming German defeat. When, in a book published in 1939, Laszlo Nemeth, regarded as the leading ideologist of populism, introduced the distinction between 'Deep-Hungarian' and 'Shallow-Hungarian' as a sort of spiritualized substitute racialism, his innovation was simply interpreted as opting for compromise between Chamberlain and Hitler – *attentisme*, as it would have been called later. The left-liberal sociologist Zoltan Gaspar, in a long review of the book, pointed out its fascist character, and indeed, an Axis-Western compromise would have entailed for Hungary, if not full-fledged racialism and fascism, a development on fascist lines and in a *Blut und Boden* spirit.

The Anschluss was immediately followed by racialist legislation in Hungary. Some young intellectuals among the 'racially pure Magyars' collected the signatures of leading gentile scholars, artists, scientists, and authors, for a protest against the nazi-inspired bill. They included the novelists Zsigmond Moricz and Jeno J. Tersanszky, the composers Bela Bartok and Zoltan Kodaly, the painter Istvan Csok – a most impressive list. Among those who refused there was only one who gave a respectable reason: Lajos Kassak. He insisted that Jews, too, should be invited to sign, 'otherwise we are agreeing in practice to what we protest against in theory'. But there were too many Jews among the men of letters; their names would have swamped the list and made it worthless.

Muzzling of the press was the other outstanding nazi-inspired act. Though prepared under the Imredy government, it came into force only later, under Count Teleki's premiership, on the outbreak of war in the autumn of 1939. One of its provisions was that 'non-licensed' periodical publications could no longer be 'tolerated'. It was these periodicals, more than either books proper or journals proper, that had upheld intellectual freedom, and now they were to vanish overnight; Vambery's radical *Our Century*; Kassak's socialist *Work*; the communists' *Thought*; and the late Attila Jozsef's *Szep Szo* – all had to stop publication. In 1941, after the death of Babits, even *Nyugat* lost its licence, although Gyula Illyes, who had for years been its assistant editor, got permission to start a new periodical, *Magyar Csillag* (Hungarian Star).

But by then most of the *dramatis personae*, if still alive, had sought refuge in the West. In Hungary itself, for the left intelligentsia only rearguard actions were possible. Two men in particular should be remembered for performing this task with exceptional wit, elegance, and honesty: Zoltan Gaspar and Geza K. Havas. Both were on the threshold of middle-age, both known to the initiated for their scholarship, originality, and style, both had spent most of their adult years in a futile chase for a job or a publisher. They were the incarnations of unsaleable left-liberalism. Gaspar, a sociologist, graduate of Law of Szaged University, had been stranded in provincial semi-employment until, ironically, the racialist law he hated enabled him to fill a tolerable post as a stopgap gentile in the capital. His *History of Twenty Years, 1918–1938* had the merit, in Havas's words, of being 'as little in harmony with the *Zeitgeist* as possible'.[15] Havas himself, as a Jew, an ex-commun-

15 Ibid., March–April 1939.

ist turned liberal, an economist who favoured Henry George's Single Tax, combined all that was officially hated. He wrote fine essays on J. S. Mill, on the Fabians, on reformers of the Hungarian Enlightenment; and he was a sensitive, if whimsical, literary critic. Gaspar was assisted by Havas, the last editor of *Szep Szo* before the guillotine fell; afterwards they brought out a collection of writings by its contributors, *Delta Almanach*. 'In my last plea' was the title of Havas's article.

Yet, to put things into proportion, these last flickers of left intellectualism were not the brightest flames of anti-nazi pathos. The centre of resistance to the nazis had shifted. In the war years it was the fanatics of a mellowed national chauvinism who performed the most spectacular deeds: Count Teleki who took his life in protest against Hungary's joining in the German attack on Yugoslavia, and Bajcsy-Zsilinszky when the Germans entered. No one was braver – or wittier – in debunking the German colonizers than Dezso Szabo, the patron of Magyar racialist silliness; and his counterpart as the intellectual leader of traditionalist counter-revolutionaries, Gyula Szekfu, contributed, together with other non-socialists, to what was generally referred to as the 'Popular Front number' of *Nepszava* (Voice of the People – the social-democratic daily) on Christmas day 1941. A number of 'fronts' were formed, and manifestos issued; the list of their supporters included moderate liberals and radicals, Christian-democrats and social-democrats, communists and fellow travellers; but their tones were pitched to conform to naive (if respectable) jingo daydreams. There was, for instance, a Historical Memorials Committee, formed to combine the commemoration of the War of Independence of 1848–9 with a more or less open protest against Hungary's commitment to the war on the nazi side. Amongst the signatories of its initial appeal were Zoltan Gaspar; the populist writers Gyula Illyes and Peter Veres; the Catholic publicists, Istvan Barankovics and Jeno Katona; the then editor of the social-democratic *Nepszava*, Arpad Szakasits; the leader-writer of the daily of the anti-nazi 'top people', *Magyar Nemzet* (Hungarian Nation), Gyorgy Parragi; the liberal literary essayist, Aurel Karpati; the sculptor, Pal Patzay; the painters Aurel Bernath and Istvan Szonyi. 'Jewish' names were conspicuously absent.

When the fifth anniversary of Attila Jozsef's death was approaching, the secretary of the bakers' union, Gyorgy Marosan, on behalf of a group of young workers, suggested that he should be re-buried in the Budapest cemetery of Kerepesi ut, alongside the country's national heroes. The social-democratic town councillors took the matter up, and the Budapest City Council, with eyes riveted on the news from the battlefield, afforded a cautious gesture of agreement. Gaspar spoke at the tomb, and later recorded the events that led up to it, in Illyes's journal. [16]

Geza Havas died in a nazi labour camp. Zoltan Gaspar went into hiding when the nazis had taken over but returned when the siege of Budapest was still on and was killed by a German bullet.

REFERENCES

There is practically nothing in English. In Hungarian, in addition to sources quoted, abundant factual information – not always with unbiased comment – can be found in the voluminous anthology of contributions by several authors, *Tanulmanyok a csehszlovak-magyar irodalmi kapcsolatok korebol* (Essays on Czechoslovak-Hungarian Literary Connections), ed. Laszlo Sziklay and others, Budapest, 1965; see also Istvan Gal, 'Anton Straka, Jozsef Attila diplomata baratja' (Anton Straka, diplomat friend of Attila Jozsef), *Filologiai Kozlony*, Budapest, Nr. 1–2, 1964. These essays throw some light on the relations between the Little Entente and Hungarian revisionism, a still sore question in the minority problems of Europe.

Until early 1939 (when I settled in London) I had often been an eye-witness and even participant of the events recorded. As the documentary literature is scanty, I have often had to rely on my own recollections and, in some cases, on hearsay. I accepted, for instance, Bela Zsolt's own story about the way Bajcsy-Zsilinszky had saved him from the labour battalion. Another friend assures me that Zsolt's escape was due to the intervention of his wife. I have left Zsolt's version, since it is characteristic of the links between the two men. Zsolt died in 1949: shortly after, his widow, learning that she was to be arrested by Rakosi's political police, killed herself.

[16] 'Poet and public opinion'. *Magyar Csillag*, 1 December 1942.

The Turkish Left

Kemal H. Karpat

The rise of a modern secular left-wing movement in Turkey, aimed at establishing a new social and political system, depended first and above all on the elimination of the traditional concepts of authority and social organization. Leftist ideas of government rest on a materialist concept of power and assume an economic explanation of social organization which is irreconcilable with the traditionalist moral understanding of government and authority. It was natural, then, that the disintegration of traditionalism and the rise of leftist thought should begin only slowly in the Ottoman Empire and become increasingly rapid in Republican Turkey. The reforms in government prepared the ground not only for modernization of the country in the general sense, but also for the development of leftist movements.

The first of these (clubs, political parties) were established during the Young Turks era (1908-18), after the power of the traditionalist dynasty had been irrevocably undermined by nationalism and secularism. The process had in fact begun much earlier, as a result of the social changes occurring after Tanzimat (1839), and especially after the Crimean War in 1853. The Young Ottomans (1865–76), especially Ali Suavi, Ziya Pasa, and Namik Kemal, held views which might have evolved into a movement of social protest, but they were stifled and diverted into the demand for a constitutional parliamentary regime after Abdulhamid II, in 1877, prorogued Parliament indefinitely and maintained the sanctity of traditional institutions. Thereafter social ideas found an outlet in literature which bore little relation to political thought. Between the years 1880 and 1908 the reformist intelligentsia, forced to flee abroad, borrowed Western political ideas without much concern for their economic and social relevance.[1] The resulting social vacuum

[1] Cf. Serif Mardin, *Jon Turklerin Siyasi Fikirleri* (Ankara, 1964), and Kemal H. Karpat. *Turkey's Politics* (Princeton, 1959), Chapters 1-3.

169

in the thought of the Young Turks reflected their aloofness from the country's realities and the inability of modern social ideas to make their way against the institutions and the philosophy of the traditional social organization.

A drastic change in these traditional political institutions therefore appeared as the primary condition for the rise of modern social thought, including its left-wing varieties. Consequently the abolition by Mustafa Kemal of the Sultanate in 1922 and the Caliphate in 1924, and of their sustaining cultural and educational bases (these had already been undermined by the secularist-nationalist policies of the Young Turks), prepared the ground for the establishment (1923) and consolidation of a Republican regime, and also removed the obstacles hampering the rise of a secular left. The Republican government, bent on preserving the unity necessary for building a national state, found it expedient to make extensive use of the traditional concepts of government and authority, but these could not be maintained indefinitely, while the social structure became diversified and evolved often in contradiction with the political ideas surviving from earlier times. The inability to harmonize the philosophy of the political system with its developing social and economic content, and to provide satisfactory intellectual explanations, caused profound tensions throughout the Republic. Fresh social ideas, being ignored or misunderstood, took the form of political hostility to a government which failed to grasp their vital meaning. Whenever conditions made it possible, as during periods of rapprochement with the Soviet Union, or when genuine attempts to introduce democratic processes were made, as in 1930 and after 1946, left-wing currents burst violently into the open.

The forms they took varied according to the degree of liberalization and the stage of social development reached. In 1930 the interval of liberalization was so short that they scarcely had time to assert themselves, and became confused with the popular protest against the ruling Republican Party. They emerged more clearly after 1946, but were soon forced underground by the government's repressive action.

A second source of leftism in Turkey must be sought in the social and cultural dislocation caused by modernization. The complex social and psychological readjustments it implied provided leftism with the opportunity to present itself as a creed offering salvation in the form of dedication to a modern form of life. Modernization, indeed, gradually undermined the traditional social and cultural framework within which the individual had found security and meaning in life. Change in a society which preserves its basic religious, cultural, and philosophical framework does not totally undermine its value system; but in Turkey the economic and social transformation, especially after 1930, profoundly affected existing values. The situation was further aggravated by the government's opposition to open debate and discussion. Given this freedom, the intellectuals would have been able to explain and justify the changes and thus adapt themselves mentally to new forms of social and political organization. Without it, they were unable to carry out their unique mission of formulating a system of ideas and thus facilitating the adjustment to the changed forms of life.

Actually it was the intellectual who became the first victim of the clash of values. The common people were still relatively secure within their traditional family relations and communal ties, which were hostile to but still protected them against outside influences.[2] But the intellectual, borrowing the outlook and values of the West, was exposed to inner conflict from the very beginning. His ideas of 'good', 'right', and 'just' differed substantially from those accepted in his immediate environment. It was usually the more sensitive and serious type of intellectual who reacted most violently to society's unwillingness to accept his own borrowed standards of 'good' and 'just', standards nourished by a kind of secular humanism which made his dissatisfaction with the traditionalist order even greater and left him mentally isolated in his own society. He turned avidly to a search for arguments and ideas to support his stand and to condemn his opponents and society at large as sinners against modernism.

Western literature offered him an easy escape into an ideal world where he shared ideas and lived among men whose way of life he wanted to make his own.[3] Later the intellectual moved from

[2] The large group of Turkish workers (over 150,000) employed in Western Europe seemed to have taken the new conditions in their stride just because their values were already formed and their intellectual unpreparedness left them immune to outside influences. See Nermin Abadan, *Bati Almanya'daki Turk Iscileri ve Sorunlari* (Ankara, 1964), p. 191 ff.

[3] A leftist escapee to the West wrote: 'I am in Europe and free. I have no hatred, only pity towards my society which tortured me and my friends and condemned us materially and morally. That society pushed aside the truly pro-

literature to social doctrine and finally began to search for political means to fulfil his social dream. The rise of leftism in Turkey was intimately associated with literature; the country's leading leftists are usually thoroughly versed in Western literature, and literary works were often used to convey political ideas to adherents and to propose practical methods of political action. The police would ascertain the political tendency of suspected leftists by raiding their libraries; Ignazio Silone, John Steinbeck, and most Russian writers were usually considered incriminating.

It was thus the intrusion of Western values upon a traditionalist system, rather than a conflict arising from the clash of economic interests, which turned intellectuals to the left, although economic arguments were later invoked as justification for a new political regime. This situation, coupled with the ruling elite's denial of freedom, and especially its dismal failure to replace fading social values with new ones genuinely in accord with new conditions, facilitated the spread of leftist ideas.

A former member of the underground communist party of Turkey (now an actor), gives an excellent insight into his conversion to marxism. He was brought up in a lower-class urban environment amidst poverty, ignorance, and bloody feuds arising from personal conflicts, while the upper class remained utterly unconcerned with the fate of the underdog. Eventually a friend, who had associated with communists, gave him Stefan Zweig's book *Mercy*, describing Zweig as a humanist. Later the reading list included Nazim Hikmet's poems and other works by left-wing Turkish writers, to be followed by occasional socialist writings. Finally the 'bourgeois' became the hated enemy opposing the establishment of the 'right' social order, and the man found himself in the left-wing underground in 1946.[4] 'I ask myself,' he writes, 'whether I would have joined the communist party . . . if I had found a little interest, affection, and understanding? . . . I ask the question in order to determine my own responsibility. I am the child of a society whose values were destroyed and its foundations

gressive citizens . . . It lives on their blood and tears . . . we have seen much and our friends have suffered much. What was our guilt? Nothing, believe me, nothing. Only our thoughts, which did not suit their minds and made them suspicious.' *Aksam*, 13 August 1960.

4 Aclan Sayilgan, *Inkar Firtinasi* (Ankara, 1962), pp. 15–27. The author entered the party in 1946 and was arrested in 1952 along with most of the underground organization.

shaken by the downfall of the Empire ... I accept my share of responsibility without going into unnecessary explanations. But those ruling society in those days must accept theirs too. It is easy to accuse and even punish a man and make him a social outcast because his values differ from society's. But this means to view lightly the problems of our country and those of the world ... I have no doubt that my generation, born with the Republic, was the victim of treachery. We saw that everything was valued politically. The politicians wrote history and made us read it the way they pleased. They defined democracy as they pleased and wanted the masses to swallow it like a pill. They praised not the power of the intellect, of creativity and culture, but that of brute force, and wanted us to become its slaves. They sacrificed what was lofty to the clamorous flattery of the masses ... A generation which was neglected and whose existence was ignored, was bound to realize that it had been deceived. It would then reject everything and would strive to find new values to replace those destroyed.'

Often left-wing ideas were taken up as a comprehensive answer to the needs of modernization. A well-integrated socio-political system, such as that of the traditionalist Islamic order, could be replaced only by a system which was equally comprehensive. This substitution of one system for another is feasible at the intellectual level if other social and political developments within the social body do not thwart or reshape the intellectuals' political ideals. The social transformation in Turkey, while offering suitable conditions for the development of a radical left, also created new interests and orientations which were in opposition to it. In this context leftism in Turkey, especially after 1940, became also part of a complex endeavour to preserve the intelligentsia's high status against the rising entrepreneurial middle class. Modernization in the Ottoman Empire and Republican Turkey aimed primarily at reforming the government institutions. The subsequent expansion of the administration necessitated a large bureaucracy, whose official role of implementing state authority was coupled with the unofficial function of providing intellectual leadership for the modernization movement. The content of this function was determined largely by the bureaucratic intelligentsia's association with and dependence on government.

The entrepreneurial groups, on the other hand, functioned initially as a subordinate economic auxiliary to the ruling bureaucratic order. But the growth in their size, power, and function within the national economy made them potential candidates for political power. Eventually, after the introduction of a multi-party system in 1945–6, they assumed their own political role and achieved power under the Democratic Party in 1950. This was followed by a marked diminution in the power of the bureaucrats who had ruled the country since the nineteenth century, while important sections of the intelligentsia were attracted to the side of the rising bourgeoisie. Furthermore, the rise of new social groups to economic and political power challenged and undermined the values and standards of the upper classes, the old Ottoman families who had led the Republican revolution, and those who grew rich in 1915–22, in the economic scramble which followed the decline of the non-Moslem middle classes. The growing importance of economic factors played a decisive part in giving a more concrete form to leftist ideology and in relating it to various social groups.

The agitated years of the War of Liberation (1919–23) saw the rise of a series of leftist groups. Of these only the young spartacist-marxists, trained in Germany, notably Sefik Husnu (Degmer) played a part in later movements. The Islamic-minded socialists took no part in the elections of 1923, while the secularist, moderate leftists were absorbed into the ruling Republican Party. After 1925 the Law on Public Order was used to liquidate all extremist movements.

The official acceptance of economic statism in 1931, and the renewal of the treaty of friendship with the USSR, enabled social questions to be discussed more freely. It was obvious that the social transformations under way needed an explanation and justification, not only to placate the intellectuals but also to influence their thinking. The review *Kadro* (1932–4) presented an amalgam of radical concepts, left and right, aiming at creating a national ideology, and possibly preventing the expansion of the radical left. But marxist political literature[5], apart from a few translations, re-

---

[5] See Kerim Sadi (Nevzat Gurken) *Felsefenin Sefaleti* (Istanbul, 1934); *Bir Sakirdin Hatalari* (Istanbul, 1934); and several other works appearing in the *Insaniyet* (Humanity) collection. See also the review *Projector*. On the *Kadro* see *Turkiye'de Kapitalism* (Tarihsel Maddecilik Yayinlari), vol. i (Istanbul, 1965), p. 154 ff.

mained confined to a few insignificant tracts, brochures, and periodicals. Underground political activities were also of limited consequence.

The really significant leftist activity after 1925 was to be found in literature. Nazim Hikmet Ran (1902–63), using also the pen name of Orhan Selim, Sabahaddin Ali (1907–48), and several other lesser names, portrayed in realistic terms the plight of the lower classes, using literature for political purposes. In an interview in 1958, Nazim Hikmet declared that 'a writer could not be politically neutral. It would be difficult to point even to a single great writer throughout history who remained perfectly neutral and passive about the problems of his time ... I believe that writers, communist writers in particular, must create a literature which will become one of the sources of knowledge of real life ... I would like to write poems, novels, plays which had this virtue for my people and for other peoples'.[6]

Orhan Kemal, one of the best contemporary Turkish novelists, tells how he was converted to such views by association with Nazim Hikmet in jail.[7] His writings also make it clear that personal friendships and family attachments often determined a writer's political and ideological orientation, and incidentally provide interesting information about the lower strata of Turkish society. Nazim Hikmet's celebrated poems *Memleketimden Insan Manzaralari* (Human views of my country), a description of various social types, are based on observation and interviews with men he met in jail. Kemal Tahir, another well-known living novelist befriended by Nazim Hikmet, told this writer in 1962 that most of his heroes were men he met in jail, while serving a sentence for his association with Hikmet. Similarly Sevket Sureyya, the leader of the *Kadro*, was awakened to the realities of Turkish life, according to his memoirs, by men he met in jail. All this suggests that the early socialist writers had only a limited knowledge of life in Anatolia, and may legitimately provoke the question whether men condemned for ordinary crimes accurately reflect Turkey's social problems.

During the war years 1939–45 conditions favoured the development of left currents; the rise of wealthy groups living in luxury gave a sharper outline to social injustice and illiteracy. At Ankara

6 Nazim Hikmet, *Anthologie Poétique* (Paris, 1964), pp. 357–8.
7 Orhan Kemal, *Nazim Hikmet'le Uc Bucuk Yil* (Istanbul, 1965).

University a team of sociologists began to study social change in Turkey in a systematic, scientific manner, publishing their results in the reviews *Yurt ve Dunya* and *Adimlar*, and took an active part in the development of village institutes, the educational institutions set up in the countryside.

The fruit of these preparations was evident in the outburst of left-wing activities following the political liberalization of 1945–6.[8] Several newspapers and reviews gave space to socialist ideas of various kinds, while the amendment of the Law on Associations in 1946, enabled left groups to organize themselves. Of about six self-styled socialist parties established at that time, only two were of any political consequence: the Socialist Party of Esat Adil Mustecapli-oglu, with a broad leftist orientation, and the marxist Workers and Peasants Socialist Party of Sefik Husnu Degmer. Of about one hundred trade unions established in 1946, at least a dozen were dominated by the left. Eventually the two parties, most of the publications, and the unions were closed in December 1946, and their leaders charged with subversive activities.

The left was once more declared illegal and identified with extremism, although a large number of so-called leftists were doing no more than seeking development and progress through ideas other than the official platitudes. This indiscriminate condemnation made it impossible to separate communists from socialists, and in fact secured for the former a dominating position. It remains true, however, that the leftists in 1946 may in a way be said to have doomed themselves from the outset by giving priority to foreign policy. They aroused hostility by their pro-Soviet attitude at a time when Stalin was exerting pressure on Turkey to obtain territory in the North and military bases on the Straits.

After 1946 left-wing activities were carried on by members of Degmer's party who escaped arrest in 1946. The underground organization under Zeki Bastimar was uncovered and its members arrested in 1952, and sentenced to various terms in jail. Their activities at home and abroad, their tactics, and especially the use they made of 'fronts' and of sympathizers (often without their knowledge), have been described by former members.[9] Open

8 The Democratic Party, established in January 1946, was supported by many socially-minded and leftist intellectuals desiring social progress. Some of them became fully identified with this party and put to good use the propaganda and organizational skills developed during their marriage with leftism.

9 Sayilgan, *op. cit.*, p. 128 ff.

activities, such as opposition to the Korean War, sporadic publications, and the *Vatan Partisi* established by Hikmet Kivilcimli in 1957, were quickly liquidated by the Menderes government.[10] Left-wing activities after the second world war were initiated by urban intellectuals, many of them from the upper classes. They attracted a number of university students (the universities remained the main centres of leftism) but were unsuccessful in gaining the support of the working class. Although using marxist slogans, they seemed to criticize chiefly conservatism and traditionalism rather than any specific social class. In fact the 'bourgeoisie' seemed to be the conservative religious small shopkeeper and the self-employed businessman relying on his own efforts for a living, rather than the banker or capitalist.

The number of convinced leftists in Turkey in the nineteen-forties probably never exceeded a thousand. Isolated from society, they appeared unable to affect the course of events. But a new generation of intellectuals was being educated in the West. Some of them, already committed to socialism or communism, assembled in Paris and organized the Progressive Young Turks, which served as a communication centre with marxist groups in Turkey; but the majority of socially-minded students in the West preferred not to compromise themselves by overt adherence to a leftist ideology and awaited a suitable chance upon their return home.

The chance came as the liberal economic policy of the Democratic Party promoted the development of entrepreneurial activities of all kinds.[11] In 1950 the industrial middle class (including their families), probably accounted for about five per cent of the total population. By 1965 the figure had risen to over twenty per cent, and exerted a powerful influence on the government. The number of wage earners meanwhile rose from fewer than 400,000 in 1950 to close on two millions in 1965. At the same time improvements in agricultural methods and an extended road programme increased

10 One of the first acts of Menderes was to stiffen the legal provisions outlawing communist activities. For legal aspects of leftist trials see Remzi Balkanli, *Mukayeseli Basin ve Propaganda* (Ankara, 1961), p. 445 ff.

11 Alec P. Alexander, 'Industrial Entrepreneurship in Turkey', *Economic Development and Cultural Change*, July 1960; Arif Payaslioglu, *Turkiye'de Ozel Sanayi Alanindaki Mutesebbisler ve Tese busler* (Ankara, 1961). There is a comprehensive symposium in *Social Aspects of Economic Development* (Istanbul, 1963).

social mobility and helped to spread social awareness. The political consciousness of the masses developed steadily as they found their place in the various occupations. The dominant motive in all these activities was economic; among the working classes it naturally expressed itself in a desire for material advancement and welfare.

This process of growth from below, initiated by the government with immediate practical motives of its own, fundamentally changed the country's social organization and the power relations within it. The bureaucracy, already affected by inflation, surrendered its political and social power to a new economic elite drawn from landed and business groups and their associates. Moreover, the intelligentsia, in the past strongly represented in the bureaucracy, saw the rise from its own ranks of professional groups either associated with the entrepreneurs as engineers and technicians, or finding lucrative employment in the service of private commercial and business enterprises. Earlier social values, based on education and dedication to state ideals, were undermined by an order based essentially on economic power. Socially and psychologically this was a far-reaching revolution. Materially and morally, it affected every section of the traditional ruling groups; the civil bureaucracy, the military, and all their affiliates. This social change occurred without benefit of intellectual justification or systematization. The automatic condemnation of all critical social ideas in the past as being conducive to socialism and communism greatly hindered the development of an adequate school of social thinking.

The intellectuals' reaction to these changes once more manifested itself in literature. The vast output of stories and novels with 'social content' after 1950, best reflects the trends of thought which eventually became the foundation of a new leftism. Writers such as Mahmut Makal, Yasar Kemal, Orhan Kemal, Aziz Nesin, Kemal Tahir, Fakir Baykurt, Kemal Bilbasar, Atilla Ilhan, Necati Cumali, to mention only a few, came mainly from the villages and the lower ranks of the urban intelligentsia.[12] They brought to public attention the unknown dimensions of Turkey's acute social problems, the widespread poverty, distress, and injustice. Gradually this type of writing found its way into the daily press. Correspondents roamed the far reaches of Anatolia and corroborated the writers

---

[12] Cf. Kemal H. Karpat, 'Social Themes in Contemporary Turkish Literature', *Middle East Journal*, Winter-Spring 1960.

with their well-documented findings. The increase in the daily circulation of newspapers (many published social novels in serial instalments) from about half a million in 1950 to a million in 1956, a million and a half in 1960, and finally to over two millions in 1965, attests to the importance acquired by the written word. Gradually the press attracted some of the left-wing litterateurs and became one of the strongholds of socialism after the revolution of 1960.

There were also a number of periodicals devoted largely to the discussion of social ideas, several of them published by village institute graduates. The review *Forum*, appearing bi-monthly in Ankara after 1954, provided probably the best systematic analysis of Turkey's problems. It often published articles by leftists but generally occupied a moderate middle-of-the-road position. This was a sensible thing to do, since it permitted the discussion of social problems without incurring the danger of being indicted for leftist propaganda.

Support and approval came from those in the bureaucracy and the intelligentsia who did not benefit directly from the Democrats' economic policy. The idea that social justice was lacking in Turkey appealed to them and they sought allies among other social groups. They hoped to win over the impoverished peasants and workers and together with them establish a new, just, and prosperous regime; but they found little response in those quarters.

The large-scale conversion of the bureaucracy and the intelligentsia to the left occurred gradually after 1954. In that year the Democrats won a great victory at the elections, and decided to speed up their development drive, based chiefly on an inflationary unplanned economic policy. Capital accumulation in private hands increased and inflation mounted, while salaries remained relatively stagnant. The dissatisfaction aroused provided the foundations of a new leftist movement not associated directly with marxism, as was the case for most earlier leftist endeavours. Furthermore, the new leftism was a response to domestic conditions, not a replica of a foreign ideology. As such it held the promise of taking shape in economic and social policies designed to broaden and modernize the Republic from within. Kemalism had built the political framework of modernism but neglected its social and economic content. The rising social currents eventually sought legitimation in the unfulfilled social promises of Kemalism, through an expanded interpretation of its populist, statist, and reformist principles.

The organized propagation of social ideas began timidly first in the Devrim Ocaklari (Reform Hearths) established early in the 1950s to defend the secular reforms against religious reaction.[13] The Ocaks attracted mostly the university students, and were in sympathy with the Republican Party. Discussions usually began with a defence of Kemalism, and after 1954 moved on to debate contemporary social and economic problems. For the most part, however, the young generation of intellectuals got their training in the youth branches of the Republican Party which, at its eleventh convention in 1954, adopted a programme which seemed to answer the intelligentsia's social yearnings. Article 36 of the programme reads:

The main source of value which must be protected and made the foundation of national existence is the citizens' effort (work). It is the duty of the state to take the necessary measures to provide employment opportunity for the citizen according to his intellectual and civil capacities, to provide jobs for the unemployed and protect labour from exploitation with due regard for the employers' rights. Our party considers the job security of every citizen an inviolable right . . .[14]

At its fourteenth convention in 1957 the Republican Party decided to expand the activities of its youth branches, since these seemed to respond best to new social ideas. They were involved in the students' demonstrations before the revolution of 1960, and played a leading part in organizing resistance to the Democrats' drive to silence the opposition. Their underground activities in April–May 1960 were inspired by a revolutionary elan which has been maintained to the present day. Until the revolution of 1960, there were about 295 Republican youth branches in the country; the number went up to about 530 in 1961, comprising roughly 25,000 energetic young members. With Inonu's support, the Republican Party committed itself to the solution of social and economic problems and especially to social justice. Unplanned economic development, it was argued, had lowered the living standards of the salaried groups, large sections of the urban population were destitute, while small groups became rich. In the elections of 1957 the Republicans increased their vote by 15 per cent, gaining 178 seats as against 31

[13] In 1963 the Ocaks had fourteen branches in ten cities with a total membership of 2,000. *Cumhuriyet*, 12 April 1963.
[14] CHP Programi (Ankara, 1954). For comparative table, see Kemal H. Karpat, 'Turkish Elections of 1957', *Western Political Quarterly*, June 1961.

in 1954. These results encouraged them to enlarge their social programme and bring to the fore the leftist members. The party's Research Bureau began to issue studies on a variety of social problems.[15] Finally, beginning in 1958–9, some party leaders openly defended socialism as the short road to development and welfare. The psychological and organizational ground for a new leftism was thus prepared. It needed only the opportunity to emerge, and this was supplied by the military revolt of 1960.

The social motivations of the military revolution were evident in its organizational structure, its policies, and especially in its attitude to social questions. The revolution was carried out by officers, mostly men in their thirties, raised in the same atmosphere and with the same aspirations as the new intelligentsia supporting them. The military government showed little favour to the groups which had grown rich under the Democrats; it stressed the importance of economic development and social justice, and its leading members, including President Cemal Gursel, openly declared that socialism might be beneficial to Turkey. Police controls over labour were lifted, and some cases of communist propaganda pending in the courts were brought quickly to an end.[16]

The period from 27 May 1960 to the elections of 15 October 1961, can be described as an intensive search for a social and economic policy capable of bringing Turkey fully into the modern age. Social evils were brought into the open and dramatized as proof of Turkey's backwardness. Newspaper reporters searched the countryside to discover villages owned by *agas* (landowners, tribal chiefs) who were described as plotting with religious leaders to keep the peasants in ignorance and to exploit them. The heartless capitalists were accused of depriving the workers of their due wages, and endless testimony was offered to show the unjust accumulation of wealth under the Democrats.

What was required to remedy these ills, it was said, was a strong regime led by a socially-minded elite. A professor summed up the situation. 'We have,' he declared, 'a unique chance in the fact that

15 By 1961 the Research Bureau had published 24 studies covering major social issues, and reproducing speeches by its members on urgent social problems.

16 See e.g. *Aksam*, 10 August 1960, *Cumhuriyet*, 5 July 1960. The case against 13 people arrested in 1958 for exploding bombs near the American Embassy while Dulles was in Ankara, was dismissed.

those (military) holding the destiny of the State in their hands . . . are an impartial body concerned only with the country's welfare. Should we miss this opportunity ?'[17] The essay competition opened by the newspaper *Cumhuriyet* about expectations from the revolution showed that the intelligentsia demanded land reform, eradication of illiteracy, better pay for all workers, an end to exploitation, economic development, etc., all to be achieved overnight.[18] However, the attempts by a few officers in the junta to capitalize on these demands and establish a strong rule was opposed by the Republican Party and the leftists at large. Both groups hoped to achieve power and use the social discontent for their own benefit.

Meanwhile several organizations known to have opposed the Democrats in the past opened their membership to socialists. The Ankara Devrim Ocagi gained several members who represented the socialist wing among teachers, journalists, and academics. A spokesman for the Ocak, accused of collaborating with leftists, answered his nationalist opponents: 'Yes, I no longer work alone in the Ankara Devrim Ocagi. A group of thirty people who have social training and know how to work as a team are steadily at work.'[19] A similar socialist orientation was evident in the powerful National Federation of Turkish Teachers Associations, as shown by its later activities and its support of left-wing parties.[20]

The establishment of a State Planning Organization in 1960 added a new dimension and a scientific justification for this new leftism or socialism, as it was now openly called. The rational use of national resources to promote rapid development, social justice, literacy, etc., could, it was said, be achieved through overall planning by the state. The idea of state planning injected a potent political ingredient into social thinking which was bound to affect the course of events.

[17] *Cumhuriyet*, 8 July 1960.

[18] Ibid., 7 August 1960. (The essays were published intermittently for about three months.) It was also reliably reported that the leftists began to publish after the revolution a review which was never distributed. It contained articles on Marxism, Leninism, and Stalinism. The review was suppressed by the police and its publishers brought into court.

[19] Letter in *Yeni Istanbul*, 3 February 1963. This organization also fought to eliminate the legal provisions outlawing communism. The Chairman, Tarik Z. Tunaya, was probably referring to this leftist infiltration when he declared: 'we are decided to fight to the end those circles who use Kemalism as a cover without being Kemalists, and who conceal their secret intentions'. *Cumhuriyet*, 12 April 1963.

[20] See letter addressed to Inonu, *Yon*, 25 July 1962.

The social ideas developed in 1954–60 and during the revolution were eventually incorporated in the Constitution of 1961. Defining Turkey as a national, secular, and social state, it recognized extensive individual rights and freedoms, and spelled out a broad social programme to be carried out by the state.[21] Thus, while providing a legal basis for social reforms, it also ensured safety for individuals to engage in political activity in order to achieve these goals. The Republican Party and some socialists dominated the Constitutent Assembly which drafted the Constitution. It was assumed that this party would come to power in the forthcoming elections and carry out a social programme through state planning, but there was among the population at large a deep aversion to any scheme likely to restore the power of the intelligentsia and bureaucracy. Entrepreneurs, businessmen, and landlords, aware that the proposed planning was aimed chiefly at their economic power, used their professional organizations and publications to fight the swing to the left. When the ban on political activities was lifted, the Justice and New Turkey parties established in 1961 came to represent their interests.

The elections of 15 October 1961 gave the Republicans the largest number of seats in the National Assembly, but not an absolute majority,[22] while the Senate was under the control of the Justice Party. With the military's support, the Republicans nevertheless formed a Cabinet under Ismet Inonu's Premiership in coalition with their chief opponent, the Justice Party. The coalition lasted about six months, breaking up chiefly because of sharp conflict over economic policy (state versus free enterprise), although outwardly it appeared as disagreement on the amnesty of jailed Democrats.[23] The subsequent government, formed in coalition with the minor parties in June 1962, again under Inonu's Premiership, was formed only after the Republicans reluctantly agreed to compromise on their social programme and to accept private enterprise as an equal. The chairman of the New Turkey Party, an ardent defender of private enterprise, was made Deputy Premier in charge of economic affairs, including the State Planning Organization. These developments opened a new and important phase in the

[21] *Constitution of the Turkish Republic*, Ankara 1961, also *Middle East Journal*, Winter 1962.

[22] The percentage of seats was as follows: PRP, 36.7; Justice, 34·8; New Turkey, 13·7; and National, 14 per cent.

[23] See Inonu's letter of resignation, *Yeni Sabah*, 1 June 1962.

history of the Turkish left. The hopes of the socialists were dashed, while the middle-class groups consolidated their power, especially after the military appeared reconciled to supporting a civilian regime.

The re-establishment of a civilian parliamentary regime appeared to have doomed the intellectuals' hopes for radical reform; among them many who had supported the Republican Party decided to initiate an independent line of action. The first result was the publication of a declaration signed by over five hundred intellectuals.[24] The signatories came predominantly from three fields: the universities (usually the lower ranks), the press, and the bureaucracy.

The declaration, which won socialist support, asserted that a rapid increase in production was the chief condition for achieving the goals proclaimed by Ataturk. Democracy could not be established so long as men were subject to hunger and unemployment. Hence, 'teachers, writers, politicians, trade unionists, entrepreneurs, and administrators, who are in a position to give a direction to Turkish society, must unite around a distinct philosophy of development ... the circles capable of determining the fate of Turkey did not possess ... a development philosophy'. The proposed development philosophy aimed at reaching its social goals through a mixed economy but relying chiefly on state enterprise. Private enterprise, besides being slow in achieving development, was wasteful, caused suffering, and in underdeveloped nations appeared incompatible with social justice. The new statism was to increase investment through forced savings (taxation) and comprehensive economic planning. Since larger economic units were essential in planning, agricultural and industrial cooperatives were to be expanded and the middleman restricted. Statism was to give high social standing to labour, eliminate exploitation, enforce land reform, and eradicate illiteracy.

Soon after the publication of this declaration several newspapers became openly (*Vatan*) or implicitly (*Cumhuriyet, Milliyet, Aksam*) the spokesmen for this new brand of socialism, and scores of books were published on the subject.[25] Ataturk was described as being a

[24] *Yon*, 20 December 1961. The French text is in *Orient* (21), 1962, pp. 135–42, the English in *Middle Eastern Affairs*, March 1963.

[25] *Cumhuriyet* chose as the subject of its annual essay competition (1963) the necessity of socialism. See also Hilmi Ozgen, *Turk Sosyalizmi Uzerinde Denemeler* (Ankara, 1963), Ali Faik Cihan, *Sosyalist Turkiye* (Istanbul, 1964). *Yon* published Nazim Hikmet's poems along with translations of marxist writings.

socialist at heart, and the entire history of the Republic was evaluated from a socialist viewpoint. The review *Yon*, heartened by its initial success (circulation went to 30,000 but then dropped considerably), intensified its attacks on Parliament, the landlords, and the rich, as well as private enterprise of any kind. The opposition to *Yon* came chiefly from conservative nationalists who appealed to traditional symbols and loyalties and condemned all socialists as communists.[26]

The socialism proposed by *Yon* as a method of action was defended on philosophical grounds by the *Sosyalist Kultur Dernegi* (Socialist Cultural Society). It was established in February 1963 by a group of intellectuals who had resigned from the State Planning Organization after Parliament had curtailed its radical authoritarian development schemes. The Society included a sizable segment of the writers for *Yon*, some independent intellectuals, and also some extreme leftists. Its aim, according to its statutes, was the scientific study of socialist ideas and their propagation. More specifically, the Society wanted to 'study in the light of science the conditions necessary for the establishment of a true democratic order'.[27] The centre of this socialist movement was in Ankara (and not Istanbul as in the past), and notably in the School of Political Science. Under its old name *Mulkiye* (est. 1859) this School had trained the elite which ruled Turkey well into the Republic. Activists in the socialist movement also included several Republican Party deputies, some former officers, and a sizable number of government officials.[28] Some of the intellectuals in *Yon* were of peasant origin (teachers educated in village institutes), but most from families of lower-ranking bureaucrats. They belonged predominantly to the generation raised in the war years. Their vehement animosity towards the rich revealed the accumulated hatred of a social order which had forced them to spend their childhood and adolescence in drab and wretched surroundings. The socialist

[26] See the publications of Komunizmle Mucadele Dernegi (Society for Struggle against Communism), and the dailies *Yeni Istanbul*, *Son Havadis*, the reviews *Dusunen Adam*, *Toprak*, etc. There were also clashes between left and right wing student groups.

[27] For two different views on this society see Namik Zeki Aral, 'Memlekette Sosyalist Cereyan', *Yeni Istanbul*, 7 February 1963; Cahit Tanyol, 'Bir Bildiri', *Cumhuriyet*, 8 February 1963.

[28] The Turkish socialists established relations with Western socialists, hoping to win their support. See *Socialist International Information*, vol. xiii, 1 June 1963.

intelligentsia, using the Kemalist idea of a classless society (he meant a society without class conflicts) interpreted it literally. The rich were condemned as the cause of social conflict and as enemies of progress.

Turkish socialism, as it developed after the revolution of 1960, seems to have been at first an effort to harmonize the relations between individual and society in a new social order, and to generate a sense of social responsibility. Its ideological sources can be traced to the Fabian school, classical Western socialism, and also to Marxist ideas revised in the light of new theories of economic development and planning as formulated in Western Europe after the war, including the views of the Dutch economist Jan Tinbergen who was adviser to the State Planning Organization. The response of rank-and-file intellectuals was generally favourable. State planning was advanced as the primary condition for achieving economic development and social welfare, and it was largely on this question that the division between socialists and their opponents turned. Consequently the need to define the nature and function of the state in socialism became imperative. Most socialists argued that the state had the prime function of establishing social justice. Subsequently, despite various traditional forces affecting its philosophy, the state would be transformed into an agency of modernization under the influence of the new intellectual elite in power. The idea of workers and peasants taking an active part in this socialist state was dealt with only later, after the need for popular support became evident. Thus the ideas of *Yon* and the Socialist Society took shape as a new elitist doctrine of power justified in terms of economic development.

Mussolini as Revolutionary

S. J. Woolf

The biographical tradition, which occupies so respected a place in English historiography, has failed to take deep root in Italy, as Delio Cantimori rightly observes in his preface to the latest, large-scale, ambitious biography of Mussolini.[1] The classic problem facing all biographers – how to narrate the life or career of the 'hero' not *in vacuo*, but in the context of the period, without submerging his individuality in too general a picture of the times – presents itself with particular force to the biographer of Mussolini. For Mussolini and Italian fascism are so inextricably interlinked that the one cannot be satisfactorily discussed without the other. Indeed, in the early years of fascism (preceding and immediately after the March on Rome), a common theme was the identification of fascism and 'mussolinism', which was developed – among those who continued to hold illusions about the legalistic and constitutional nature of fascism – into an ingenuous (or sophistic) distinction between 'good' and 'bad' fascism, the former represented by Mussolini, the latter by the provincial squadrists whom Mussolini was temporarily unable to bring to heel.[2] In later years, in the years of 'il Duce del fascismo', the eulogistic biographies of Mussolini – which attempted to legitimize by marriage the concubinage of his earlier socialism with his fascist career – in part reflected, in part entered into the general propagandist attempt by the regime to graft itself on to the historical evolution of Italy and present itself as the natural, almost inevitable heir, the virtual culmination of the forces which had led to the Risorgimento and the unitary state: in the work and thought of Mussolini, for example, according to one such propagandist, Mario Missiroli, fascism emerged logically from socialism, as the solution to the historical problems

[1] R. De Felice, *Mussolini il rivoluzionario 1883–1920* (Turin, 1965).
[2] E.g., *inter alia*, E. Ciccotti, *Il Fascismo e le sue fasi* (Milan, 1925).

187

created by the Risorgimento.[3] In general terms, fascist biographers have tended to subordinate fascism to Mussolini, and so create the image of an Emersonian – or even Carlylean – hero, moving in isolation, in the rarefied atmosphere of such heroes, towards his destiny.[4] Anti-fascist biographers, on the other hand, have concentrated on 'explaining' – and so denigrating – Mussolini in psychological terms, either on the individual level, or as a reflection of the collective moral and psychological weaknesses of the Italian people; or, otherwise, have tended to submerge his personal career in an examination of the historical phenomenon of the origins of fascism.[5]

Renzo De Felice, in his introduction to the first volume of his projected four-volume biography of Mussolini, shows himself fully aware of the difficulty of achieving a satisfactory balance, and states clearly the premises of his own solution to these problems. Moreover, the vast new documentation he has been able to consult, thanks to the liberality and intelligence of Italian archive regulations and the generosity of private individuals, as well as the plethora of material which has appeared since the war, has suggested to him the possibility of a new interpretation of the life of Mussolini. In effect, this biography, while not definitive (an impossibility, given the present state of research), will clearly remain of fundamental importance for many years to come. It is on both these counts – the claim to present a new technique in the tradition of Italian biographical historiography, and a new and more balanced interpretation of Mussolini's life in the early crucial years (this first volume reaches the end of 1920, a date deliberately chosen by De Felice as marking a break with what he regards as the 'traditional' periodization of Mussolini biographies), that this weighty contribution to Italian contemporary history deserves to be considered.

De Felice's aim is to write a biography which, while preserving the individual characteristics of its subject, should also provide an insight into the significance of early fascism. He is concerned, that

[3] M. Missiroli, *Italia d'oggi* (Bologna, 1932); idem., *Studi sul fascismo* (Bologna, 1934).

[4] E.g., A. Beltramelli, *L'uomo nuovo (Benito Mussolini)* (Milan, 1923); M. G. Sarfatti, *Dux* (Milan, 1926); Y. De Begnac, *Vita di Mussolini* (Milan, 1936).

[5] P. Monelli, *Mussolini piccolo borghese* (Milan, 1950); G. A. Borgese, *Goliath. The march of fascism* (New York, 1937); G. Dorso, *Mussolini alla conquista del potere* (Turin, 1949).

is, like all good biographers (and Croceans), that the particular illuminate the general. In fact, he says, this biography may be considered as representing 'a sort of first reflection of the way and the measure in which Mussolini's socialism and then his fascism were seen and evaluated by his contemporaries' (p. xxv). The method to achieve this end is twofold: to narrate Mussolini's development as viewed, if not by Mussolini himself, at any rate by his contemporaries – avoiding, that is, as far as possible, the historical benefit of hindsight – so as not to predetermine the course of this development; and to insert Mussolini's life in a 'fan-like perspective, which opens up gradually as Mussolini's horizons broaden and his figure aquires a greater importance until it assumes a national and European role, which consequently is to be inserted in a context which is no longer local, of the party, or national, but international'.

The biography is thus based, on the one hand, on an attempt to outline the sources and development of Mussolini's thought, which, if somewhat schematic at first (e.g., the simple enumeration of writers to whom Mussolini was indebted in his formative years from 1902 to 1909, with little attempt to show the *ways* in which their writings affected his thought), grows increasingly fuller for the later years, and proves of great value in the discussion of Mussolini's *volte-face* in favour of intervention in October 1914 (pp. 221–87), of the sources and elaboration of his ideas of 'productivism' and 'national syndicalism' (pp. 402–18), and of the disparate sources (especially the syndicalist ideas of partial expropriation of De Ambris) of the first fascist programme of June 1919 (pp. 513–19). On the other hand, the narration of Mussolini's actions in their successive phases is preceded by increasingly detailed descriptions of the political scene in general, and in particular of the environment in which Mussolini acted, not to justify certain solutions as 'necessary', but to 'explain what were the alternatives and possibilities, the errors and solutions which a given situation presented' (p. xxiv).

To what extent does De Felice achieve his stated purpose? Mussolini's inner development, according to the author, cannot be explained in terms of any single theme or key, psychological or other (e.g., the hardships of his early life to account for his driving ambition; or his 'petty-bourgeois' nature). His character and actions often seem contradictory because he was driven not by one, but by a series of convictions, which he adopted with emotional intensity at successive moments; the lack of a single over-riding belief or ideology left him uncertain, more open to outside influences (all the more so, given his acute sensitivity to changes in the political climate): 'in all the crucial moments of his life he lacked the capacity to decide, to the extent that one can say that all his most important decisions were virtually imposed upon him by circumstances, or were taken tactically, by degrees, adapting them to the external reality, which is not very different. In many ways he was, in fact, to use one of his early pen-names, *l'homme qui cherche* and not *l'homme qui va*, who finds his path day by day, with no idea of where he will arrive, but "feeling" like a true politician what was his right direction' (p. xxiii).

It is this unstable quality, the sixth sense of a politician possessing – in the last analysis – no deep ties, which, according to De Felice, lends coherence to Mussolini's career. An extreme socialist revolutionary, more concerned with the long-term problems of the revolution, with arousing a sense of class consciousness, than with the immediate realities and possibilities of the day-to-day struggles of the proletariat, he displayed – as the reformist Claudio Treves noted accurately – 'the classic concept of revolutionary idealism, of absolute diffidence, and almost of explicit condemnation of the economic organization of the working-class movement' (p. 117). With an unsophisticated concept of marxism, strongly influenced by Sorel, Nietzsche, revolutionary syndicalist and anarchist thought, but also open to the heterogeneous cultural ideals propagated by the intellectuals writing for the periodicals *Leonardo* and *La Voce* and by the positivist rationalism of Salvemini's *L'Unità*, it is not so surprising that Mussolini should have lost his initial faith in the socialist internationalism of neutrality, when both these moderate democratic intellectuals and Corridoni's revolutionary syndicalists raised the cry for intervention against the central European imperialist powers, and when his own Socialist Party showed itself incapable of seizing the opportunity and formulating an imaginative policy.

It is in these terms that De Felice explains Mussolini's dramatic break with the Italian Socialist Party in October 1914. His later drift towards the right is explained in 'internal' terms by the transformation of Mussolini's original belief in a war for revolutionary ends to a dominating conviction (especially after Caporetto) that the war must be won at all costs, and in 'external' terms by the increasing inability of the democratic and revolutionary interventionists to avoid the taint of association with the reactionary nationalists. By the end of the war, Mussolini's socialism had been transformed into 'productivism' or 'national syndicalism', supported by the example of Jouhaux in the French CGT. To all effects he was no longer a socialist; the class struggle had been replaced by collaboration, with the syndicates to mark out the new path within the framework of the national unit. Although the fascio formed by Mussolini in March 1919 possessed a distinctly revolutionary programme, its founder's failure to create a left-wing interventionist bloc, and its collapse in the November 1919 elections, meant inevitably the completion of Mussolini's parabola (and that of the fascio movement) from left to right, from revolution to reaction.

De Felice's detailed reconstruction of Mussolini's evolution has the undoubted merit of offering a clear and logical – though by no means a very novel – pattern of development. But even from so bare an outline as has been sketched above it should be clear how dependent this reconstruction is, on the one hand, on De Felice's interpretation of Mussolini's ability as a politician to remain in control of changes in the political climate, and, on the other hand, on his explanation of how Mussolini's actions did not control, but were, in fact, determined by external events. There is, indeed, an implicit dichotomy, a contradiction, between these two criteria, which emerges clearly in the difference of approach between the earlier and later parts of this biography.

In the first part – that dealing with Mussolini's career as a revolutionary socialist and his position during the war – De Felice's total condemnation of the Socialist Party leaders and their policies, of the empty verbosity of the maximalists on the left of the party and the unimaginative, implicitly collaborationist attitude of the reformists on the right, of their negative mentality during the war, has the effect of exalting the figure and stature of Mussolini as the 'new man', the one person able to break with the past and lead the Socialist Party on to a new and more fortunate path. He emerges as a figure of national importance, capable of influencing critical situations, as, for instance, during the Reggio Emilia congress in 1912, or when he adopted the interventionist cause in 1914, or by his destruction of Bissolati and the democratic interventionist forces in 1919. He emerges, moreover, as a man of far greater insight than his socialist colleagues, maximalist or reformist, in his 'feel' for the attitudes and needs of the masses in the immediate prewar years, or in his realization of the necessity of Italian intervention in the war. Logically, the programme put forward by the socialist interventionist forces which Mussolini supported (the Unione Socialista Italiana) is judged by De Felice – in contrast to the ineptitude of the neutralist Socialist Party – as marking a progress in the development of Italian socialism, as a programme striking in its modernity and realism (p. 385).

But with the end of the war, the weakness of Mussolini's position and the mass support given to the official neutralist Socialist Party would seem to contradict this image. Mussolini's failure to create an ex-combatant force, his inability to achieve a left-wing interventionist bloc, the ignominious collapse of the fasci in the 1919 elections, all present a startling contrast to his earlier control, his earlier political ability. This contrast is explained by De Felice almost in terms of the *force majeure* of external events, which even Mussolini could not resist. Thus, De Felice paints a picture of the isolation and helplessness of the interventionist forces once the war had begun, through Salandra's refusal to utilize their support and through Bissolati's weakness in the Boselli government; of the revolutionary attitude of the masses after the war; of the collapse of all the democratic interventionist forces through Bissolati's tactical errors and the rising tide of nationalist feeling which swept away the middle-class basis of these democratic forces; of the inevitability of the reaction of the bourgeoisie against the maximalist threat. In this increasingly large-scale *mise-en-scène*, the figure of Mussolini tends to disappear, his actions become determined by these external events, which leave him isolated, with little or no space for manoeuvring, in a trap from which he managed to escape – as much through the refusal of the revolutionary groups (such as the Republican Party) to accept him, and through the independent action of the agrarian fasci, as through his own deliberate decision – only by turning decisively to the right in 1920.

There is an undoubted conflict between this earlier image of Mussolini's political acumen and his later, often curiously inept, conduct. To give the credit for the former to Mussolini, and explain the latter by events outside his control is inconsistent, and in consequence not convincing. It reflects an inadequately critical tendency, which makes of Mussolini a greater, a more important political figure than he was in these years. Nobody who has studied his career would deny his political ability, his aggressiveness, his determination to dominate and not be dominated. But clearly he was not always so able a leader. Convinced of his ability to 'feel' and to lead the masses, his conduct was, at least in part, based on his belief in his capacity to move with, if not slightly ahead of, changes in public opinion, to let himself be carried with, and to dominate, the tide. In 1914–15 he calculated wrongly: he did not carry the masses with him, and paid the price of his mistaken choice in the postwar years. In 1918 he mistook the ambitions of the bourgeois officer class for those of the whole combatant force – and once more erred: he found himself cut off from the masses, and because of his equivocal behaviour increasingly mistrusted by the interventionist revolutionary groups. His conduct was not coherent because he was too ready to change it for tactical reasons. It might almost be said that ultimately for Mussolini tactical ends had replaced strategy. It could be argued that his political career was finished by the end of 1919, and that he was merely fortunate to be carried to success in 1920.

Methodologically, as can be seen, this biography of the early, crucial phases of Mussolini's career does not live up to the ambitious premises stated by the author. Inevitably, these methodological difficulties reflect on the content of the volume. To what extent can it be said that the vast documentation he utilizes offers a 'new' interpretation of Mussolini's activities ? This is not the place for a detailed examination of the numerous episodes in Mussolini's early life, but it is worth noting how relatively few important 'new' facts emerge from this exhaustive research into the police archives. In fact, what is striking is how the contemporary suspicions and accusations against Mussolini, which circulated so widely – for instance, about the subsidies paid to the *Popolo d'Italia* from foreign sources and industrialists, or about the appropriation by Mussolini for his electoral campaign of part of the funds raised by the *Popolo d'Italia* for D'Annunzio at Fiume, or about his agreement with Giolitti in 1920 – find detailed confirmation. What merits discussion in this book, indeed, are not any 'new' revelations, but the author's analysis of the stages of, and reasons for, Mussolini's conversion, and his reconstruction of certain aspects and moments of the general political scene in Italy.

The 'inner' process of Mussolini's conversion is dealt with at length and efficiently by De Felice. Mussolini's uncertainties about the neutralist cause almost immediately after the outbreak of the war, and his readiness to absorb outside suggestions (in particular from the revolutionary syndicalist groups), his search for a new path for the Socialist Party, and his final decision to back the interventionist cause, are well described. The subsequent difficulties of Mussolini's position are analysed with skill: on the one hand, the problem faced by the revolutionary and democratic interventionists of maintaining themselves distinct from the nationalist interventionists; on the other, the enormous psychological and practical impact of Caporetto, hardening nationalist feeling, even among the democrats and revolutionaries, and leading to the creation of committees of internal defence against the neutralist 'saboteurs', which were formed in common by all the interventionist forces of 1914–15, but which were dominated by the right-wing nationalists. After so shameful a defeat, Italy *had* to win her own war. Mussolini himself expressed this attitude strikingly in a letter to Soffici immediately after the defeat: 'God . . .; on the Isonzo I was satisfied with Istria, Fiume, and Zara; now that we are on the Piave, I want all Dalmatia!' (p. 380).

By early 1918 Mussolini had already moved far from the socialist cause, and was replacing the class struggle with his theory of 'productivism'. His path from then until his famous speech of 3 January 1925, in which he acknowledged his responsibilities, followed, according to De Felice, a fairly steady trajectory, uncertain in the following two years, but from 1920 gaining force from its own momentum. Until the 1919 elections, he was still trying to create a new force on the left, and it is in these attempts that De Felice finds the reason for Mussolini's detachment from the original fasci movement, his readiness to discuss and accept decisions, the relative subordination of his contribution compared to that of the futurists and of De Ambris (cf. De Felice's interesting discussion of the sources and formulation of the 1919 fasci programme, pp. 506–19). With the crisis of the fasci movement caused by electoral failure, the stalemate of D'Annunzio's occupation of Fiume, and Mussolini's concern lest he find himself isolated by the formation of a Giolitti-Catholic-reformist socialist government, the transformation of Mussolini from the early revolutionary into the supporter of the forces of order was complete.

This, in brief outline, is De Felice's analysis of the stages of Mussolini's conversion. It is without doubt a far more convincing interpretation of Mussolini's progress than that offered by any previous biographer, including Megaro. It cannot, however, be considered in isolation, but only as an integrative part, the focal point, of the author's reconstruction of the general political scene.

De Felice's investigation and description of certain political circles, hitherto obscured rather than illuminated by the repeated generalizations of historians – such as of Corridoni's revolutionary syndicate (UIL), or of the reformist interventionist socialist groups in the war – merit praise. But, inevitably, it is his discussion of the origins of fascism that attracts the major attention. He bases his account of the conditions and factors which gave rise to fascism on the conclusions of the most recent historiography, and consequently offers no radically new interpretation, but tends to confirm generally accepted conclusions and integrate them in his biography. He lays great emphasis on precision in dating, which enables him to correct implicitly Salvatorelli's definition of fascism as a petty-bourgeois movement by accentuating the undoubted left-wing, revolutionary character of the original fascist movement, which, according to De Felice, underwent its real metamorphosis at the second congress of the fasci at Milan in May 1920 (pp. 593–8). This, however, is as well known as the dating of the revival of the movement to 1920. No new elements are offered to explain this revival: its underlying causes remain, for De Felice, the support and connivance of government and official circles (his long exculpation of the liberal ruling class on the grounds that it was based on an erroneous judgment of fascism rather than on any positive philo-fascist feeling seems irrelevant in this context), the crisis of the revolutionary maximalist psychosis, and the reaction which followed this crisis. In fact, fascism succeeded, ultimately, not because it was by nature reactionary, but because its very lack of an ideology, its practical relativism, made it peculiarly malleable to the imprint of the prevailing conditions in the country. Ottavio Dinale, a revolutionary syndicalist close to Mussolini in the early years, described this process in December 1920 with accuracy: 'Despite the bombastic words of the programmes approved by their congresses, in which all the ingredients of the new or old revolutionary medicines were immersed, because the fasci lack a real and true political content and a doctrinal basis, they are obliged to accept the caprice of circumstances passively, and their vaunted *praxism*, which should have been the generating fluid of elasticity, becomes a solid cement which binds them together and fixes them in the iron framework of the facts of every day, until it transforms them, at first a little at a time and almost unknowingly, then suddenly and consciously, into a real and true counter-revolutionary organism, the white guard counterplaced against the red guard' (p. 660).

In this general picture of the origins and early stages of fascism, of the increasing convergence between this politically neutral, relativistic movement and the rising reaction of the agrarians, Mussolini's own progress assumes a somewhat secondary importance. For, as De Felice points out, the agrarian fascist movement developed virtually autonomously, independent of Mussolini and the central committee of the fasci at Milan, while in the central committee itself Mussolini's followers, such as Michele Bianchi and Cesare Rossi, assumed increasingly independent attitudes. But the nature and impulse of this new fascist movement – or rather movements – are not explained by De Felice. He does not differentiate the history of these local fasci, in Emilia, Romagna, the Marches, Tuscany, according to their regional or local origins and patterns or conditions of development. Yet only such a differentiated study could ultimately explain the weak position of Mussolini and the success of the revived fascist movement. The choice of 1920 to end this first volume may be appropriate to mark a stage in Mussolini's 'private' evolution (though the war, Caporetto, or 1925, in De Felice's own words, mark more decisive stages), but it is not so satisfactory in integrating Mussolini's evolution in that of fascism. We must await the next volume of this biography for a full discussion of these problems.

harper ⚜ torchbooks

HUMANITIES AND SOCIAL SCIENCES

American Studies: General

CARL N. DEGLER, Ed.: Pivotal Interpretations of American History   TB/1240, TB/1241
A. S. EISENSTADT, Ed.: The Craft of American History: Recent Essays in American Historical Writing
Vol. I TB/1255; Vol. II TB/1256
CHARLOTTE P. GILMAN: Women and Economics. ‡ Ed. with an Introduction by Carl N. Degler   TB/3073
MARCUS LEE HANSEN: The Atlantic Migration: 1607-1860. Edited by Arthur M. Schlesinger   TB/1052
MARCUS LEE HANSEN: The Immigrant in American History   TB/1120
JOHN HIGHAM, Ed.: The Reconstruction of American History △   TB/1068
ROBERT H. JACKSON: The Supreme Court in the American System of Government   TB/1106
JOHN F. KENNEDY: A Nation of Immigrants. △ Illus.
TB/1118
LEONARD W. LEVY, Ed.: American Constitutional Law: Historical Essays   TB/1285
RALPH BARTON PERRY: Puritanism and Democracy
TB/1138
ARNOLD ROSE: The Negro in America   TB/3048

American Studies: Colonial

BERNARD BAILYN, Ed.: The Apologia of Robert Keayne: Self-Portrait of a Puritan Merchant   TB/1201
BERNARD BAILYN: The New England Merchants in the Seventeenth Century   TB/1149
JOSEPH CHARLES: The Origins of the American Party System   TB/1049
LAWRENCE HENRY GIPSON: The Coming of the Revolution: 1763-1775. † Illus.   TB/3007
PERRY MILLER: Errand Into the Wilderness   TB/1139
PERRY MILLER & T. H. JOHNSON, Eds.: The Puritans: A Sourcebook   Vol. I TB/1093; Vol. II TB/1094
EDMUND S. MORGAN, Ed.: The Diary of Michael Wigglesworth, 1653-1657: The Conscience of a Puritan
TB/1228
EDMUND S. MORGAN: The Puritan Family   TB/1227
RICHARD B. MORRIS: Government and Labor in Early America   TB/1244
KENNETH B. MURDOCK: Literature and Theology in Colonial New England   TB/99
WALLACE NOTESTEIN: The English People on the Eve of Colonization: 1603-1630. † Illus.   TB/3006
LOUIS B. WRIGHT: The Cultural Life of the American Colonies: 1607-1763. † Illus.   TB/3005

American Studies: From the Revolution to 1860

JOHN R. ALDEN: The American Revolution: 1775-1783. † Illus.   TB/3011

MAX BELOFF, Ed.: The Debate on the American Revolution, 1761-1783: A Sourcebook △   TB/1225
RAY A. BILLINGTON: The Far Western Frontier: 1830-1860. † Illus.   TB/3012
W. R. BROCK: An American Crisis: Congress and Reconstruction, 1865-67 ○ △   TB/1283
EDMUND BURKE: On the American Revolution. ‡ Edited by Elliott Robert Barkan   TB/3068
WHITNEY R. CROSS: The Burned-Over District: The Social and Intellectual History of Enthusiastic Religion in Western New York, 1800-1850   TB/1242
GEORGE DANGERFIELD: The Awakening of American Nationalism: 1815-1828. † Illus.   TB/3061
CLEMENT EATON: The Growth of Southern Civilization: 1790-1860. † Illus.   TB/3040
LOUIS FILLER: The Crusade Against Slavery: 1830-1860. † Illus.   TB/3029
FELIX GILBERT: The Beginnings of American Foreign Policy: To the Farewell Address   TB/1200
FRANCIS GRIERSON: The Valley of Shadows: The Coming of the Civil War in Lincoln's Midwest: A Contemporary Account   TB/1246
JAMES MADISON: The Forging of American Federalism. Edited by Saul K. Padover   TB/1226
BERNARD MAYO: Myths and Men: Patrick Henry, George Washington, Thomas Jefferson   TB/1108
JOHN C. MILLER: Alexander Hamilton and the Growth of the New Nation   TB/3057
RICHARD B. MORRIS, Ed.: The Era of the American Revolution   TB/1180
R. B. NYE: The Cultural Life of the New Nation: 1776-1801. † Illus.   TB/3026
FRANCIS S. PHILBRICK: The Rise of the West, 1754-1830. † Illus.   TB/3067
TIMOTHY L. SMITH: Revivalism and Social Reform: American Protestantism on the Eve of the Civil War
ALBION W. TOURGÉE: A Fool's Errand. ‡ Ed. by George Fredrickson   TB/3074
A. F. TYLER: Freedom's Ferment   TB/1074
GLYNDON G. VAN DEUSEN: The Jacksonian Era: 1828-1848. † Illus.   TB/3028
LOUIS B. WRIGHT: Culture on the Moving Frontier
TB/1053

American Studies: The Civil War to 1900

THOMAS C. COCHRAN & WILLIAM MILLER: The Age of Enterprise: A Social History of Industrial America TB/1054
W. A. DUNNING: Reconstruction, Political and Economic: 1865-1877   TB/1073
HAROLD U. FAULKNER: Politics, Reform and Expansion: 1890-1900. † Illus.   TB/3020
ROBERT GREEN MC CLOSKEY: American Conservatism in the Age of Enterprise: 1865-1910   TB/1137
ARTHUR MANN: Yankee Reformers in the Urban Age: Social Reform in Boston, 1880-1900   TB/1247

---

† The New American Nation Series, edited by Henry Steele Commager and Richard B. Morris.

‡ American Perspectives series, edited by Bernard Wishy and William E. Leuchtenburg.

* The Rise of Modern Europe series, edited by William L. Langer.

¶ Researches in the Social, Cultural, and Behavioral Sciences, edited by Benjamin Nelson.

§ The Library of Religion and Culture, edited by Benjamin Nelson.

Σ Harper Modern Science Series, edited by James R. Newman.

○ Not for sale in Canada.

△ Not for sale in the U. K.

History: Renaissance & Reformation

History: Modern European

3

Intellectual History & History of Ideas

Literature, Poetry, The Novel & Criticism

Myth, Symbol & Folklore

RELIGION

Ancient & Classical

Biblical Thought & Literature

The Judaic Tradition

Christianity: General

Christianity: Origins & Early Development

Christianity: The Middle Ages and The Reformation

NATURAL SCIENCES
AND MATHEMATICS

Biological Sciences